IMAGES
of America

WARREN COUNTY

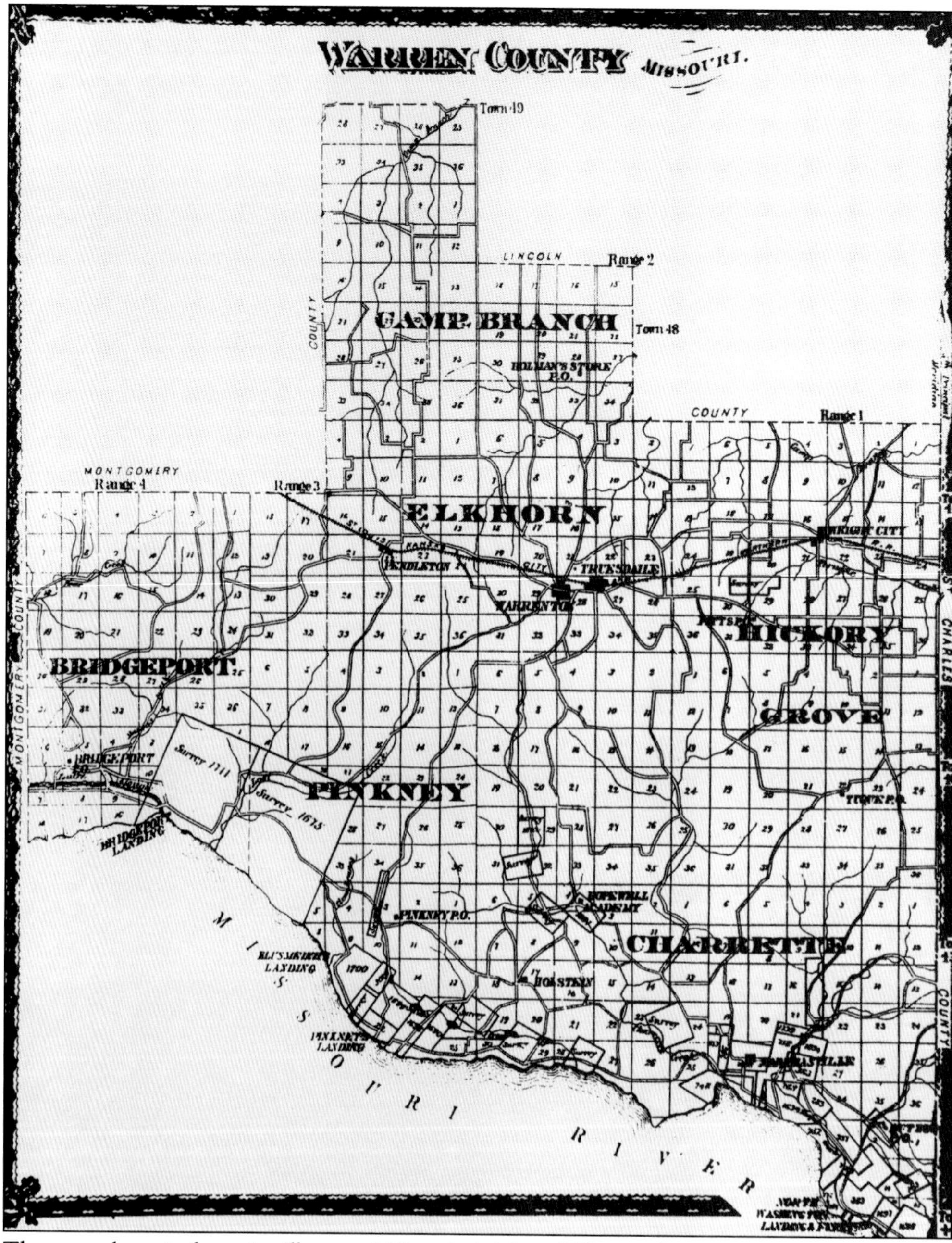

The map above is from *An Illustrated Historical Atlas of Warren County, Missouri*, by Edwards Brothers of Missouri, published in 1877. (Collection of the author.)

ON THE COVER: The Dutzow Coronet Band is, from left to right, (first row) Ed Feldmann and Gus Berg; (second row) Fritz Dickhaus, Ben Nagel, August Riefenberg, and Charles Rexroth; (third row) Professor Husler, Anton Diermann, Otto Hinnah, Henry Rohe, George Schulz, John Schopp, and Alvin Dickhaus. (Collection of the author.)

IMAGES
of America

WARREN COUNTY

Dorris Keeven-Franke

ARCADIA
PUBLISHING

ISBN 978-0-7385-8290-0

Published by Arcadia Publishing
Charleston, South Carolina

Printed in the United States of America

Library of Congress Control Number: 2011926679

For all general information, please contact Arcadia Publishing:
Telephone 843-853-2070
Fax 843-853-0044
E-mail sales@arcadiapublishing.com
For customer service and orders:
Toll-Free 1-888-313-2665

Visit us on the Internet at www.arcadiapublishing.com

I dedicate this to my mentor, Ralph Gregory, whose generosity, love of local history, and desire to share it continues to inspire me

Contents

ACKNOWLEDGMENTS

For the past 25 years, I have had the pleasure to share my love of local history with so many individuals. It would be impossible to thank them all; however, some deserve extra special thanks. When the *Warren County Tribune* first asked me to write for them in 1991, I learned just how passionate the citizens of Warren County are about their history, and an exciting exchange began with so many generous and kind people, many of who I miss dearly today. My friend George "Watson" Giles has spent countless hours pouring over old maps and land records with me, and without his assistance, this book would never have been possible. Other mentors over the years have included Walter Kamphoefner and Steven Rowan, whose help, comments, and criticisms have helped me many times. Most importantly, I have to thank the friendly discussions and debates with Ralph Gregory and admit how he always inspired me to question, dig, and then share, leading me write those countless columns for local newspapers. Finally, I must acknowledge and thank my family for all of their support over the years.

Remember, history can never be told exactly right, because we each hold dear to our hearts our own way of remembering.

Unless otherwise noted, all images appear courtesy of the author's collection.

INTRODUCTION

Long before it was officially named Warren County, the area was home to American Indians and French-Canadian fur traders who used the broad Missouri River as their thoroughfare. The Sac and Fox tribes clashed with the larger Osage but to no avail. Local landmarks' names still give testimony to the early settlers' association with the Osage, who intermarried with the residents of the early settlement La Charrette.

A long-established rendezvous point used by the fur trading industry, La Charrette was so deep rooted by 1796 that the Spanish government sought to establish its own settlement, St. John, along John Long's survey on the opposite riverbank. By the early 1800s, the settlement had grown large enough to hire a schoolteacher for the area families.

The story was that it was called La Charrette because the fur traders actually hauled their fur skins in carts. From beavers to elk, the area was filled with abundant game. When pioneer and trailblazer Daniel Boone arrived in the area in 1799, the settlement was well established. Members of Boone's family, the Callaway family, and his wife's family, the Bryans, would eventually build homes in the area.

Capt. Meriwether Lewis had the La Charrette settlement in mind as his original 1803 destination for a winter training camp of his corps, revealed in a study of his exchange of letters with Pres. Thomas Jefferson. However, as the official transfer of the newly purchased Louisiana Territory had not transpired yet, the Spanish refused Lewis permission to access to any land west of the Mississippi. When Lewis and his coleader, William Clark, arrived with their troops in May 1804, they met with fur trader Regis Loisel, who was actually working as a spy for the Spanish government to learn more about Lewis and Clark's plans after departing this "last settlement of whites" on their way west. Maps and other information was exchanged; however, there is no mention in the journals of a visit with Boone.

Daniel Boone had been given a large land grant by the Spanish government in exchange for bringing settlers to this frontier. He served as syndic, also known as a judge, settling disputes amongst his neighbors. He still loved to hunt and trap, and apparently, he roamed the area, visiting the homes of his children. Boone, a frontiersman, had already left his mark on American history by time he wrote his sister, saying, "I live with my daughter and Flanders Callaway" near Tuque Creek. When his wife, Rebecca Bryan, died in 1813, she was buried in her family's nearby cemetery, high upon a hillside overlooking the Missouri River. In September 1820, Boone was alongside her. He would reside there many years before a marker was erected. Years later, Kentucky would come to claim its hero, and the question still circulates from time to time if, perhaps, the wrong grave was opened. Some area residents claim today that the American hero still lies on the Warren County hillside.

The Louisiana Territory had been divided into districts, and the area had become part of the St. Charles District in December 1812. Settlement was rapidly increasing as huge wagonloads of families moved west along the Boone's Lick Road, which connected with the Sante Fe and Oregon Trails even farther west. Along the river, towns were being platted and vying for the distinction of being named county seat.

In 1818, Marthasville was platted by settler John Young and named for his wife, Martha. On the hilltop directly north of La Charrette, the young town had a better vantage point than the low-lying valley, which was often flooded, eventually washing away the earlier settlement. Marthasville was the only stop on the US postal route that settlers in the area called "the light horse trail." The US postal route was also established in 1818; it followed Boone's trail to the Boone family's western salt-making settlement, called a salt lick, and the even-earlier Osage Trace.

Further west of La Charrette along the Missouri River, a town named Pinckney was platted by Fredrick Griswold, becoming the county seat of Montgomery County in December 1818. Carved out of the St. Charles District, it contained what would later become Warren County. Pinckney grew rapidly, with lots not only for homes but also a courthouse, a jail, and even an academy. Streets were laid out, and frame houses were built. The earliest steamboats would stop for wood alongside the landing. Several churches were built, and the town was booming. However, after the town was flooded in the Great Flood of 1824, talk began of the need for a more centrally located county seat. Petitions circulated, and the Montgomery County seat was moved to Danville in 1824. Years later, during the Civil War, Confederate guerrillas would raid and set fire to the town, destroying area records for the years prior to Warren County's own organization.

Daniel Boone's fame had spread far and wide through his biographers—writer Timothy Flint's biography of Boone had been translated into German by the late 1700s. An impressionable young man in Germany named Gottfried Duden may have read of the frontiersman's exploits, inspiring him to purchase land in the area in 1819. By that time, Boone's son Nathan was surveying land for what would potentially become part of the state of Missouri and had perhaps suggested the purchase, along Lake Creek, when he noted in his surveyor's journal that it was the only farmable land in the area.

In August 1821, the State of Missouri was established after much debate as a slave-ownership state. That decision was part of the long march leading up to the Civil War. Most of the residents at the time were slave owners who had moved west from Virginia, Kentucky, and Tennessee.

Duden arrived in the autumn of 1824 with his cook and a young farmer named Lewis Eversmann. In the beginning, they lived with the family of Jacob Haun, who had also purchased his farm when depositing the funds for Duden's purchase. Haun was a second-generation American, his father having come from Germany as a child. They had come west with the Boone clan and had served with Nathan Boone's Rangers in the War of 1812.

The cabin on Duden's farm, built by Haun's brother-in-law Dabney Burnett, wasn't suitable for Duden and his maid, so they lived with Haun until a larger cabin could be built. Young Eversmann, however, wasted no time building a cabin on his portion of the land that he and Duden had purchased after their arrival. Soon, he met Anna McLean at the house of her sister, who was married into one of the area's largest tobacco plantation owners, the Hancock family. The McLean family had settled on the southern side of the river in what was formerly St. John and would eventually become Washington. With his marriage to Anna McLean, Eversmann would not only be the first permanent German settler but a slave owner as well.

Both McLean and Nathan Boone would take Duden hunting and show him the area's farms. Duden spent time researching and writing a glowing description of the area on the hillside north of Haun's cabin. Fascinated with the life of the area's residents, he would later write about the earlier Ramsey massacre by the Sac Indians at the close of the War of 1812. Duden collected stories of gathering maple syrup in the sugar camps, brush fires, and the life of the American farmer, all the while living a leisurely life as a writer.

Duden's neighbors were surprised to see him leave for Germany and questioned why he didn't stay, since he planned to return. He tried to explain that he needed to return to Germany in order to share how the area was a perfect place to begin anew, explaining how his country was full of famine due to overpopulation and political struggles. He hoped he could encourage his fellow countrymen to settle here on the western frontier. Duden's collection of letters would become *A Report on a Journey to the Western States of North America*, with 1,500 copies published at the author's own expense in Germany in 1829. It was a small book with a big impact.

In Germany, Duden's book was reprinted and republished by emigration societies. It was taken up and read throughout Europe. It shared a vision of life among American settlers, who had meat on their tables every day, more land than they could ever hope to farm, and no king to answer to or go to war for. Soon, Duden's book was taken up by societies organized to emigrate in groups, as Duden had suggested.

The first small group, referred to as the Berlin Society, arrived in the summer of 1832 and purchased several hundred acres of land communally. The land adjoined the farm of Gottfried Duden to the north. There were less than 10 families in this group, and each was led by university-educated young men unprepared for life on the American frontier. When their benefactor, Baron Johann Wilhelm von Bock, arrived, ownership of the society's land was transferred to him, and plans began for the village of Dutzow, named after his former estate in northern Germany. Bock planned for this to be a truly German settlement, with streets named for famous Germans like Schiller and Mozart. On Bock's land was a mill as well as a distillery that was declared to make the best apple brandy in the area. Meeting and billiard halls were built, and a windmill was experimented with.

In 1833, enough settlers had arrived that Warren County could be carved out of the former Montgomery County. With no county seat within its borders, the first order of business for the commissioners was to establish one. And there began a new debate. Named for Joseph G. Warren, a hero of the Revolutionary War fought just over 50 years before, the county was filled at that time with slave-owning families who had moved west in the past 30 years.

With a large amount of those families living in the southern half of the county along the Missouri River, they wanted the seat to be established near them at the town of New Boston, where there was already a mill, church, and general store. Area residents anxiously waited for the commissioners to make the establishment official, which they soon did.

Further north, however, there were those who wanted to see a more central location established as the county seat. And for that reason, a wealthy St. Louisan named Henry Walton came forth to establish Warrenton. This was a popular choice, as court was already being held at the home of Mordecai Morgan, who lived along Big Creek. And since Morgan's home didn't lie within the new city of Warrenton, his farm was the city's first official annexation. The debate raged on, with county residents demanding that court be moved out of Morgan's cabin and down to New Boston. The clerk refused. Newly appointed commissioners decided to put the decision to a vote of the residents, and on January 5, 1837, voters officially moved the county seat to Warrenton.

By that time, huge changes were occurring in the demographics of the young county. Germans were filling the valleys by the thousands. After reading Duden's book, they hoped that a better life for their families could be found in Missouri, and so they came. Some felt betrayed, as Duden had described the climate as mild, which it had been during the years he had visited. Others criticized Duden, feeling that his descriptions had been too glowing. One early settler who had come in 1834, Fredrich Steines, wrote home, "While all is not exactly as Duden has described, in some ways it is much better." Duden felt misunderstood, and his life had been threatened, causing him to change his plans for returning to the United States. Duden left the care of his farm and his cattle to Lewis Eversmann and his plans for settlement to others, but he continued to own his Warren County farm until his death.

Young Germans Paul Follenius and Friedrich Muench had met while students at the University of Giessen. Filled with revolutionary ideals, they and their fellow students tried to enact change. When those efforts failed, they turned to the report of Gottfried Duden. They shared their plan for a huge society that would establish a new German state. In 1833, they published a pamphlet calling for members of the newly established Giessen Emigration Society. The response was overwhelming, with nearly 2,000 applications to join. However, membership was closed at 500, and they came in two contingents. The society was made up of all classes of Germans, and the members were required to have enough funds to establish themselves and purchase farms.

Unforeseen events led to a disastrous change in this group's plans. The two contingents were slated to depart Bremen in early May, with Follenius and his group to arrive on the ship *Olbers* at the port of New Orleans. Cholera was epidemic, and Follenius fell ill and nearly died. Members of the group began to scatter, thinking settlement plans were abandoned.

Meanwhile in Germany, a long and unforeseen delay with Muench's group lasted for five weeks. Not knowing the condition of the other half of the society, they hurried and were able to book passage on the ship *Medora* into Baltimore. Another strange turn of events led them to meet up with Bock in Cincinnati, where they were devastated to hear of the rest of the society's sad fate. Eventually, both Follenius's and Muench's groups met up in Warren County. Many of the members of the society eventually settled together along Lake Creek near Dutzow and Duden's farm. Many established themselves and became prominent leaders in the community.

Friedrich Muench continued the work of Duden, promoting Missouri to his fellow countrymen. Encouraging Germans to immigrate to Missouri, where they could raise their families "where the sun of freedom shines," he wrote countless books in German on a wide range of subjects. Born in a small village as the son of a Lutheran minister, he followed in his father's footsteps. In Missouri, he adopted the creed of the Freethinkers and coedited the Hermann, Missouri, newspaper *Der Lichte Freund*. Muench suggested to his Cincinnati friend Eduard Muehl that Muehl should bring his newspaper to Missouri, where it became the first to publish Harriet Beecher Stowe's *Uncle Tom's Cabin* in German for its readers.

As a viticulturist, Muench surveyed the state of Missouri for native rootstock to improve the wine culture with his son-in-law Gordian Busch in 1851. A frequent columnist in agriculture newspapers, he eventually wrote *American Wine School* as a handbook for those in the Missouri wine industry.

Concerned for the country's issues regarding slavery, Muench, a staunch abolitionist, was drawn into the political issues of his day. In the mid-1850s, he traveled as far as New York giving speeches regarding the problem. In Chicago, he supported Abraham Lincoln's nomination for president in 1860. Despite his and his family's lives being continually threatened for his activities, Muench was elected to represent the first district in the Missouri State Senate by Warren, St. Charles, and Montgomery County residents in 1862. He was respected, honored, and greatly admired for the tenacity of his beliefs.

So strong was his belief in Missouri and Warren County that Muench was encouraged by his friends to write *The State of Missouri* in German. With Missouri footing the bill, Muench returned to Germany in 1859 for three months to promote Missouri with his book. By this time, the majority of Warren County's residents were either German-born or of German descent. The book was later followed with second and third editions.

Today, Warren County maintains pride in what began as a French Canadian fur trade settlement and became a final destination of America's pioneers. Part of today's beautiful Missouri Rhineland, it also takes pride in the German culture and heritage that it grew with. It is now one of Missouri's richest historical counties, brimming with stories of pioneers and determination steeped in America's heritage.

One

La Charrette

The actual beginning of the La Charrette settlement is lost in the sands of time, washed away with the years of flooding along the changing Missouri River bottom. French Canadian fur traders had settlements all along the Mississippi River at Kaskaskia, St. Louis, and Portage des Sioux where they swapped and traded with the American Indians. The Osage tribe was the most prominent, leaving its mark nearby in caves and along cliffs. The Osage quite often intermarried with the French as well, after many years of friendly relations.

The Osage had been pushed westward into the path of the Pottowatomie, Sac, and Fox tribes, causing uprisings and attacks on the encroaching settlers.

The early land grants reveal the French pattern—a common field behind the homes, each with a narrow strip of property connecting it to the river, which was the highway at that time. All commerce and travel depended on the river and was subject to its rise and fall. It was here that the Corps of Discovery and its leaders, Lewis and Clark, would stop in May 1804, referring to it as "La Charrette."

By the time of the War of 1812, tensions amongst the pioneers and the Osage had risen, so the local settlers created an unofficial Fort Charrette for their protection. Whenever trouble was brewing, a large horn was blown, calling all the area residents together inside its walls. Being so distant and far into the frontier, the worst event, the Ramsey massacre, actually took place after the treaty to end the War of 1812 had been signed in the east. As the Ramsey family lived on the fringe of the Charrette settlement, it was a surprise when they were set upon in the early morning in the spring of 1818. Indians killed Ramsey's wife and three young children.

As more settlers arrived, tensions moved further west, and the area gave rise to Warren County's oldest town, Marthasville.

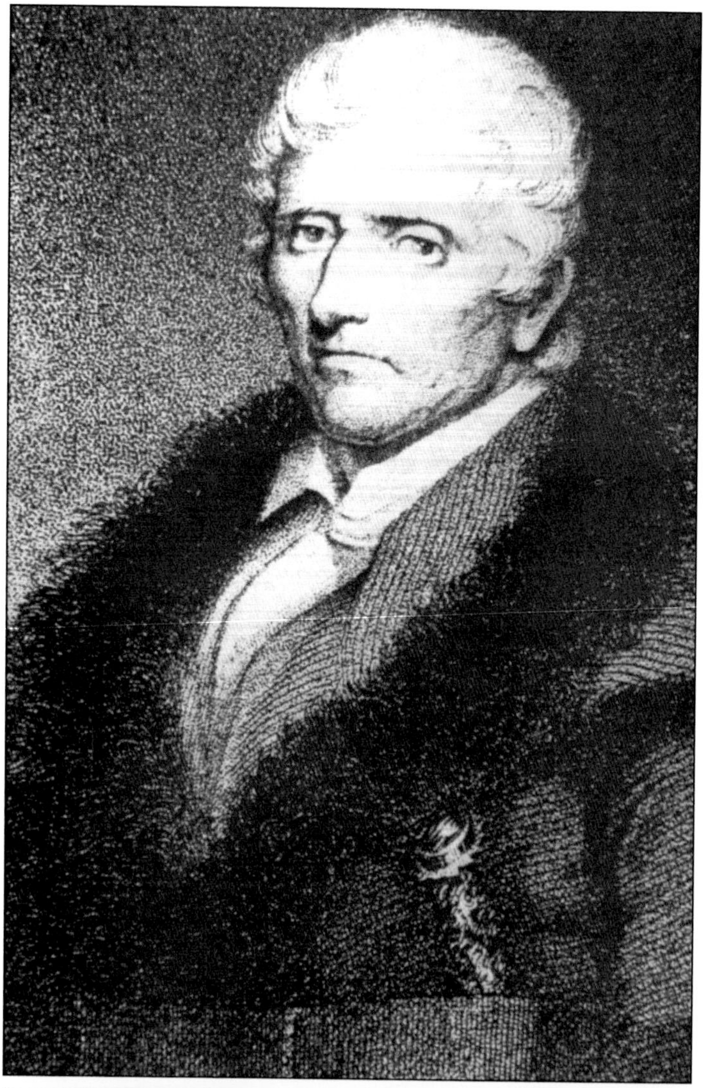

Daniel Boone was born in Pennsylvania in 1734 and spent the last 20 years of his life in Missouri, where he died and was laid to rest in 1820. He was an American frontiersman and folk hero, famous for trailblazing the settlement of Kentucky and the Wilderness Road through the Appalachian Mountains. His exploits gained him fame as far as Europe when his biography was published there in 1784. In 1799, he settled here at the invitation of the Spanish government, owners of the Louisiana Territory at that time. Well respected, Boone was appointed as a local syndic, or judge. After his wife, Rebecca, died in 1813, he lived at La Charrette with his daughter Jemima and her husband, Flanders Callaway. He died while visiting his son Nathan but was brought back to La Charrette for his funeral and burial alongside his wife.

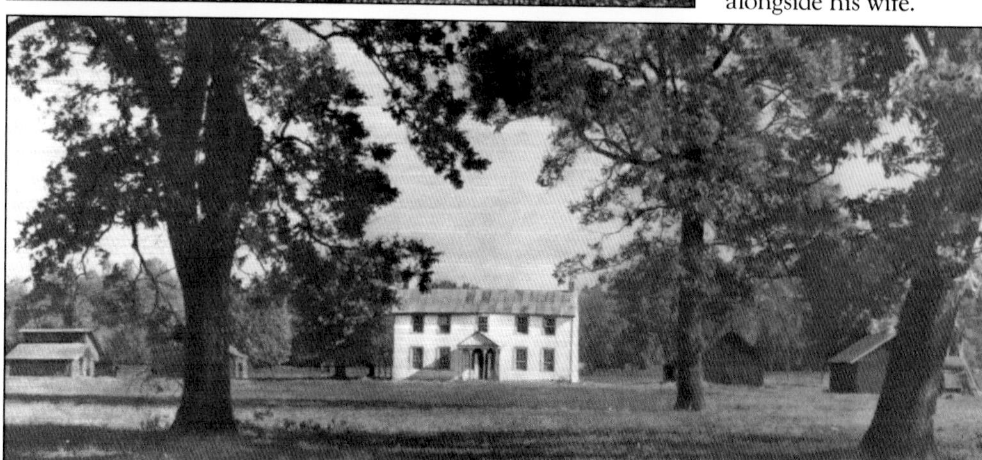

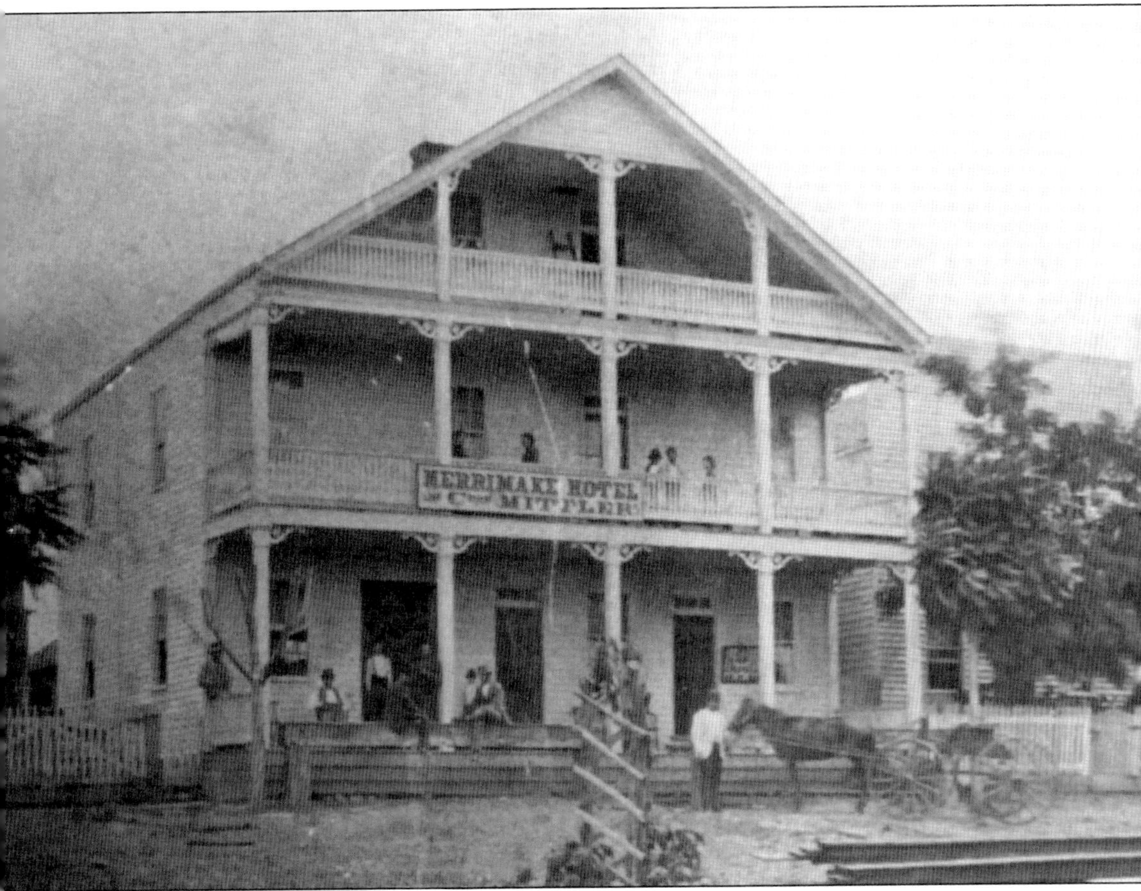

In 1817, Dr. John Young established the town of Marthasville on the hilltop north of La Charrette, naming it for his wife. On June 21, 1817, he advertised lots for sale in the *Missouri Gazette*. It had changed from a small fur trader's outpost to a thriving town. While many of the early residents had moved west, slave-owning residents who had come west from Virginia and Kentucky still attended the local auctions. The residents petitioned to be a stop on the postal route—the "light-horse trail along the Osage trace"—meaning that overland travelers could move easily along a well-established road. The town was growing, as this three-story Merrimake Hotel, established by Charles Mittler, who had settled here in 1839, demonstrates. Boasting over 350 residents, the town was a favorite stop for travelers along the Missouri River.

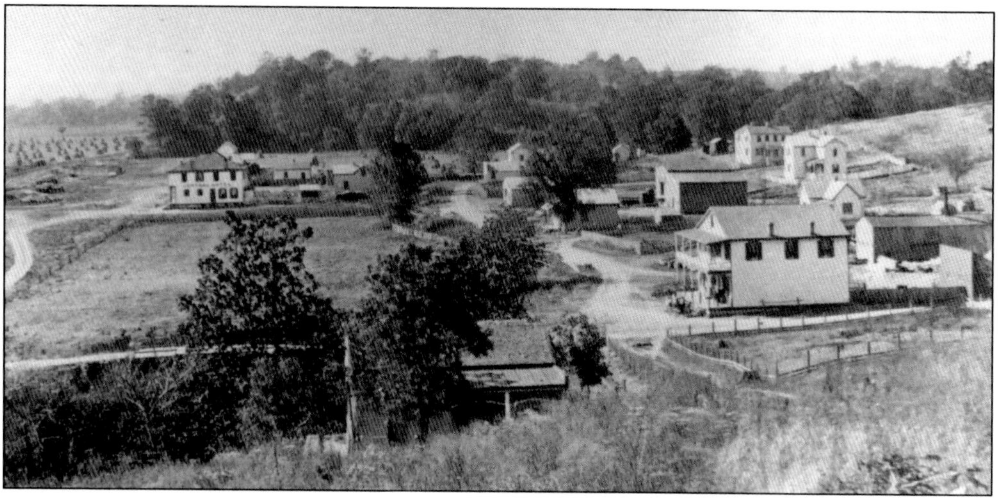

In 1892, the Missouri, Kansas & Texas Railroad, nicknamed the "Katy," arrived in Marthasville. The town changed from a river town to a railroad town and grew, as farmers could now ship their crops even faster. This also brought the town of Marthasville, platted on the hilltop, to the river bottom once again. The earlier La Charrette settlement had been lost over the years to the floods that quite often ravaged the bottomland. The railroad crossed the flat bottomland faster, since it did not have to climb or tunnel hillsides.

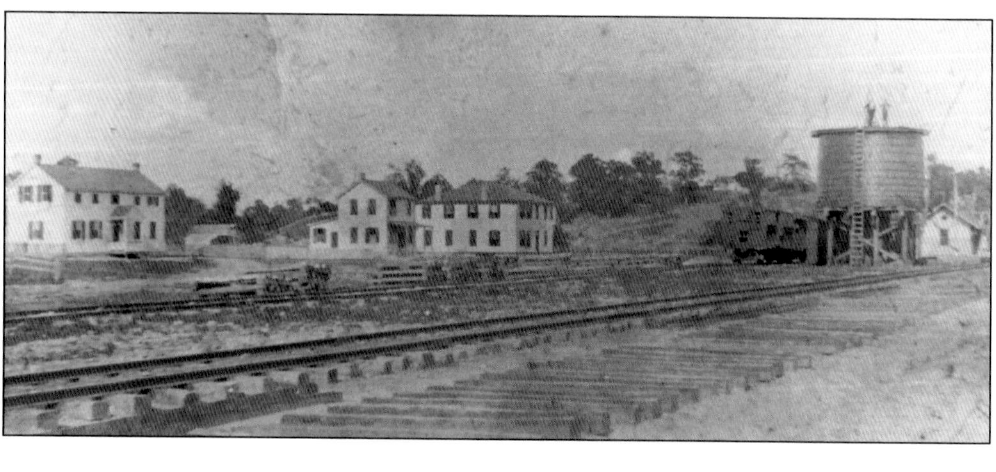

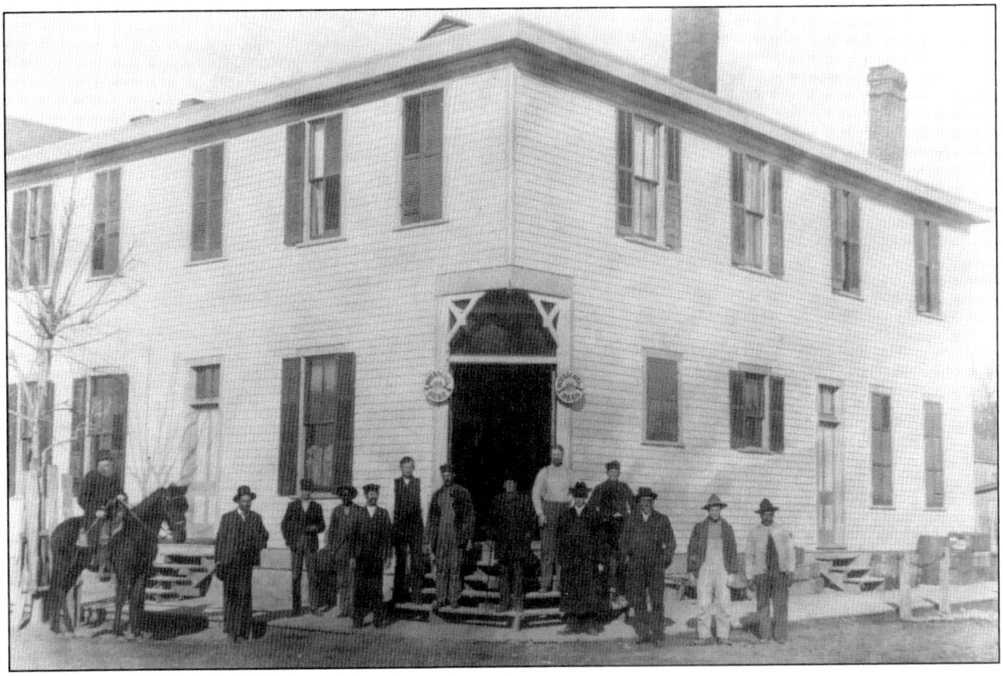

With the arrival of the railroad came thriving businesses like the large Central Hotel, as seen here. Railroad engineers and workers called the hotel home while track was laid heading west to towns like Bernheimer and Case. With the saloon, the clientele seems to be all male. At some point, perhaps when the railroad workers moved west with the track, it became more of the town's meeting hall.

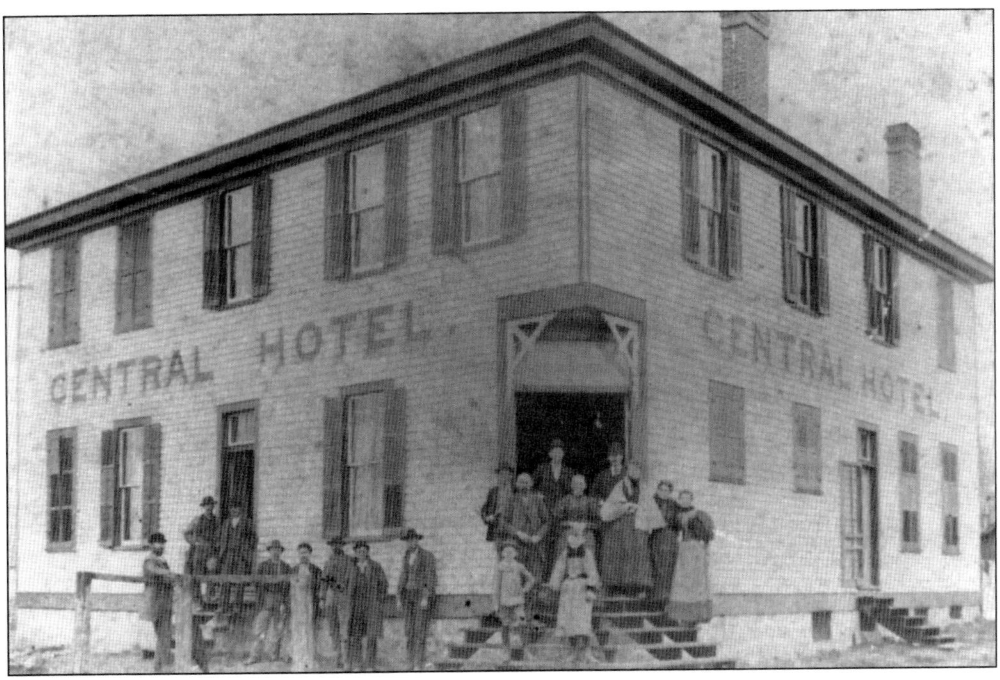

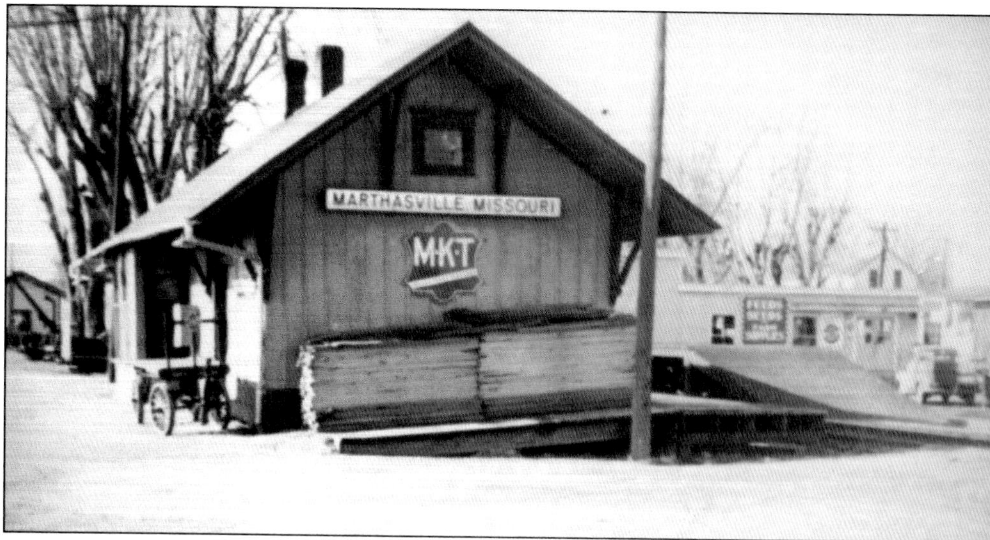

By the time the railroad arrived, earlier towns along the Missouri River were fading. The horse-powered ferryboat *Tilda Clara* had ferried passengers from Franklin County's town of Miller's Landing to Warren County towns such as Treloar and Pinckney for years. Pinckney had been established as Montgomery's county seat in 1818, much to Marthasville's despair. The town had grown rapidly as a county seat with a private academy, a mill, several churches, frame houses, a courthouse, and a jail. In 1824, a huge flood caused residents to clamor for a more centrally located county seat, having it moved first to Danville and then to Lewiston. With that, the town of Pinckney began to fade, suffering again in the Great Flood of 1844. With the flood of 1881, the river changed course, and the early town of Pinckney, once in Montgomery County, became part of Franklin County. A new post office was established, but the town never regrew.

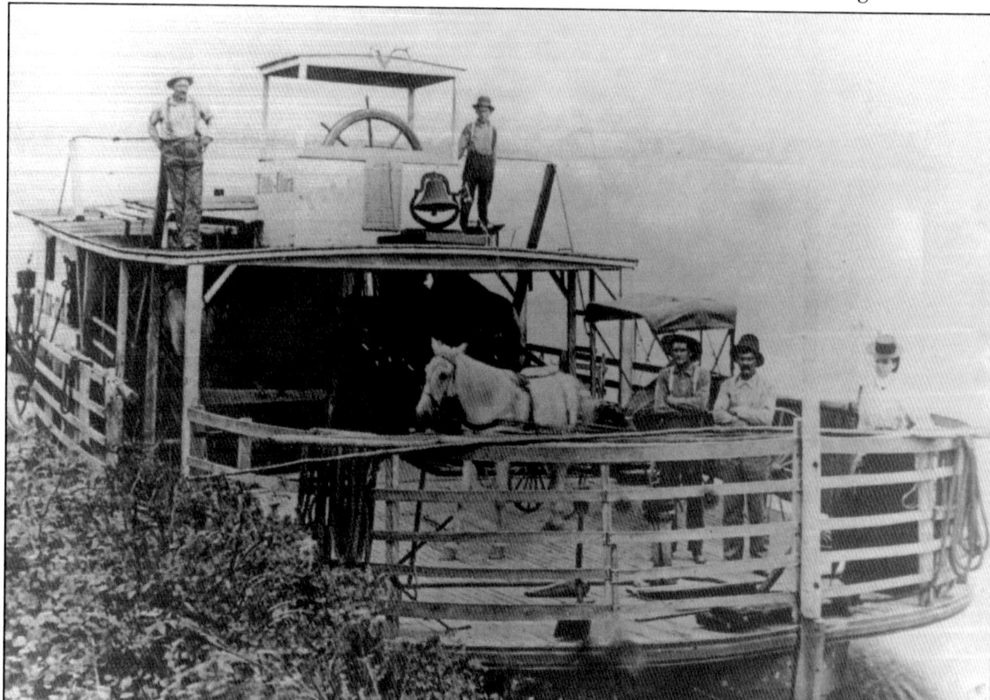

Two

THE GERMANS ARRIVE

When the story of Daniel Boone and the abundance of this new frontier reached war-torn Europe, some took notice. After years of famine, over population, and political intrigue, Germans were immigrating to Russia, England, and South America in search of a better life. A wealthy young attorney named Gottfried Duden purchased land in Warren County just east of Marthasville, along a stream called Lake Creek, in 1819. In 1824, he arrived in Missouri with his housekeeper and a companion, Lewis Eversmann.

Duden lived with farmer Jacob Haun and his family from 1824 until 1827. He and Eversmann purchased land, and each soon had a house built on his portion. Duden spent his days leisurely traveling the area, simply observing as area residents built homes, created farms, and raised families. He went duck hunting with Nathan Boone, Daniel's son. The life he lived was uncomplicated, and his descriptions were romantic.

Duden returned to Germany, and in 1829, he published the first edition of *A Report on a Journey to the Western States of North America*, which gave a glowing description of his life in Missouri. His small self-published book was taken up by thousands of Germans in search of a better life. Duden's advice was to form emigration groups, believing there was safety in numbers.

The first such group, the Berlin Society, arrived in 1832. Germans from the Osnabrück area arrived next, in 1833. By then, a group of 500 Germans had formed in Germany known as the Giessen Emigration Society. They arrived in 1834, hoping to create a German state. While this goal was not a feasible, what they did create was better.

As these early arrivals sent word home, more soon arrived from Germany. Warren County was soon the most predominately German county in the entire state, with over 50 percent of its population of German descent by 1861, when the Civil War began. Missouri would become one of the most popular states for German immigrants, with St. Louis an anchor of the nation's German triangle with Milwaukee and Cincinnati.

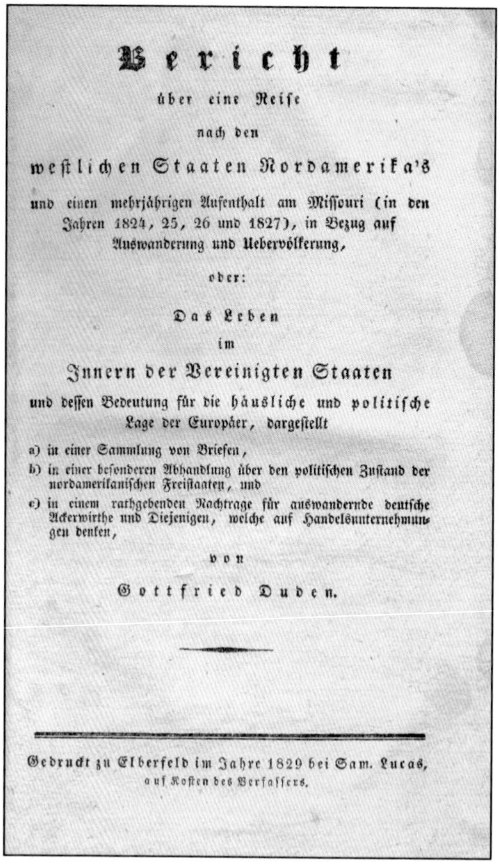

Bericht

über eine Reise

nach den

westlichen Staaten Nordamerika's

und einen mehrjährigen Aufenthalt am Missouri (in den Jahren 1824, 25, 26 und 1827), in Bezug auf Auswanderung und Uebervölkerung,

oder:

Das Leben

im

Innern der Vereinigten Staaten

und dessen Bedeutung für die häusliche und politische Lage der Europäer, dargestellt

a) in einer Sammlung von Briefen,

b) in einer besonderen Abhandlung über den politischen Zustand der nordamerikanischen Freistaaten, und

c) in einem rathgebenden Nachtrage für auswandernde deutsche Ackerwirthe und Diejenigen, welche auf Handelsunternehmungen denken,

von

Gottfried Duden.

Gedruckt zu Elberfeld im Jahre 1829 bei Sam. Lucas, auf Kosten des Verfassers.

Attorney Gottfried Duden (1789–1856) published 1,500 copies of his report (left) at his own expense. Additional editions soon followed by him and emigration groups throughout Europe. Though he planned on returning to his Missouri farm, the criticism that surfaced following his first edition made him change his plans. Abandoning his Missouri dream, he lived out his life in Bonn, Germany, where he is buried. By 1834, the wealthy Baron J.W. von Bock (below), credited with creating the Berlin Society, platted the village of Dutzow, named for his former estate in Germany. He planned for Dutzow to be a truly German city. Bock was a friendly, jovial eccentric with grand plans, but he died poor. Bock's farm and village adjoined Duden's land, once a mecca for German immigrants.

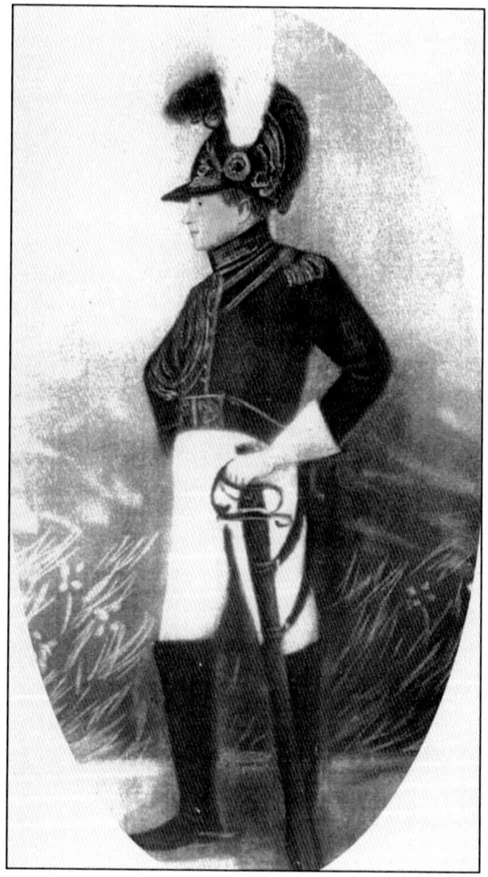

Paul Follenius (1799–1844) was a cofounder of the Giessen Emigration Society. His older brother, Karl Follen, and friend Friedrich Muench were embroiled in the German student revolutions in the 1830s. After his brother fled for the United States, he and Muench were students together at the University of Giessen. As Gottfried Duden suggested, they created the Giessen Emigration Society in 1833. In 1834, Follenius led his contingent in through New Orleans, where many of the members contracted cholera. On their way to St. Louis, so many became ill, including Follenius, that the group splintered. Follenius eventually moved onto Duden's farm and purchased the farm of Jacob Haun, where Duden had first stayed in 1824 and 1825. Follenius, also an attorney, was not destined for the farmer's life and died of typhoid following the Great Flood of 1844.

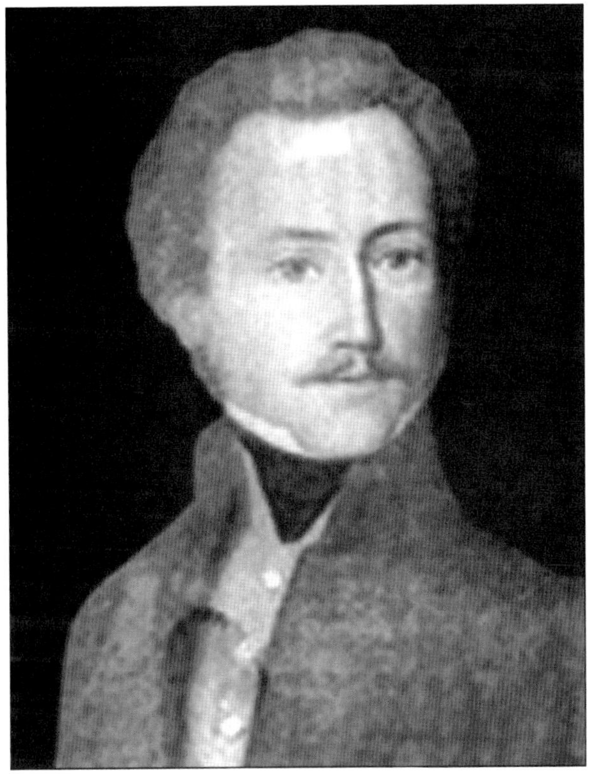

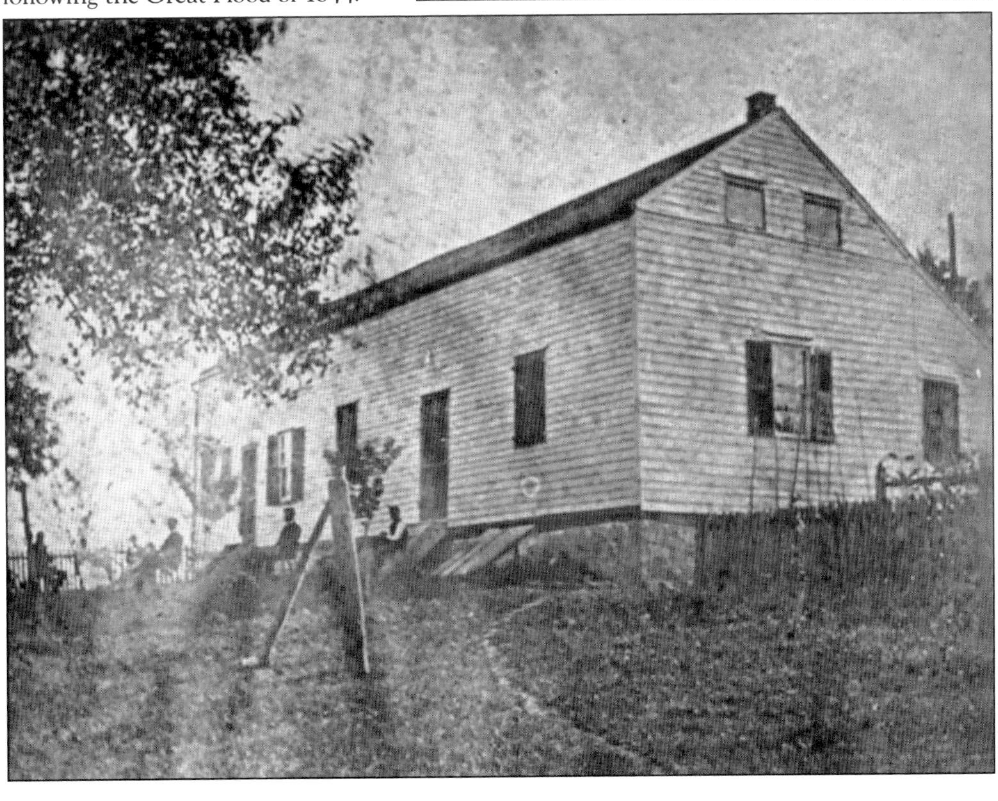

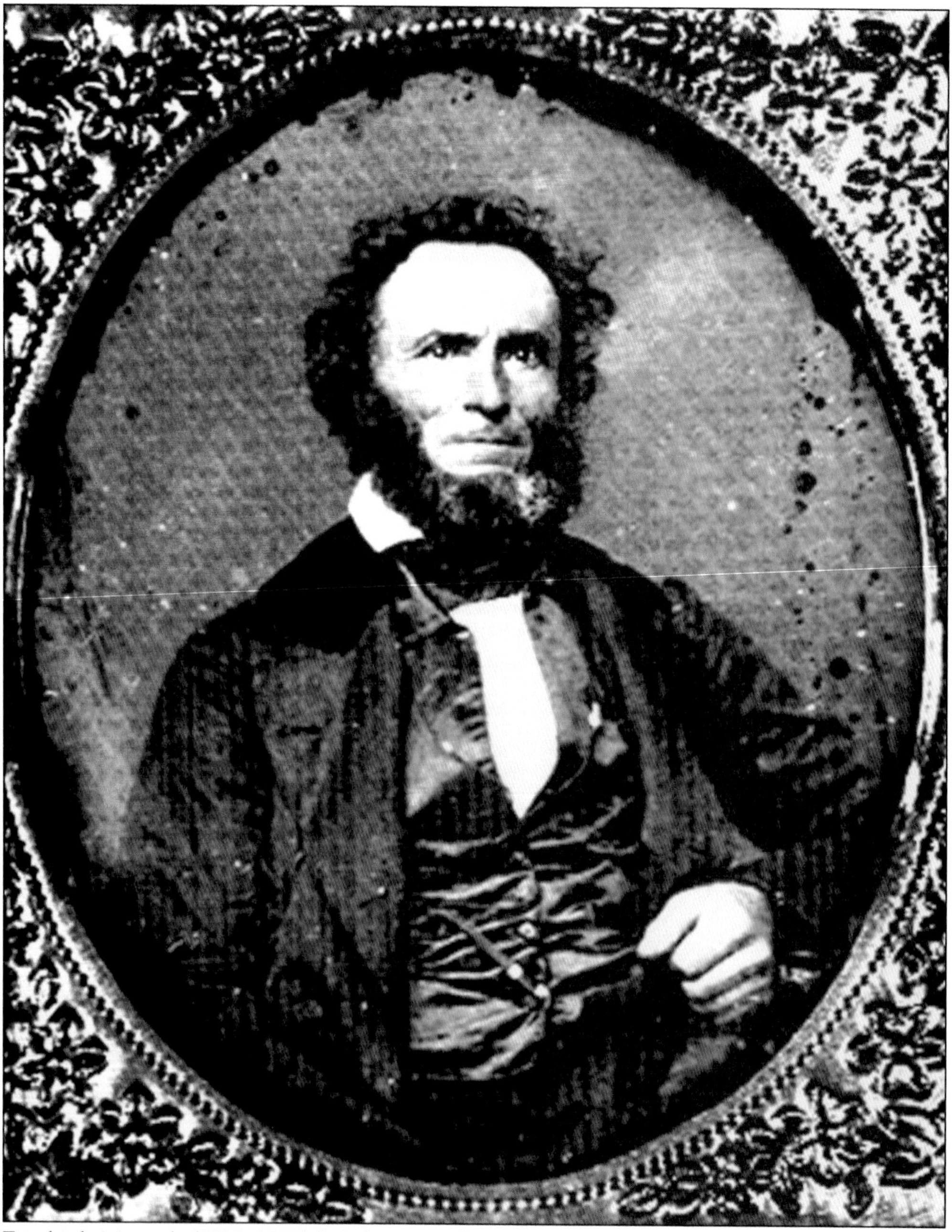

Friedrich Muench (1799–1881) led the second contingent of the Giessen Emigration Society to Missouri through Baltimore. They had been delayed five weeks in Germany, unable to find passage when their ship did not arrive. By the time they arrived in Warren County, Follenius had arranged for Muench to purchase an adjoining farm. After carving a home from the wilderness, Muench began writing in German and English for fellow emigrants, covering subjects all the way from viticulture and wine making to philosophy and religion. Agriculture and emigration were favorites, and he also tried his hand at poetry and short stories. In 1859, he wrote the first edition of *The State of Missouri*, providing advice to his fellow Germans about the state. In 1862, he was elected to the Missouri Senate representing the first district, which included Warren County.

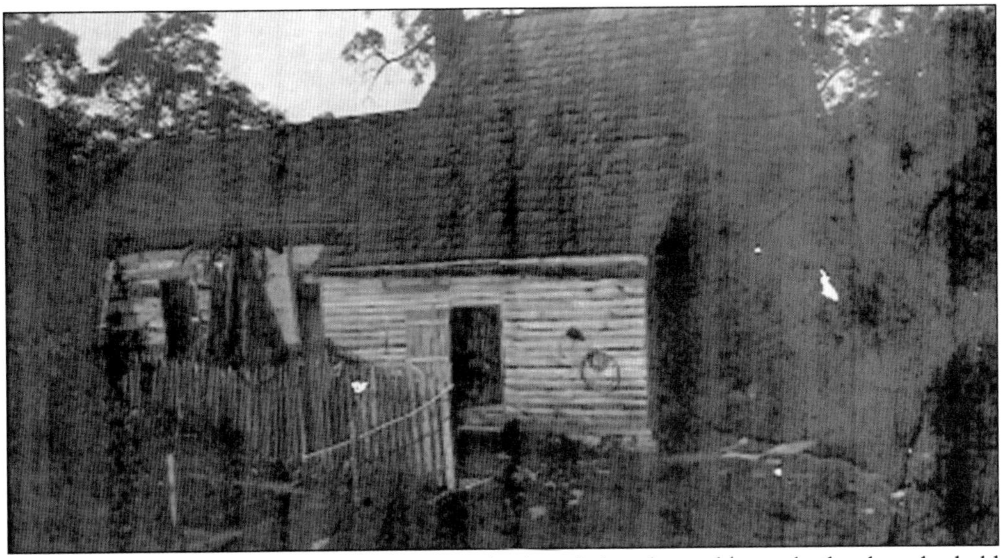

Friedrich Muench's first home was soon weatherboarded and an addition built where he held school for the local children. Upstairs was his book-lined study, where he wrote hundreds of articles and two more editions of *The State of Missouri.* A staunch supporter of Lincoln, Muench suffered threats to his life, home, and family from the remaining slave owners in his neighborhood, but he refused to leave. His son Berthold was killed at the Battle of Wilson's Creek, the first major battle of the Civil War in Missouri. Seen below are his sons Ferdinand, Hugo, and Julius and their families. Julius married and continued living on the farm, where he raised his family. In 1881, when Friedrich Muench was called to dinner and did not come, it was discovered that he had passed away in his beloved vineyard with pruning shears in hand.

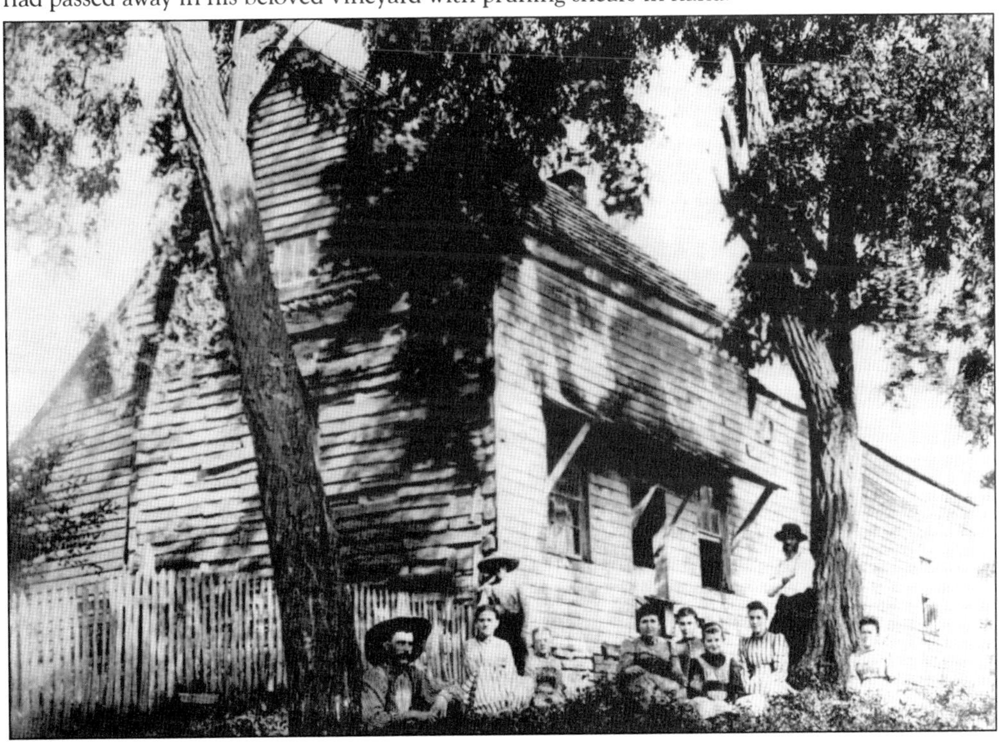

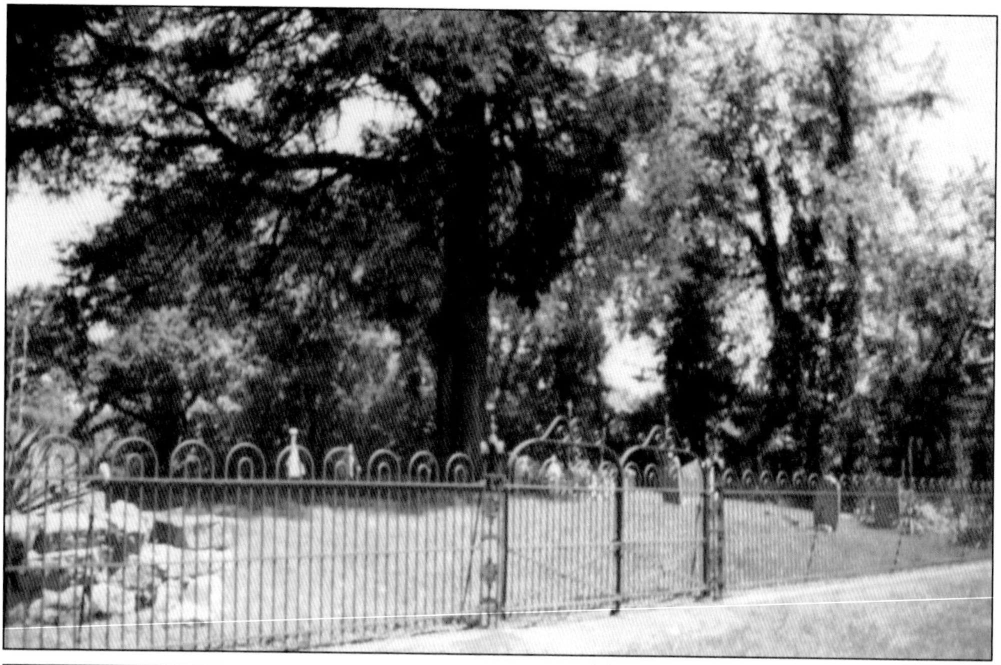

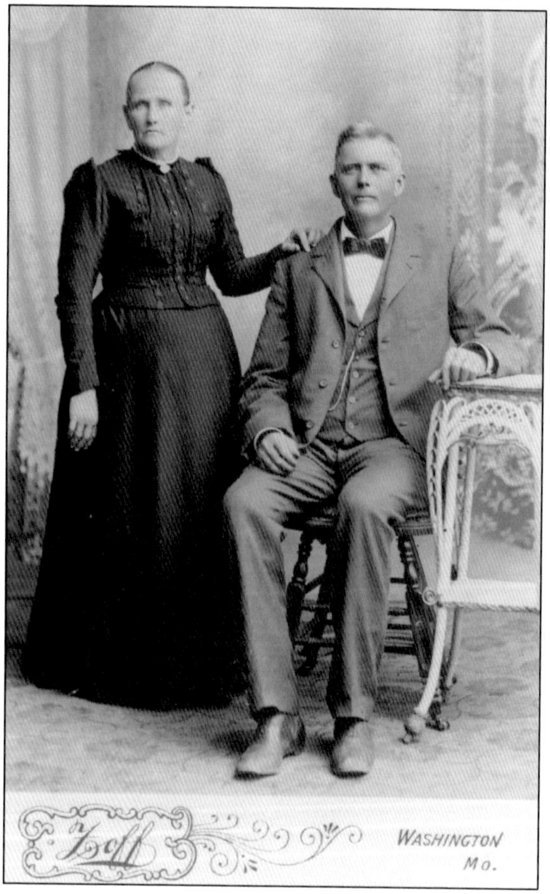

Although Friedrich Muench was ordained as a Lutheran minister at the University of Giessen in 1818, after reaching Warren County, he chose never to commit to a church because he didn't want the responsibility of ministering to a flock. However, his daughter Pauline's diary tells of how "PaPa" would speak every other Sunday to the local German families needing that connection in their lives, such as John Mittler, seen here with his wife, Louise Berg, whose family had emigrated with the Giessen Emigration Society in 1834. This property, with its cemetery still there in Dutzow, was owned by Friedrich Muench and others and is where the little log building Muench spoke at stood. Muench had adopted the Freethinkers meeting style, and coedited the German *Der Lichte Freund* (the Friends of Light) newspaper. The Freethinkers, or Freethought, was a philosophical viewpoint based on rational scientific thinking. Muench wrote many articles on his philosophical viewpoints that were published in German in both the United States and Germany.

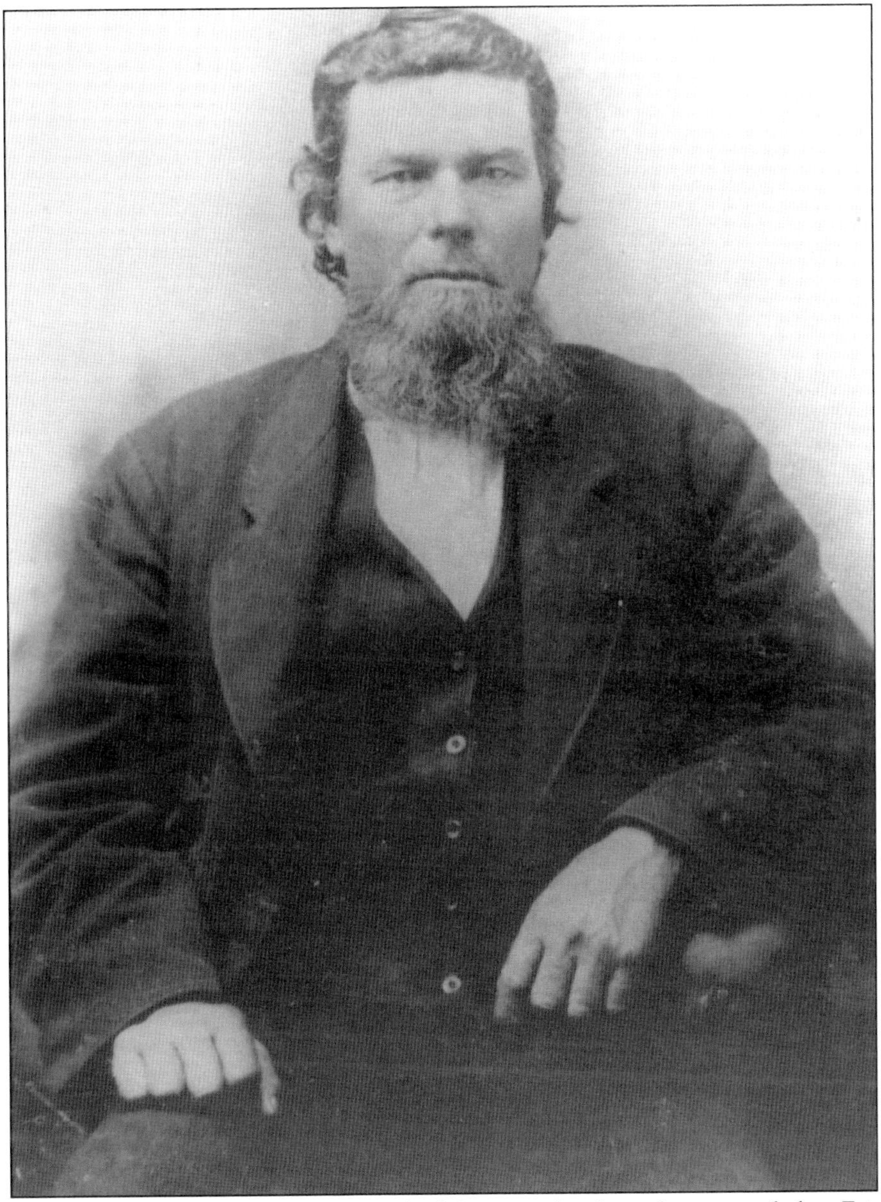

The Giessen Emigration Society consisted of German families who responded to Friedrich Muench's pamphlet A *Call for Large Scale Emigration*, which circulated in 1833. The privately passed circular spelled out the membership requirements for the group, to which thousands applied for membership. The group was closed at 500, and both contingents arrived in Warren County during the summer of 1834. The group is sometimes referred to as a failure, as it did not achieve its original goal of creating a German state within America. However, as those families and others like them wrote letters home to Germany, chain migration began. As Walter Kamphoefner suggests, it was these letters written home that ultimately brought thousands of Germans to the United States during the 1800s. By the 1850s, Warren County and the adjoining counties of Franklin and St. Charles were predominately German. Where once the early American friends and families of Daniel Boone lived, the area was now mainly German, with residents like John Fuhrer (seen here), born in 1830 in Germany.

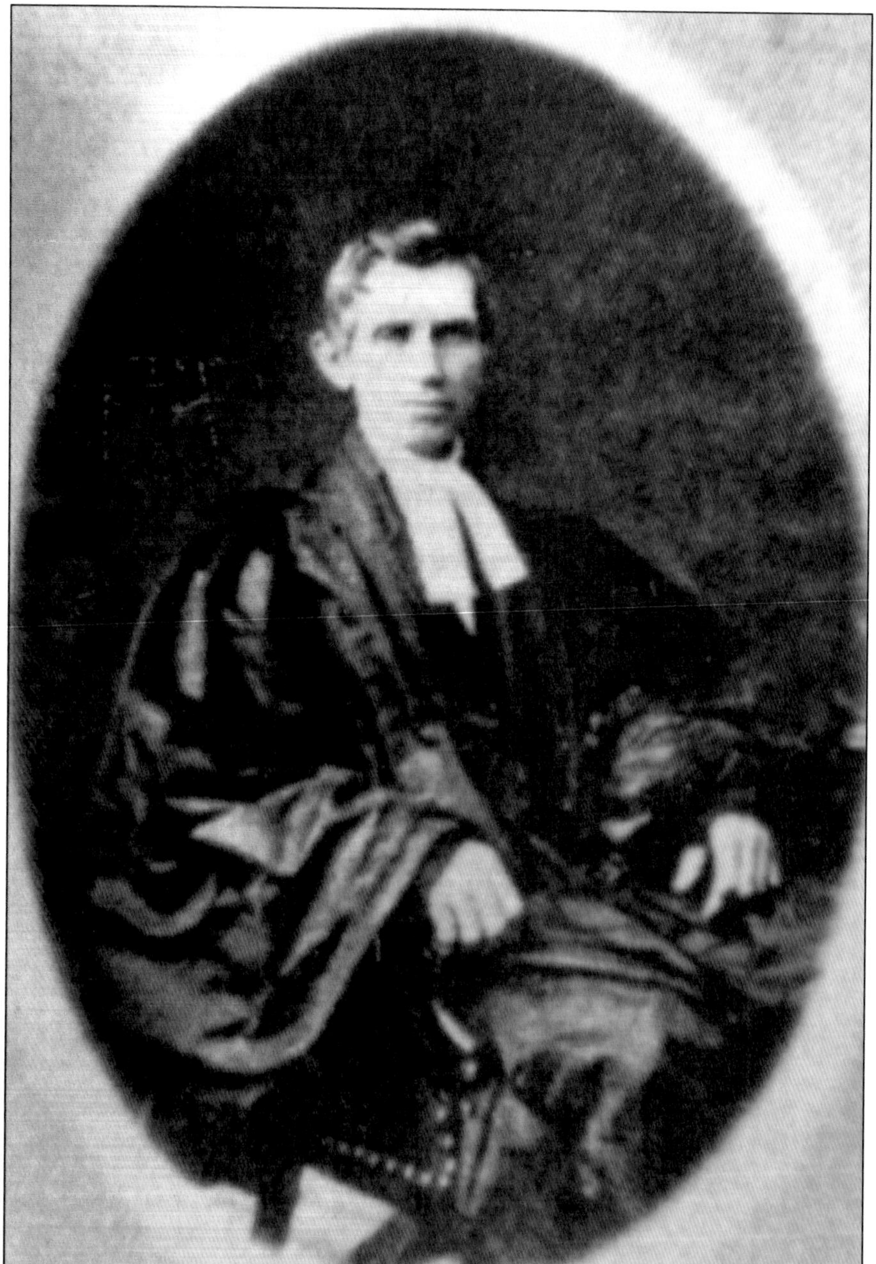

One of the earliest followers of Gottfried Duden, Hermann Garlichs (1807–1864), was a struggling German gentleman farmer when he was asked by his neighbors to minister to their religious needs. He returned to Germany, became ordained as an Evangelical minister, and married Adelheid von Borries. Upon his return, he served families in the Dutzow area as a circuit preacher. In 1836, he relinquished those duties to serve at Holstein and Upper Charrette in Warren County. By 1841, he was instrumental in founding the Synod of the West by forming the first German Evangelical Church Society of the West. This brought the Evangelical and Reformed Churches to many Warren County towns. Garlichs left Missouri in 1846, but the work he began was carried out by other German ministers like him.

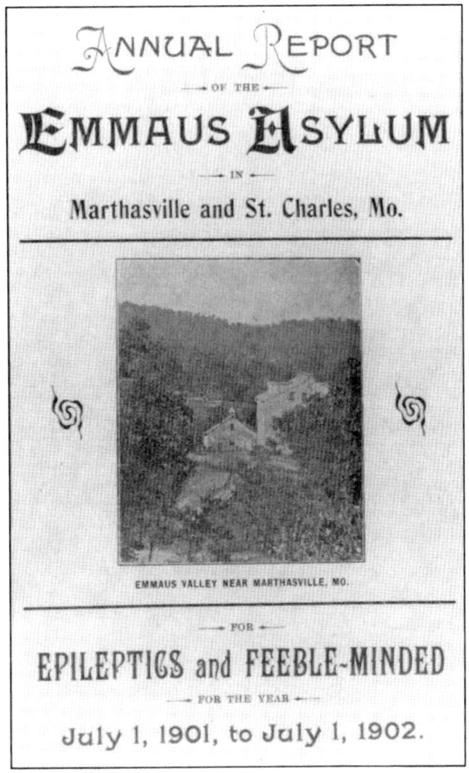

ANNUAL REPORT

OF THE

EMMAUS ASYLUM

IN

Marthasville and St. Charles, Mo.

EMMAUS VALLEY NEAR MARTHASVILLE, MO.

FOR

EPILEPTICS and FEEBLE-MINDED

FOR THE YEAR

July 1, 1901, to July 1, 1902.

The German Evangelical Church Society in the West would soon open the Marthasville Seminary on 59 acres of land donated by Heinrich Nienkamp on July 4, 1849. From the beginning, it was the responsibility of the students to support the school, and one way they did this was with the publication of their German newspaper the *Friedensbote*. Soon, the college's building was expanded and a large hall was added for prayer meetings and chapel exercises. With the Civil War came many difficulties, and in 1883, the seminary was closed. After 10 years of lying vacant, the Eden Theological Seminary purchased the beautiful property to open the German Evangelical Emmaus Asylum for Epileptics and Feeble Minded. The institution would be one of the first such asylums in the United States. C.F. Sturm and Rev. J.W. Frankenfeld were early leaders at the Emmaus Asylum.

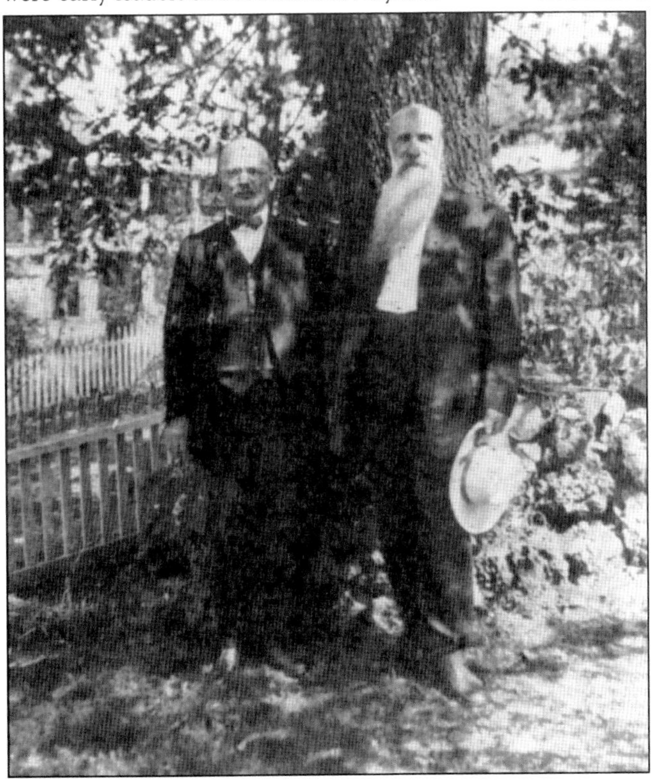

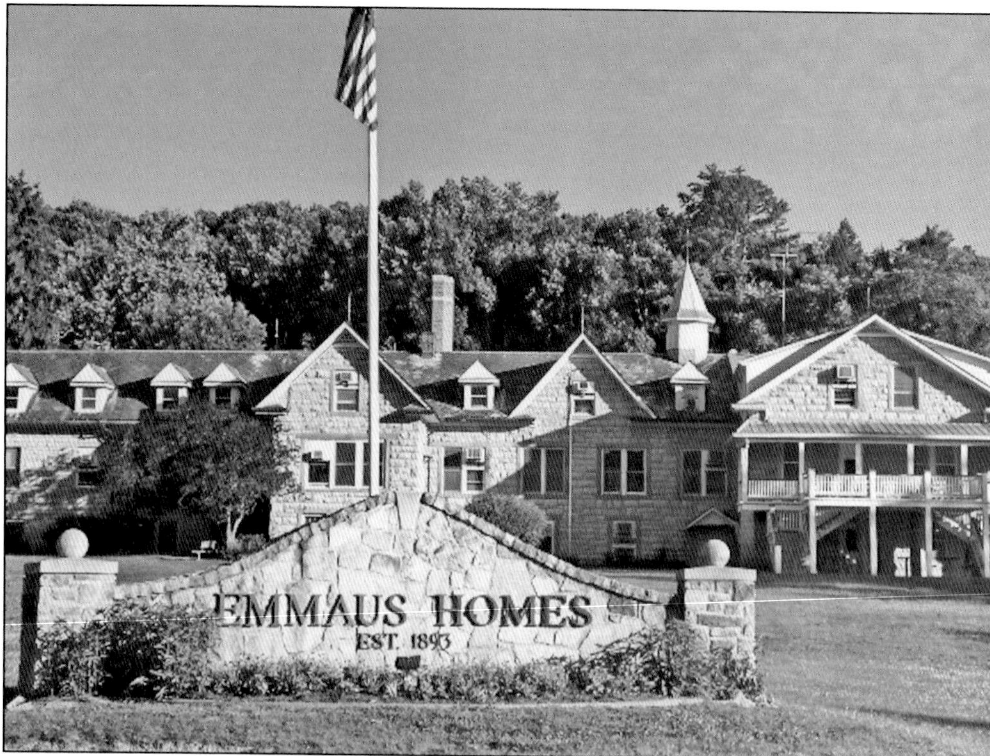

By 1897, all of the early buildings had been repaired, while others were added to the Emmaus Asylum. This is the large main building of the campus, featuring a new chapel with a large steeple and clock tower, one of the first additions to the campus. In 1918, Emmaus had served over 390 residents. Dormitory buildings were added in 1927, but in 1930, a fire destroyed one of the oldest buildings, which was one of the original four of the early seminary. Other buildings have been added to the beautiful campus, which that lies on 100 acres in a valley near Marthasville. The residents and staff are an integral part of the community. As society has come to better understand developmental disabilities, Emmaus's programs have changed and grown. Programs have been developed that address needs of individuals on a variety of levels. Today, it is a mission of the United Church of Christ's Council for Health and Human Service Ministries and serves far beyond the Dutzow community (below).

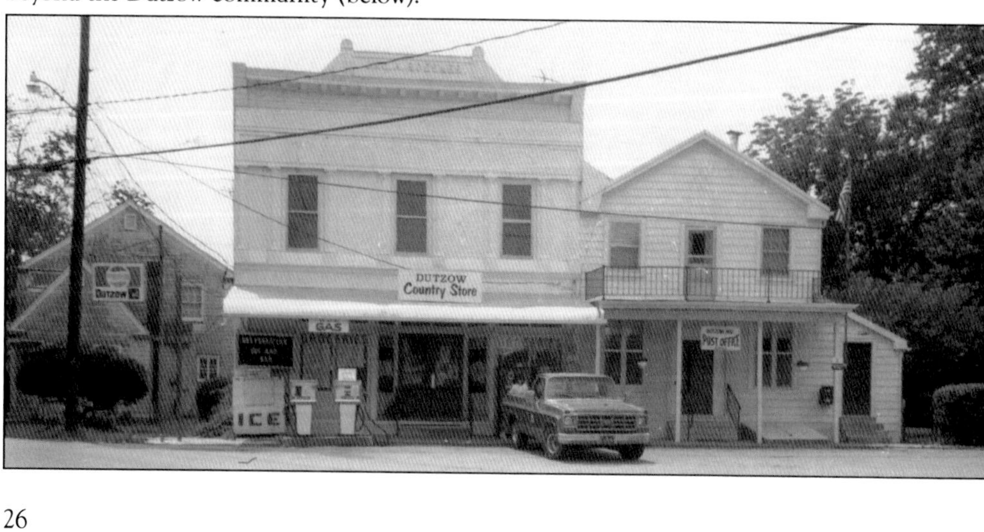

Three

The Civil War

The Civil War in Warren County was a synopsis of the conflicts of the entire state. Early Southern and slave-owning families had filled the state up until German immigrants began arriving in the early 1830s. The immigrants were staunch supporters of individual freedoms after departing Germany for those same reasons. Strong Union supporters, the immigrants' battlefield experiences of their youth combined with their fondness of gymnastics practiced in their local Turnverein halls made them excellent soldiers. Many early families had intermarried with the German immigrants by that time, leaving many families divided amongst themselves by Union or Confederate sympathies. Slave patrols watching for runaways commonly guarded the roadways.

The first shots fired in Warrant County were when Confederate guerrillas attacked a train full of Union soldiers on July 5, 1861. That ambush resulted in the loss of Thomas Edwards. A retaliatory ambush on July 15 led to the arrest of several locals, resulting in the death of Joseph Sublett in a Union prison. By August, angry guerrillas attacked the Wabash, Pacific & St. Louis Railroad and burned the Red Hill Bridge at midnight.

The 3rd Cavalry Missouri State Militia was mustered into service at Warrenton on January 25, 1862, and stationed at Camp Annie, located in Hummel's Pasture, just east of the town near the railroad. In the spring of 1862, Brig. Gen. John Pope encamped 10,000 troops in Warrenton, taking the home of slave owner John Pulliam as his headquarters. The tobacco merchant's home on Main Street served as the site for the local slave auction. Later, the home would become the Colonial Hotel, which still stands today.

In August 1862, the alarm was raised again. H.A. Schoppenhorst was in command of Warren County's Home Guards. A resourceful captain, he housed his men in the courthouse where they used the cupola to stand watch. When food became scarce, he ordered his men to the potato patch, earning him the local nickname of the "Potato Captain."

The Germans were resourceful Union troops, and it was through their efforts that the Confederates in the county were never allowed control.

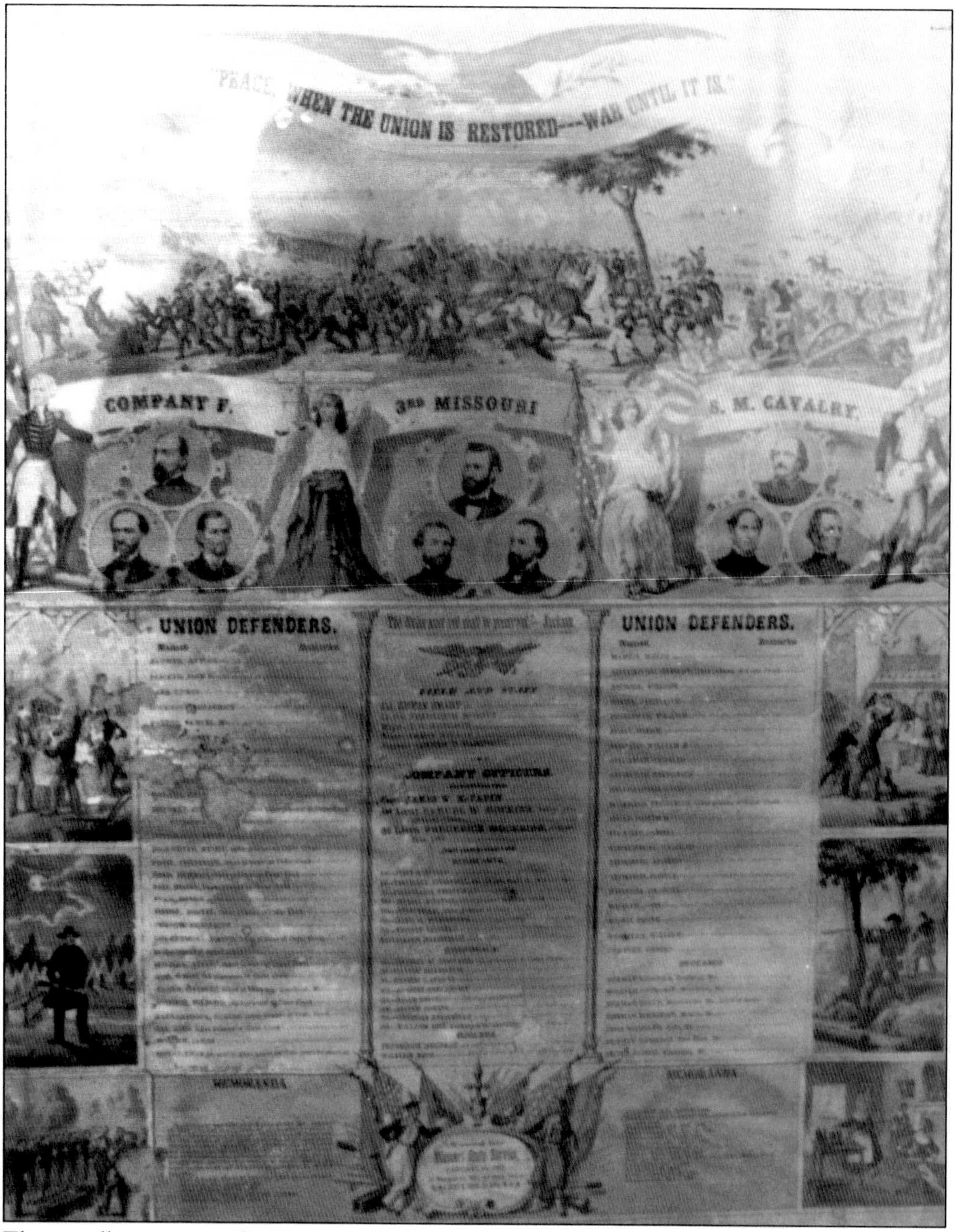

This enrollment poster for Company F of the 3rd Cavalry Missouri State Militia reads, "Peace, when the Union is restored—war until it is." Posters like this proudly displayed the names of the local men who were serving, including the field, staff, and company officers. It also listed the deceased, and in the memoranda at the bottom, it also listed the major events the company had taken part in. Surrounded by patriotic symbols, it surely filled its viewer with strong emotions for supporting or joining their troops in action. In October 1864, things reached a crisis for the 3rd Cavalry as Confederate general Sterling Price was making a final attempt to take Missouri. Many of the troop's enrollees had just finished a three-year stint and were ready to go home to their families when word reached them of the attack on Danville.

Leonidas Dryden purchased land from Mordecai Morgan to establish his home at Warrenton. Dryden, a prominent attorney, received Mandy (below) and her children (right) as a wedding gift. Warrenton was a desired Confederate location. After word came of "Bloody" Bill Anderson being killed at Montgomery County's seat, Danville, on October 27, 1864, the Confederates attacked Warrenton in retaliation. After dark on October 29, a force of 900 troops attacked the railroad there, throwing the train from the tracks. Union colonel Fredrick Morsey had sent a warning to the troops coming from St. Louis of the ambush that was planned. Morsey had received word of the attack at Danville from his son William, who was teaching at the Danville Female Academy when it occurred.

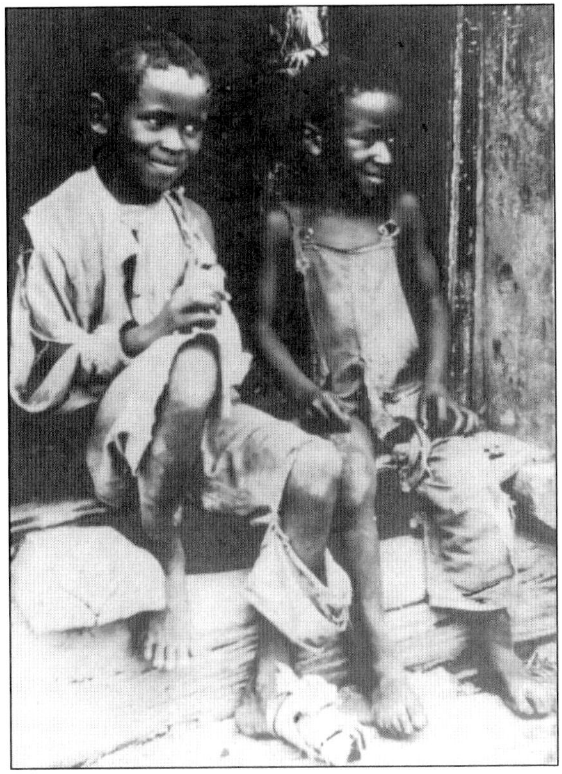

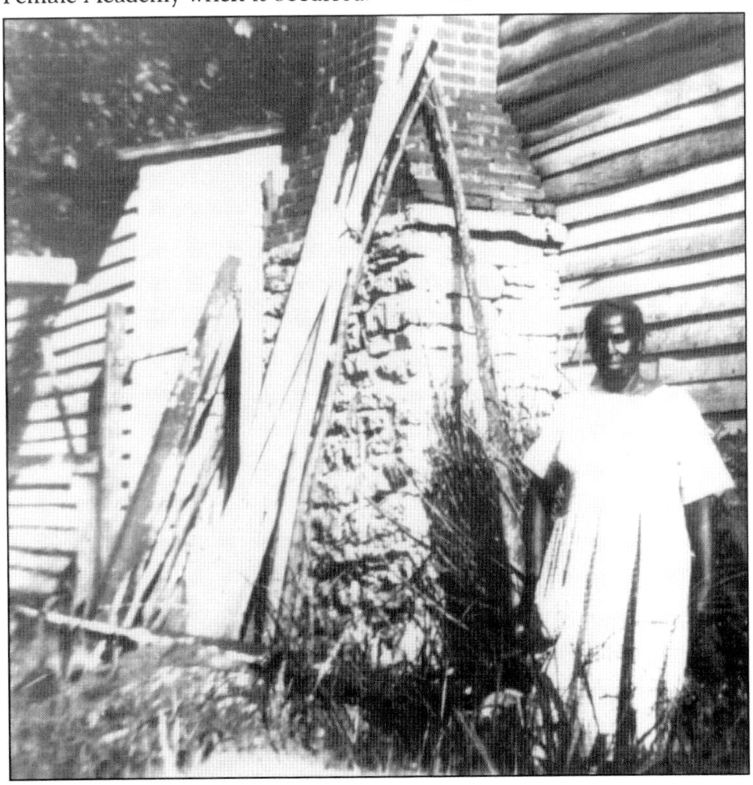

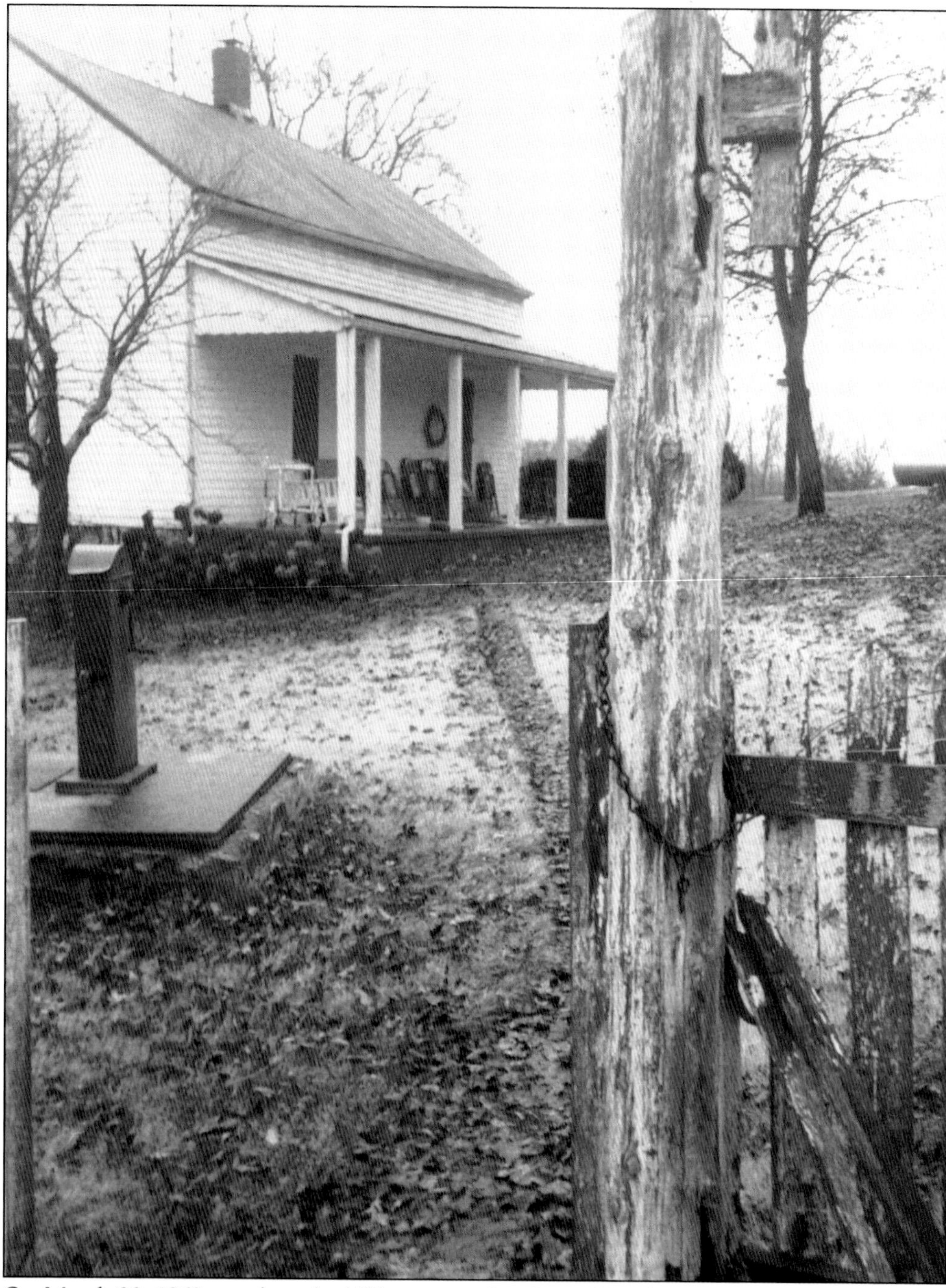

On March 20, 1862, word reached Warrenton that James Henderson, a leading recruiter for the Confederate army, was at the farm of Dr. Warner Brisco, who lived about a mile north of Marthasville. Henderson had lost his wife and most of his family in a steamboat explosion, for which he blamed the Union army. He and his son were injured and had come to their friend Dr. Brisco for medical assistance. Capt. James W. McFadden and Company F of the 3rd Missouri Cavalry, stationed at Warrenton, learned about Henderson's activities and hiding place. Determined to capture Henderson at Brisco's home, the 3rd Missouri quietly surrounded the farmhouse.

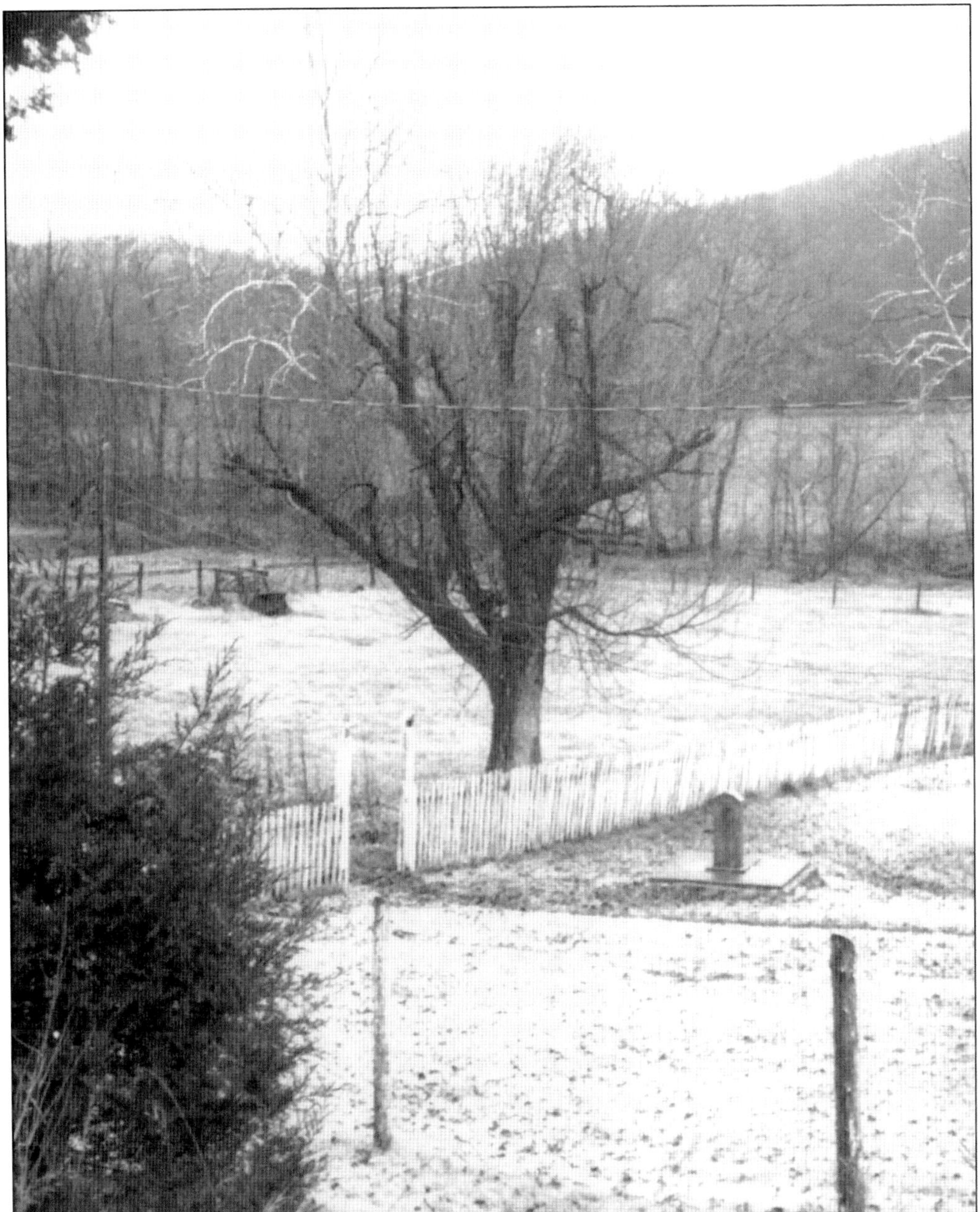

The 3rd Missouri Cavalry stationed themselves on the surrounding hillsides in thickets of trees outside of Dr. Warner Brisco's house, but word had somehow reached Confederate recruiter James Henderson about what was going to happen. A demand for surrender was given. Henderson and his son donned the clothing of Brisco's wife and daughter and attempted to escape the house. The son dashed for the barn, where the horses were stabled. As Henderson attempted to reach the barn, a volley of shots opened upon the man, wounding him. One lodged in the fence's gatepost. Henderson fell wounded as he ran through the gate. The entire company had opened fire upon the man and the house. The house was riddled with bullets, and the windows were broken. Henderson was taken to Warrenton for medical attention but died within days. His son survived, and the house still stands today with a musket ball embedded in its wall.

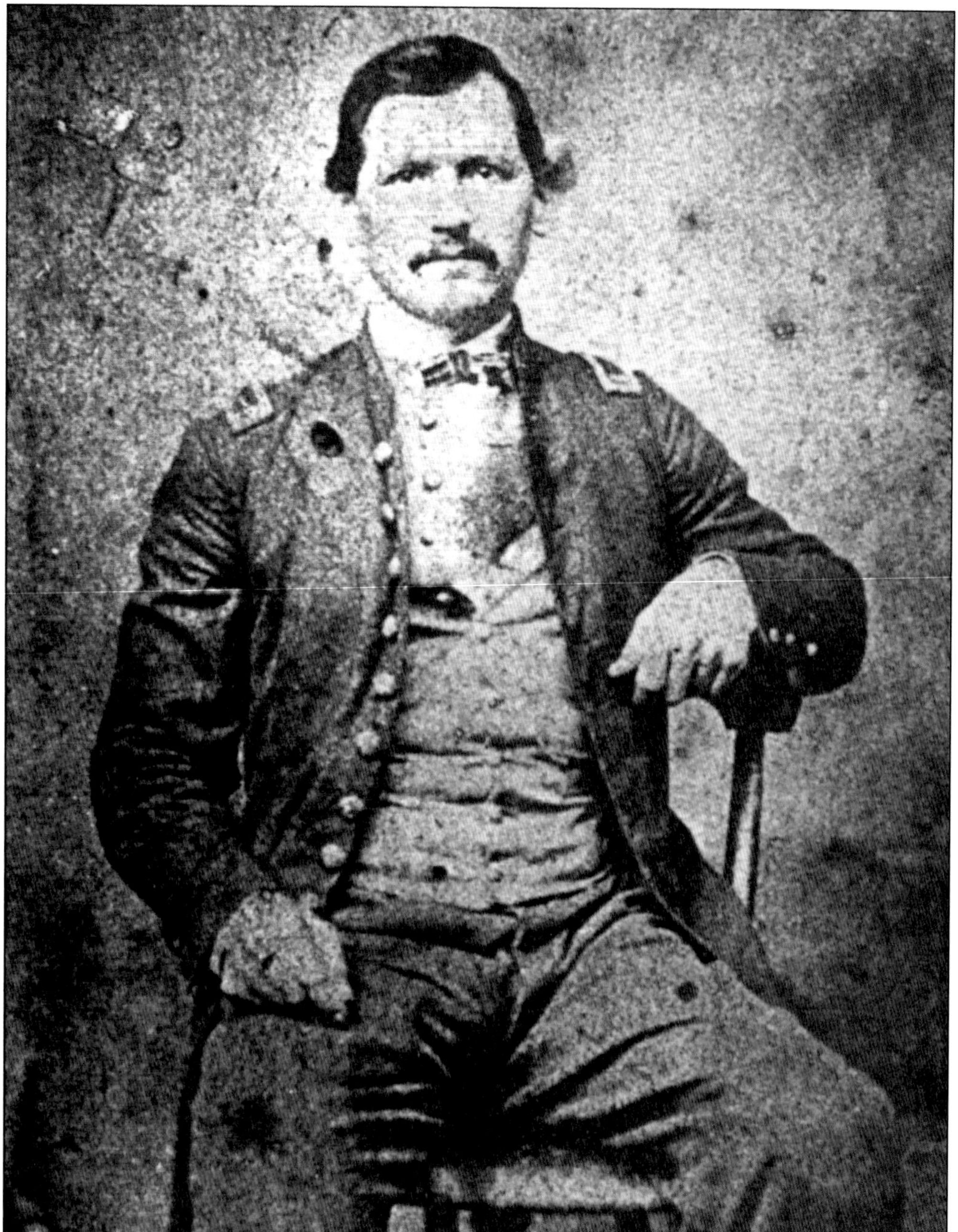

J. Gottlieb Hummel and his wife, Marie, emigrated from Germany in the late 1850s, to purchase land near her brother, Christian Strecker, in Warren County. When the Civil War began, Gottlieb enlisted in the Union army in a volunteer regiment composed solely of German-speaking soldiers. He had begun his military training in Germany. His commission papers were signed by Abraham Lincoln, and with some additional training, he quickly advanced to lieutenant. In a battle near Antietam, Maryland, he was wounded in the leg, which resulted in amputation. In 1863, he returned home to Warrenton and to his wife and children Wilhelm, Louis, Martha, and August, but he died in 1868 from pneumonia.

Four

Central Wesleyan

With the Civil War came thousands of widows and fatherless children. German Methodist churches realized the need for an orphanage and purchased 940 acres from the William Truesdale estate on April 14, 1864, with the intention to build one. The German Methodist Conference formed its first board of trustees, placed the orphanage inside Truesdale's former plantation house, and constructed a new two-story building next to it to be used as a school. In 1865, the organization registered its name as the Western Orphan Asylum and Educational Institute, and the first child was welcomed in by July 20. In March 1870, the name of the institution was formally changed to become the Central Wesleyan College and Orphan Home. A primary school began at the orphanage, but with no upper school, students from the orphanage would just proceed on to the new college for free.

The entire complex, college, and orphanage had one superintendent, Rev. Philip Kuhl, who began work in 1865 and was lovingly known as "Papa Kuhl." Farming operations provided financial support for the orphanage, and the farm was laid out on about half of the 300 acres that the institution had retained. Sales of about 600 acres of the land purchased had provided funds for building projects and other improvements. Crops of wheat, oats, and hay were grown and harvested, while cattle, hogs, chickens, and horses were also raised on the farm.

In June 1884, the orphanage and the college were separated and each given their own charter by the State of Missouri. The college retained 30 acres, and the orphanage was given the balance. By 1921, the orphanage had housed over 665 children. The college, which had opened its doors on October 3, 1864, with a class of 179, had grown rapidly, and soon it became a thriving, integral part of Warrenton.

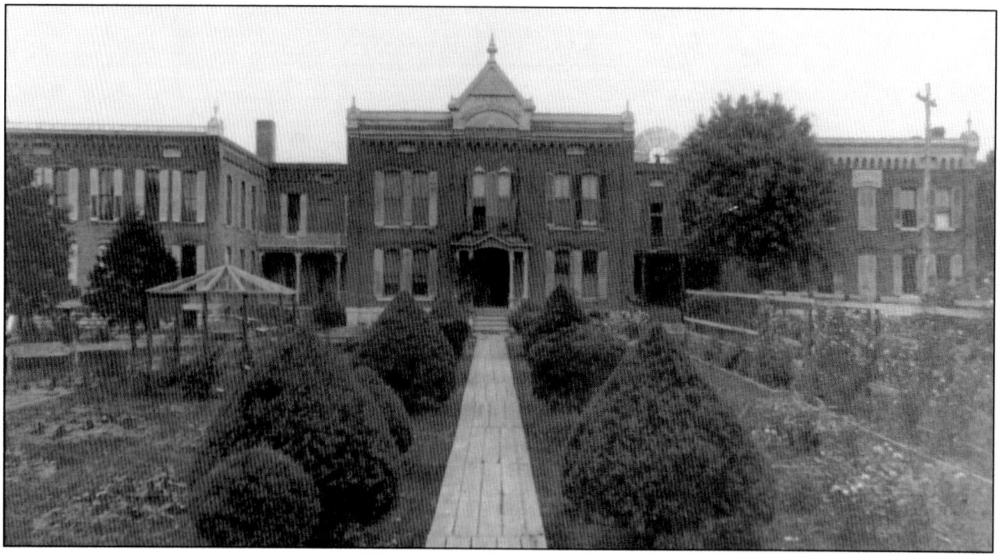

The purpose of the orphanage was "to establish and maintain a home for orphans and such other children as may be received into the home, to take care of them physically, mentally, and morally, to feed clothe and educated them, and to provide as far as possible for their present and future welfare." The center building seen above was originally the home of William Truesdale and had a windmill behind that originally powered the water system. The addition to the left was constructed first to house dormitories and classrooms, followed by the addition to the right. The image below shows the cafeteria, kitchens, and laundry building. Everything was arranged with neatness and served a purpose.

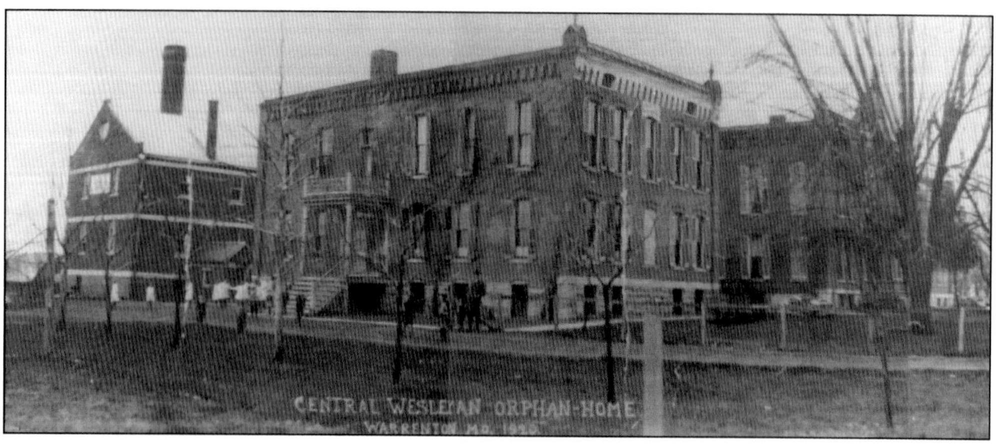

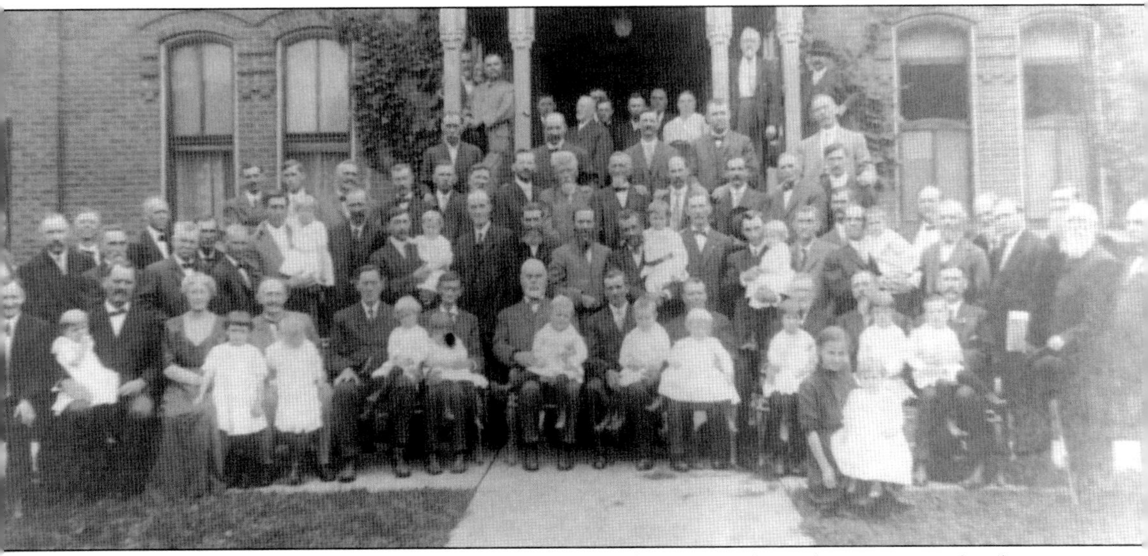

The Western Orphan Asylum and Educational Institute charter stated, "In the reception of orphans and children, neither shall the reception of scholars depend upon their religious profession, but the school shall be open to all students possessing a good moral character."

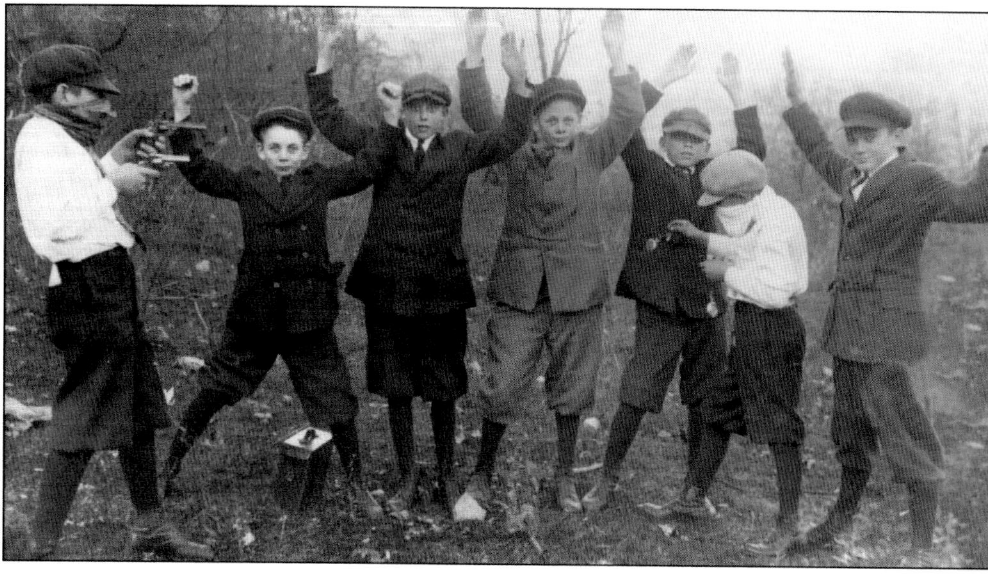

During the first school year, there was an attendance of about 190 pupils, including orphans. That next year, troops of US soldiers made a descent upon the community but were quickly informed that it was not a slave owner's plantation home. Occasionally, the students were required to serve military duty by guarding the town. The young boys in these photographs are apparently enjoying a game of make-believe, followed by a good tug-of-war contest.

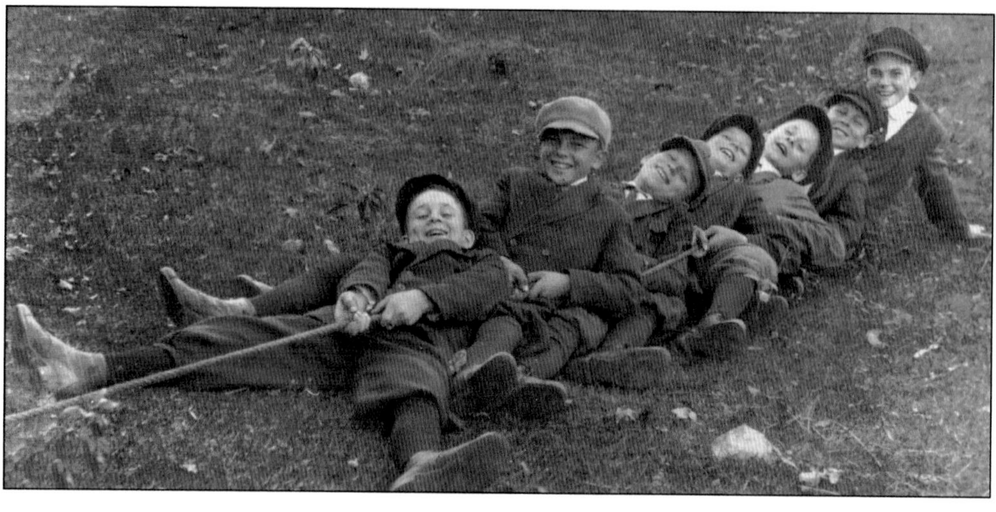

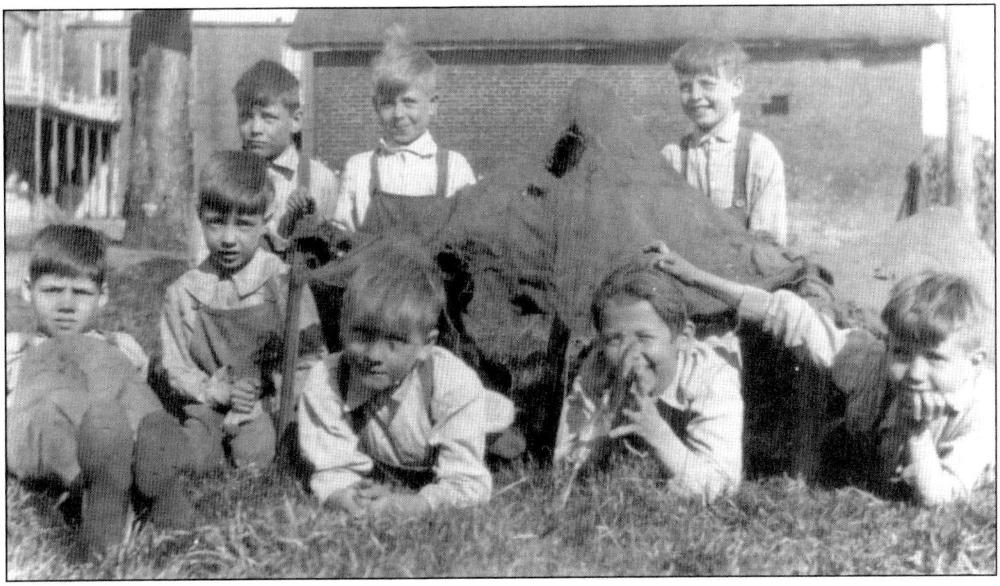

Dr. Koch, who was connected with the school from the beginning, soon received the aid of three assistant teachers. The school portion opened, offering the following courses of study: primary, classical, scientific, commercial, and normal. In 1878, the college boarding department was separated from the orphanage, and Rev. C. Heidel was appointed superintendent of the orphanage and farm. The orphanage would continue under its own auspices, separate from the college.

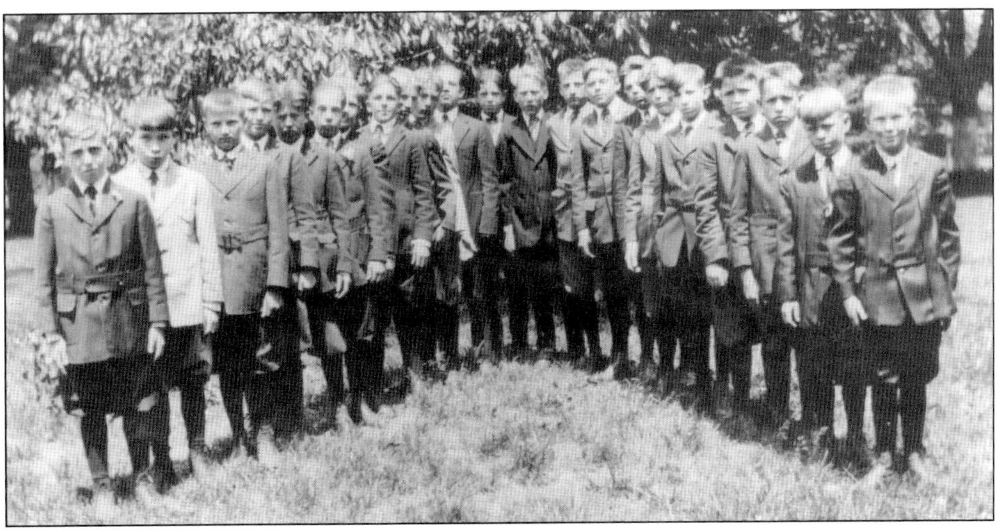

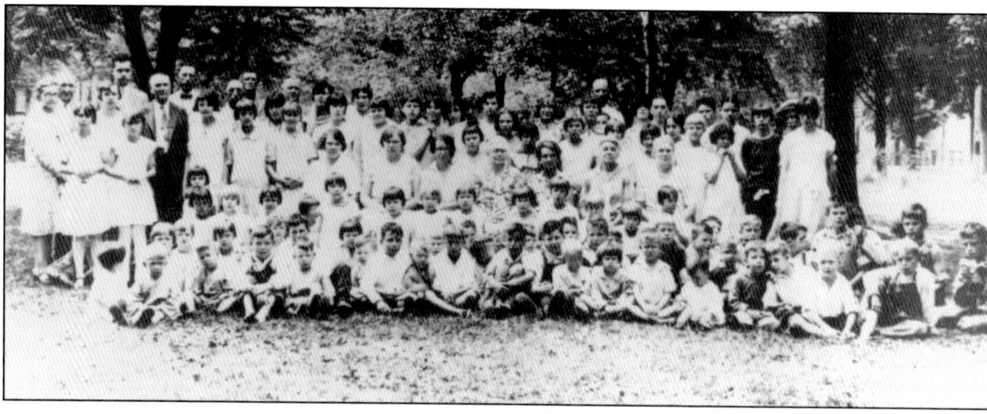

By 1902, there were about 100 orphans at the home, but the number began to fall back after that. The orphanage dorms were replaced by cottages that offered a more family-style residence. By 1929, the Northern German Methodist and the English Methodist Conferences merged. Because of the economic times and all of the mergers and changes, the orphanage was forced to close in 1939.

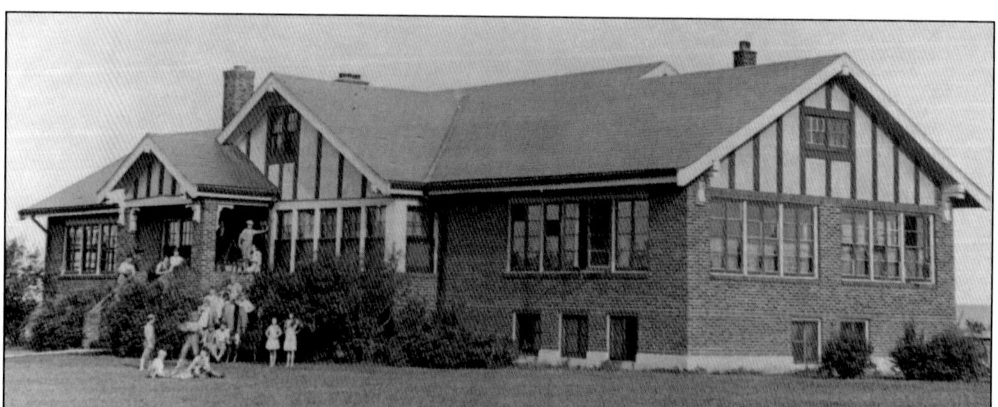

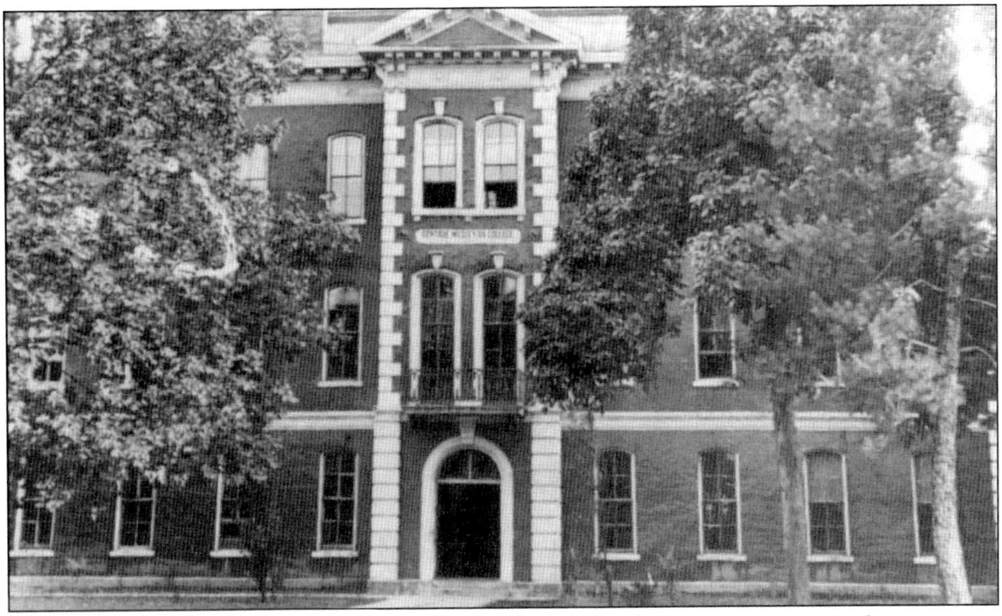

In 1883, steps were taken for a separation of the college and orphanage, and by 1884, the separation was complete. The Central Wesleyan College had a completely separate board of trustees, with the first board of directors appointed by the St. Louis and Western German Conference of the Methodist Episcopal Church. In 1875, the three-story Main College Building was constructed, but a few years later, it was damaged by a huge tornado that swept the county. The school's first small chapel, the Jubilee Chapel, was replaced in 1913 by the College Methodist Episcopal Church. Both the Hinners pipe organ and the large Gothic stained glass windows in the west wall of the Jubilee Chapel were installed in the new church building.

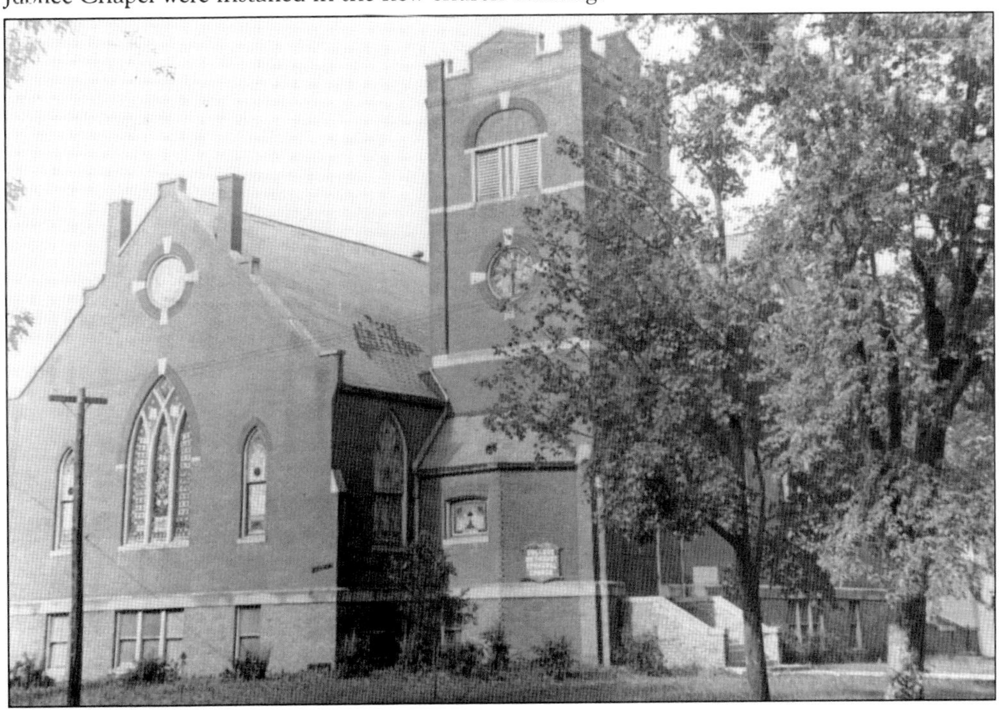

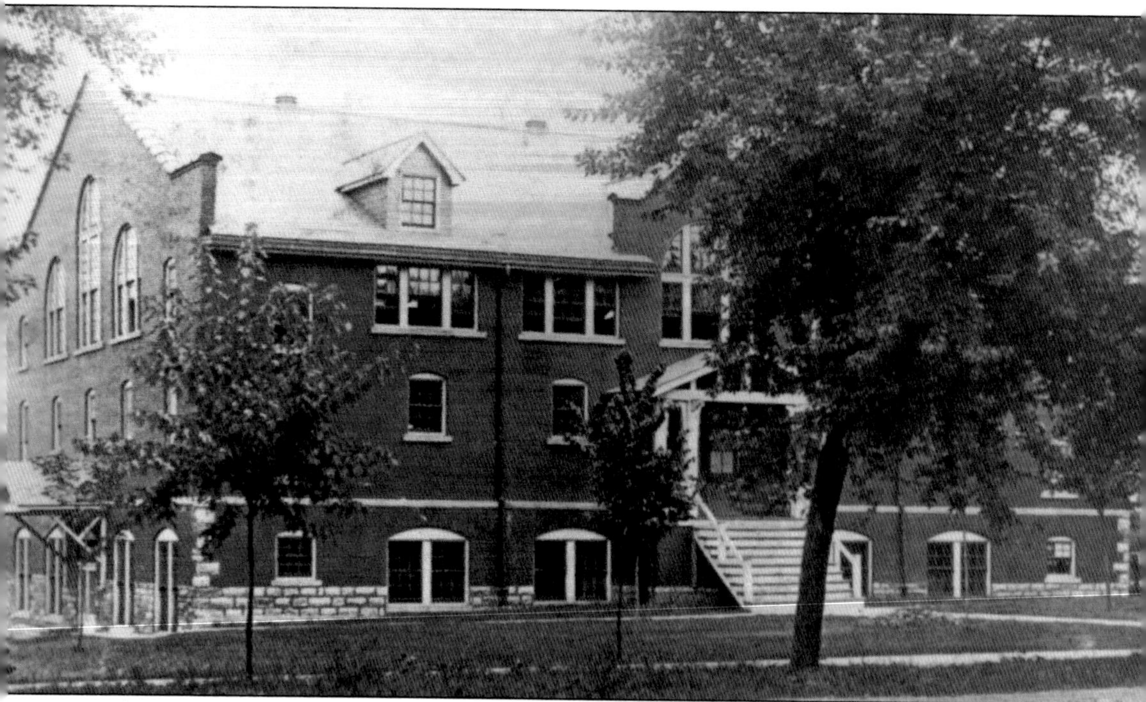

The gymnasium was reputed to have been one of the best when it was constructed in 1909. The first game played on January 16, 1909, was against rival Kemper Military Academy, and was won by Central Wesleyan, 49-16. The lower basement level under the gymnasium held science labs with classrooms.

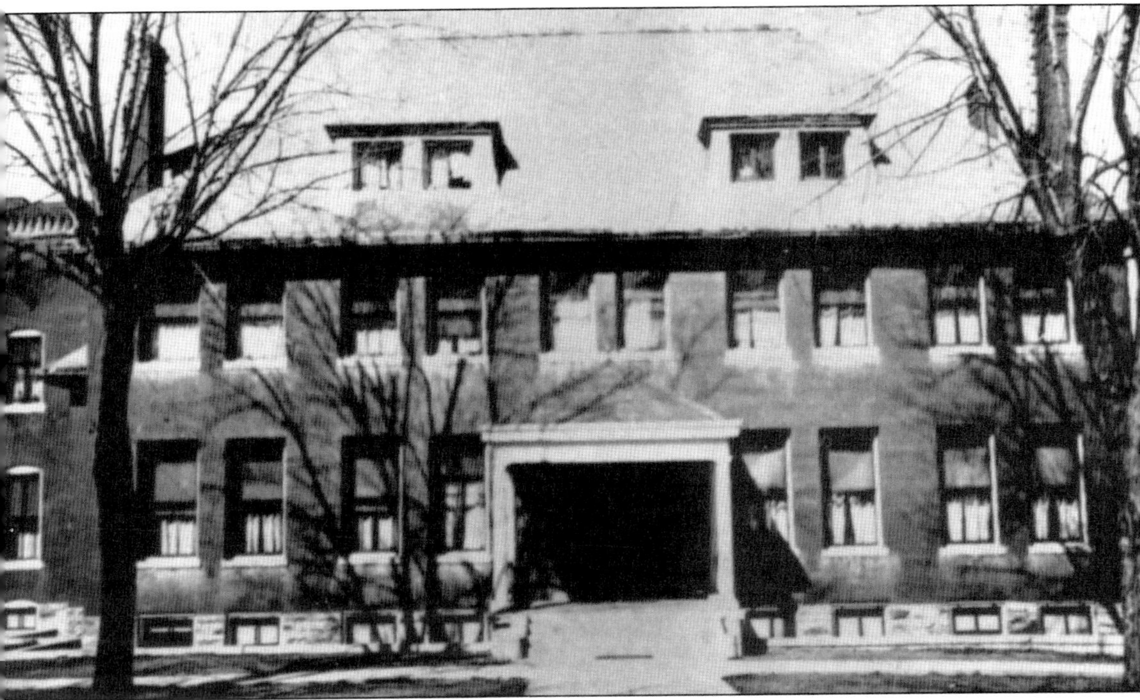

This women's dormitory, built in 1894, contained the campus's large dining hall. Dorm rooms were shared at the cost of $31.50 for the nine-week term in 1910. At that time, tuition was $9 per course of study. Eventually, the Depression and the merger of the Northern German Methodist and the English Methodist Conferences caused hard times, forcing the college closed its doors for the final time during spring term of 1941.

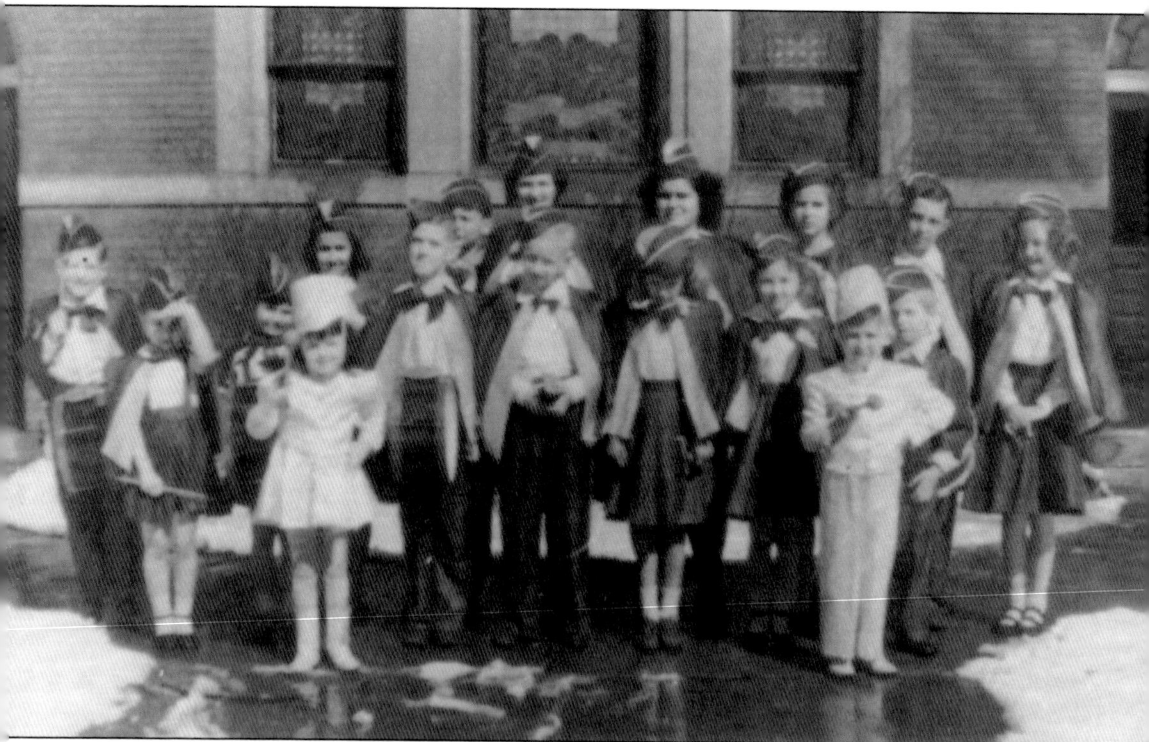

The college buildings continued to serve as the community's central hub for all the social events. In 1949, the Rhythm Band of the New Truxton School demonstrated its talents for everyone's enjoyment.

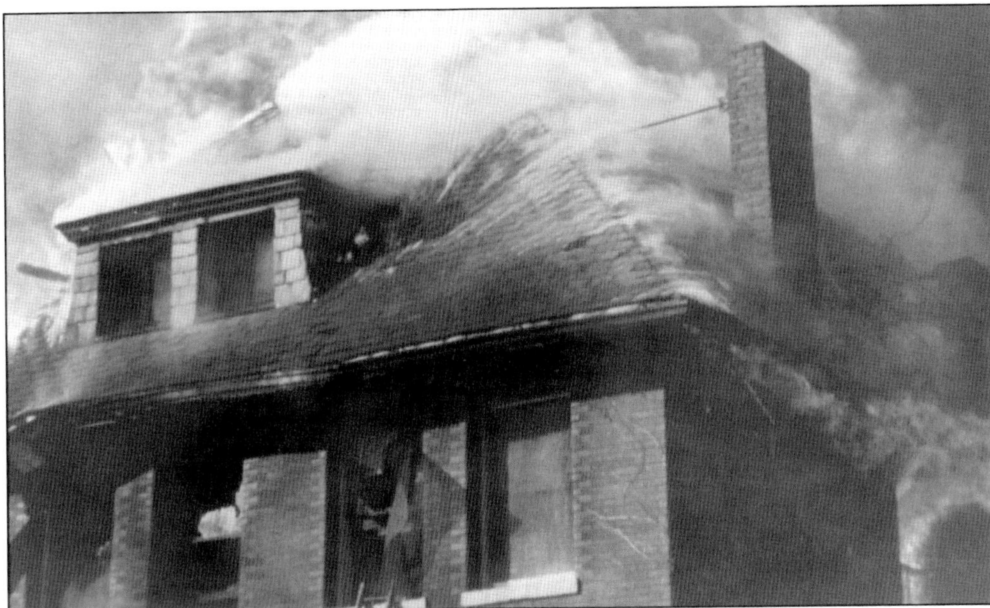

At 2:30 during a peaceful Sunday afternoon on February 17, 1957, one could find many friends and family visiting at the local Katie Jane Nursing Home, housed in the former girls' dormitory of the Central Wesleyan College. There were a total of 194 residents when a sudden fire engulfed the building that day, leaving behind a death toll of 72 persons. Seventy-one people died that day, with one individual passing away the day after. Heavy black clouds of smoke filled the sky when volunteer firefighters arrived minutes after the alarm was sounded. Rescuers worked frantically, pulling residents out of doors and windows, and the entire community sprang into action. The event, the deadliest nursing home fire in Missouri's history, led to sweeping reforms in the industry.

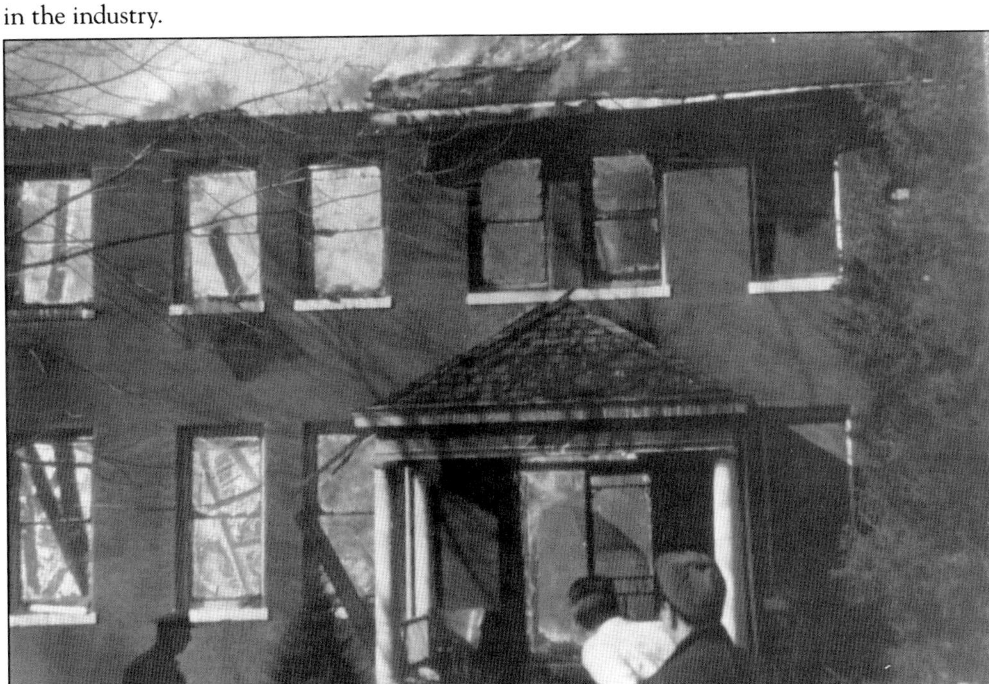

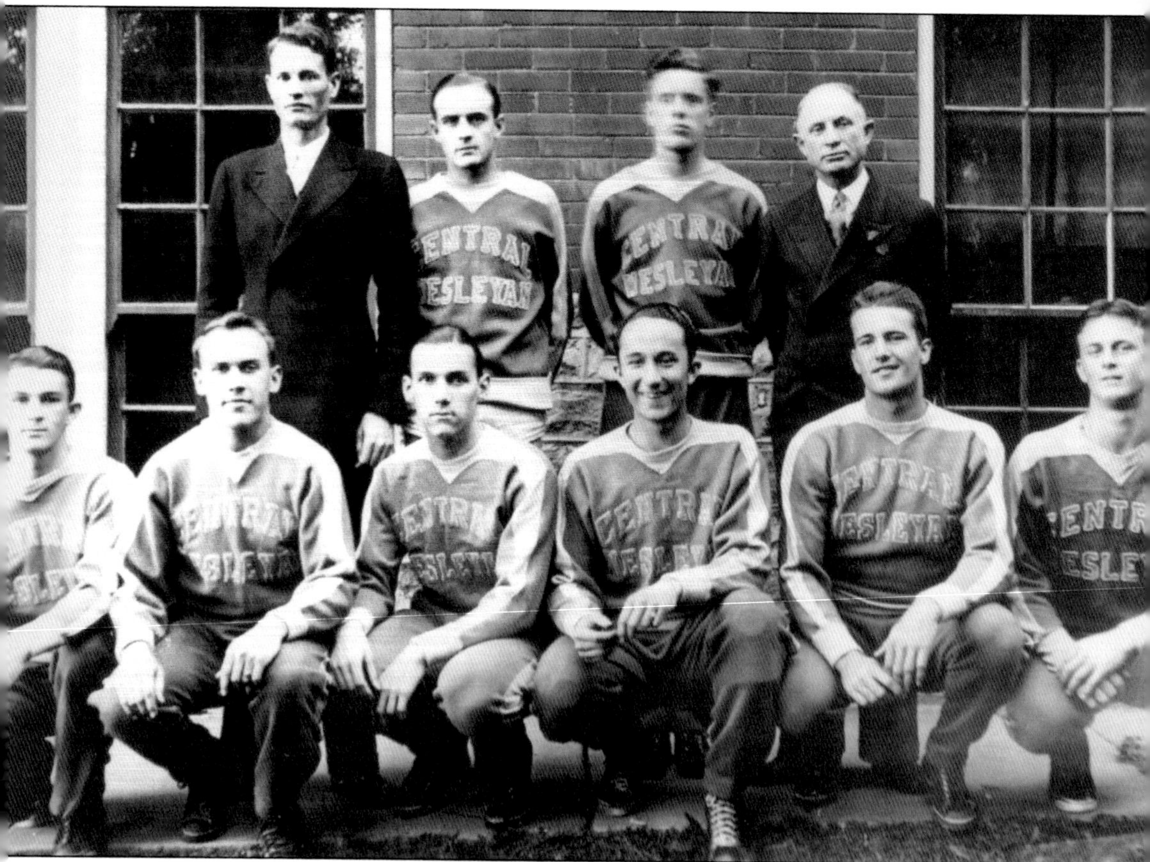

Gone are the days of track teams and basketball teams, memories of plays in Kessler Hall, the blue and white school colors, the football games, and school songs. The community had struggled through the lean times, supported the college programs, and sent its finest young people to be educated, both academically and spiritually. The college had become an integral part of Warrenton and Warren County. Many of the city's and county's most important events had been held on the campus. Daily life centered around the events at the college. Warrenton and Warren County were known statewide for being the home of the Central Wesleyan College. A very intrinsic part of Warren County's history was gone forever with its doors closing.

Five

Cities, Towns, and Communities

While every community is important to those who live there, some cities and towns have played a more prominent role in Warren County's history than others. Beginning in 1818, the town of Pinckney was established as the seat of Montgomery County. Pinckney was a thriving town with streets named Commons, Market, Main, Front, and High intersecting Mulberry, McKinney, Main Cross, and Sharp. There were several thriving businesses, a mill, and both Methodist and Evangelical churches. The courthouse and jail were also busy locations. The Pinckney Academical Society had established a school. However, the town's location would be its downfall, as it sat directly along the shifting Missouri River. In 1824, a major flood overtook the town, with the river cutting a course to its north, and all business within the important town was halted. The court was briefly moved to Lewiston. As the river receded, an outcry arose, with residents clamoring that the seat of justice be moved to a more central location and away from the danger of flooding. Although the town rebuilt, Montgomery moved its county seat to Danville. Pinckney rebuilt and survived the Great Flood of 1844, but its final death blows came with the floods of the 1870s and 1880s. When the waters receded, the Missouri River had changed its course, staying within that newly created northern channel and leaving the town of Pinckney inside Franklin County. While many towns have come and gone in Warren County's history, none of them did it quite like Pinckney.

Many of Warren County's lost and forgotten communities can only be found in the chronicles of the post office. Many find their beginning when one enterprising merchant opens his mercantile and an application for a post office is made. Some towns, like Tuque, Abbatis, and Brandts Spring, never made it much past that point.

Other towns began with the arrival of the railroad as a necessary stop on the line. Towns like Bud, Gore, and Case were created for such reasons. Some grew while others disappeared, but all were considered home at some point in time.

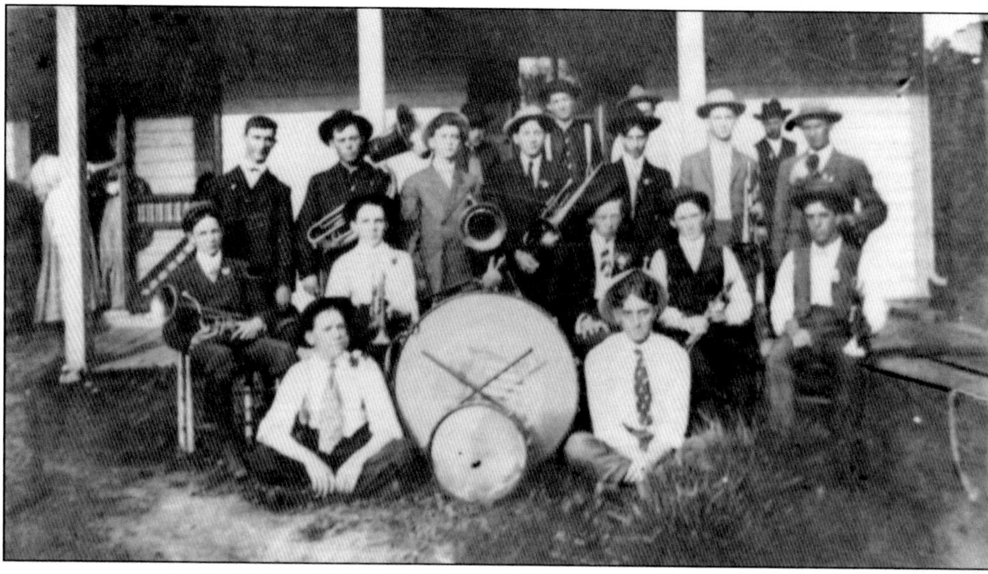

The picture above is the Wright City Band musicians, which included Fritz Krome, bass violin; William Kemner, lead violin; Louis Blattner, lead violin or cornet; George Blattner, second violin; and F.W. Schnadt, cornet or trombone. Sometimes, Mr. Schramek or Mr. Pagel would join in with their clarinets. Below is the Nieburg Manufacturing Company in 1906, when it was the only three-story structure with an elevator in Warren County.

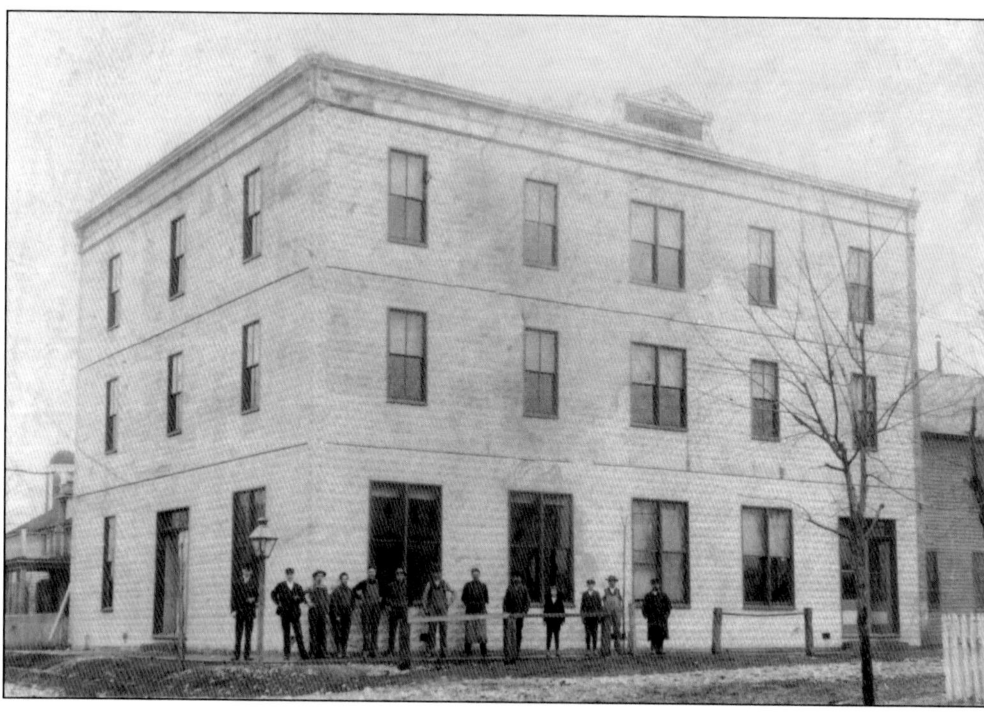

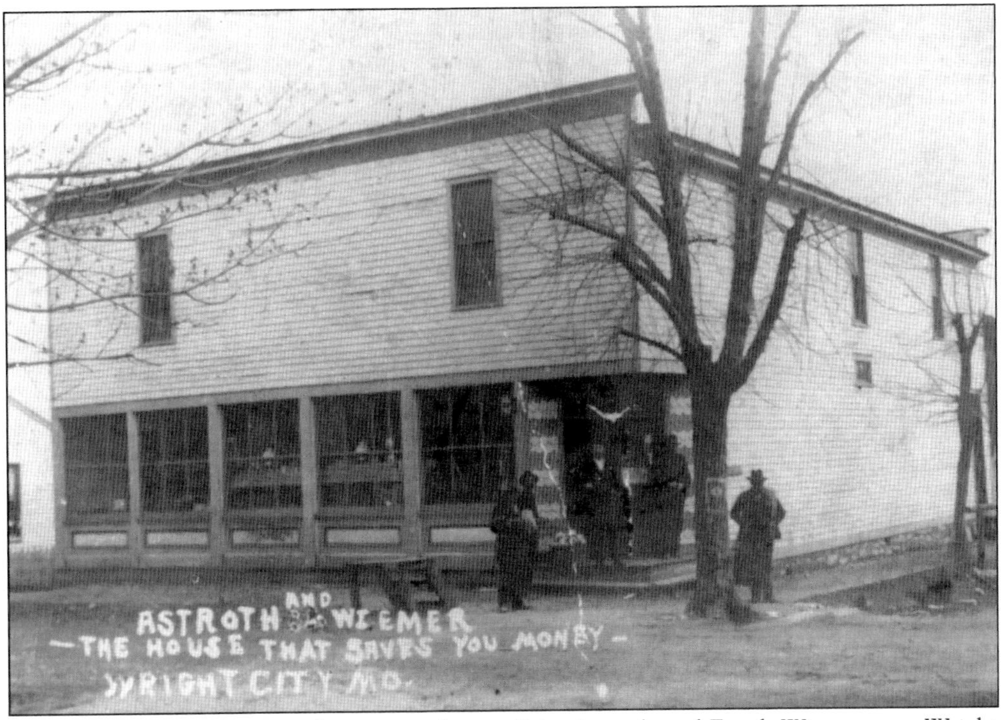

Second-generation German Americans August Fritz Astroth and Frank Wiemer gave Wright City "the store that saves you money." Frank Wiemer had begun the business earlier with his first partner, Frank Strack. The buggy seen below was made by the experienced mechanics at the Nieburg Manufacturing Company in Wright City, Missouri, and was durable, made of seasoned material, and strictly first-class. Fredrick Nieburg began making wagons in 1857 on his 80-acre farm west of Wright City in Pitts. He also constructed made-to-order coffins with the deceased's measurements, which sometimes required working late at night to deliver the order.

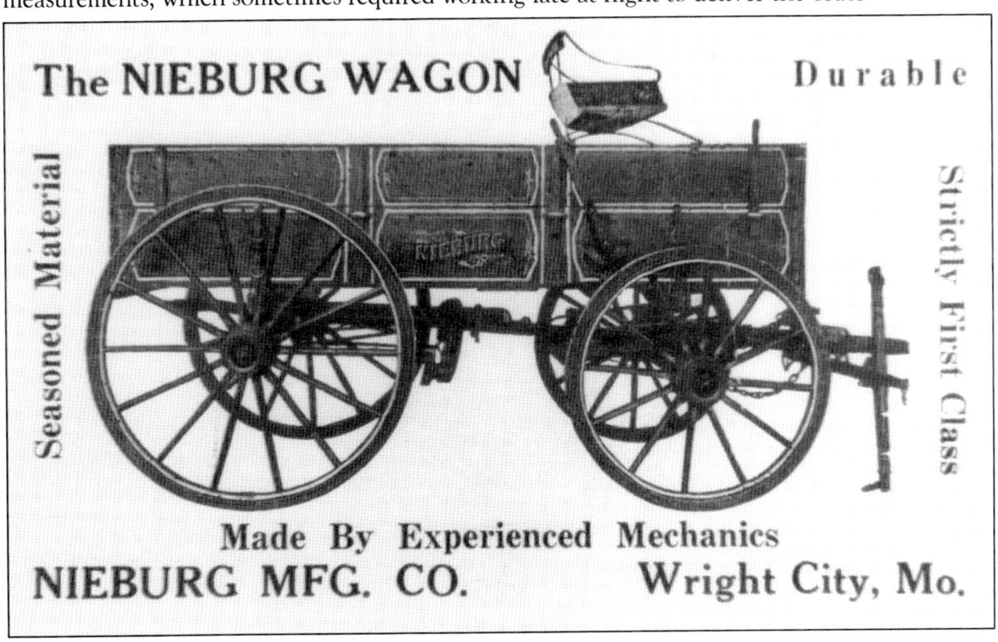

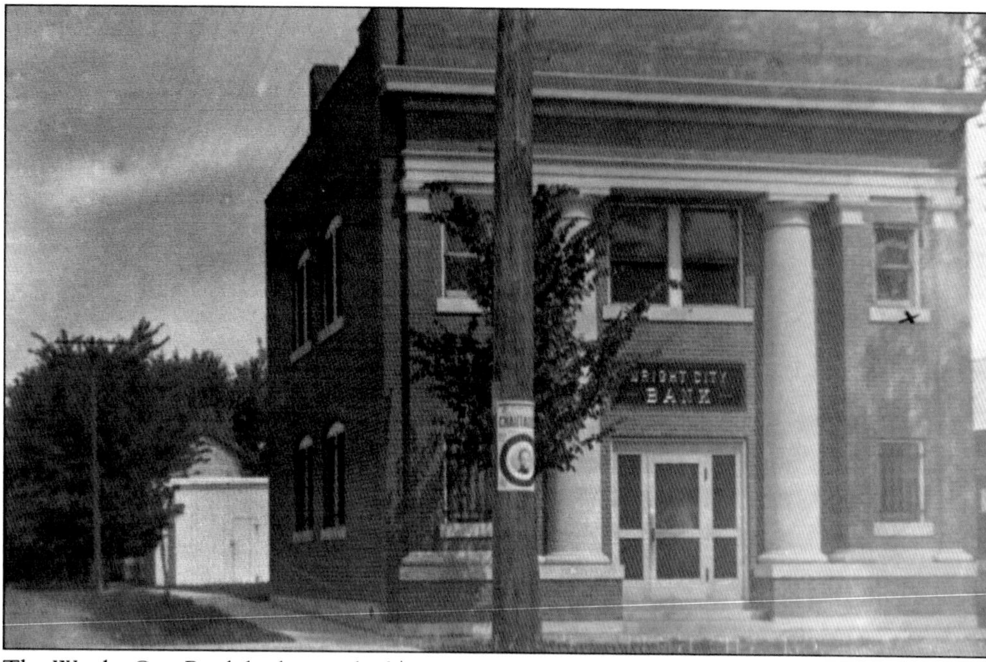

The Wright City Bank had capital of $35,000 in 1914, making it a proud asset for the city. The board of directors was a list of who's who at the time: G.W. Schaper, C.G. Nieburg, E.A. Flusmeier, F. Krome, H.H. Strathmann, and J.H. Eversmeyer. Wright City also enjoyed businesses like Richard J. Gempp's Saloon, where posters advertised the August Busch Lager beer for sale inside. Richard had been born in St. Louis to early German immigrants and opened his first saloon as a young man in Truesdale. By the early 1900s, he had opened this saloon and was also serving as the town's justice of peace. This must have saved time if there were any incidents at the saloon—they could instantly be brought to the attention of the local magistrate.

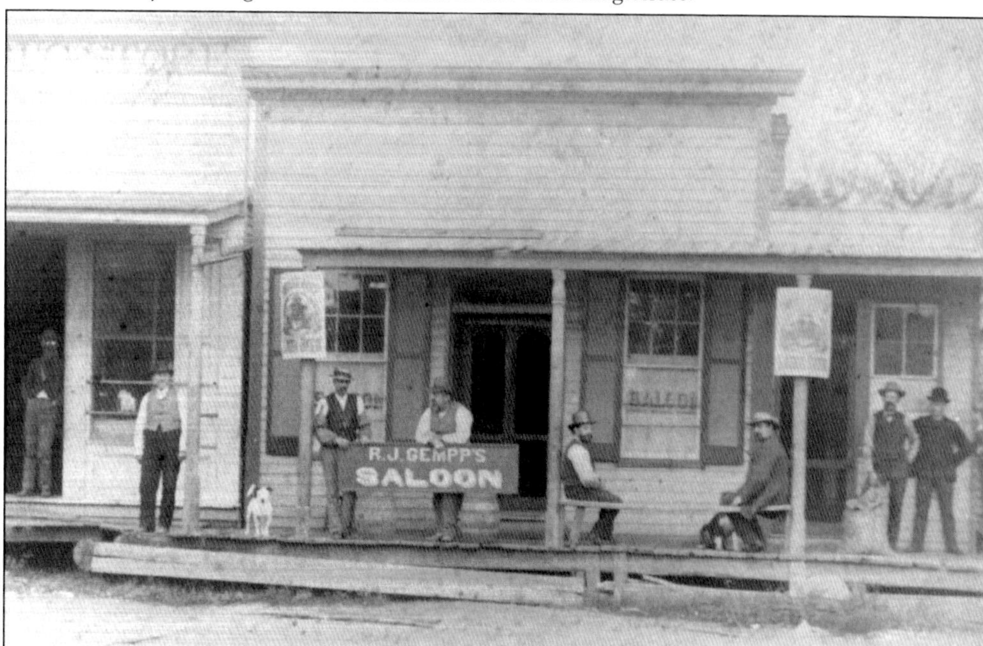

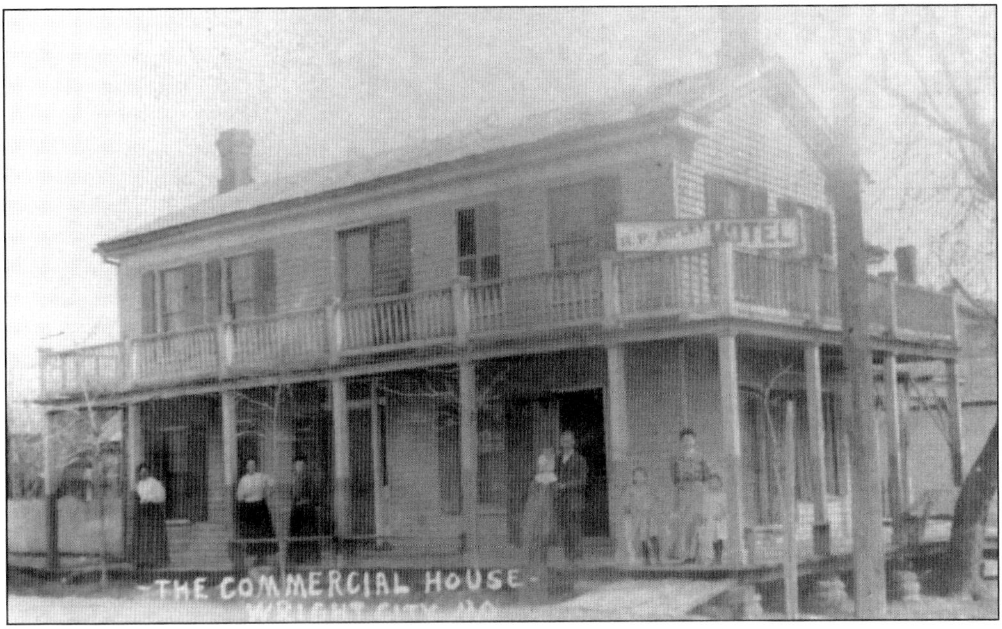

Robert P. Aspley was born in Kentucky and had moved to Lincoln County, Missouri, as a farmer before opening the Commercial House Hotel in Wright City. In the image above, his wife, Margaret, and their daughter stand near the office door alongside the workers to the left. Another local businessman was Capt. Ernst Fredrick Ordelheide, whose store also housed the post office and the telephone exchange. Capt. Ordelheide had emigrated from Germany at age 18, and shortly thereafter, he served as captain in Company E of the 3rd Missouri Cavalry under Col. Fredrick Morsey.

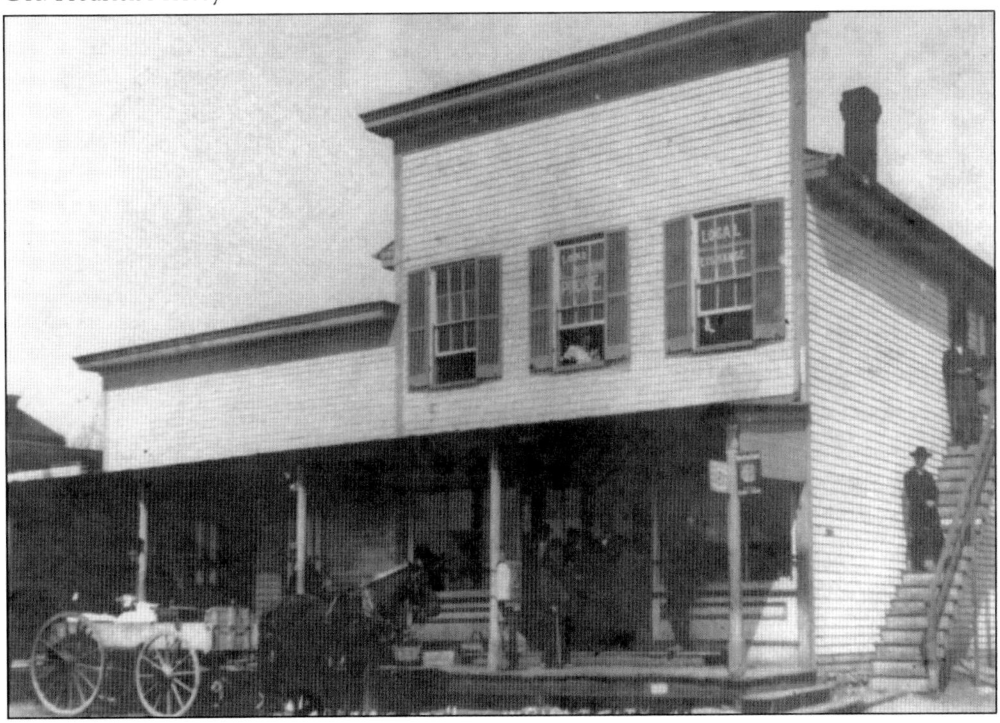

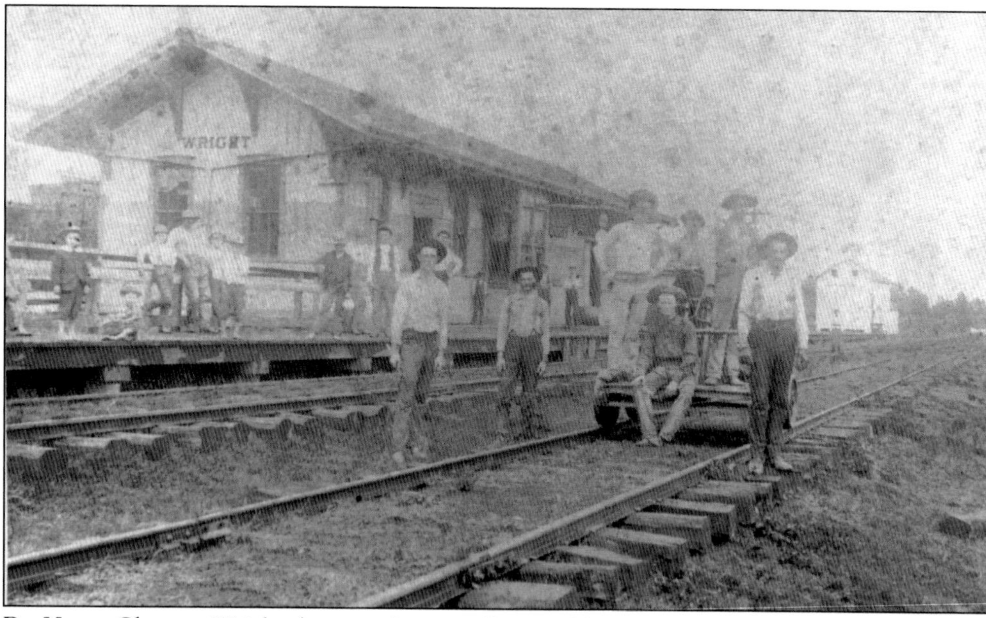

Dr. Henry Cleggett Wright, born in Augusta County, Virginia, in 1805, came to Missouri as a boy in 1822. In 1832, he purchased 100 acres of land, where he built his home; he purchased 80 acres more in 1845. A large slave owner, he also served in the state legislature and one year in the state senate. He used his influence for a depot for the St. Louis, Kansas City, & North Missouri Railroad to be located in his new town of Wright City in 1857. J.V. Hayes drew up the plat and surveyed the original town, which consisted of 15 blocks north of the track. Seen above is the Wright City depot. With the railroad came business, such as the Nieburg Wagon Company, as seen below. In 1859, the company was established in Pitts, but it moved to Wright City in 1874.

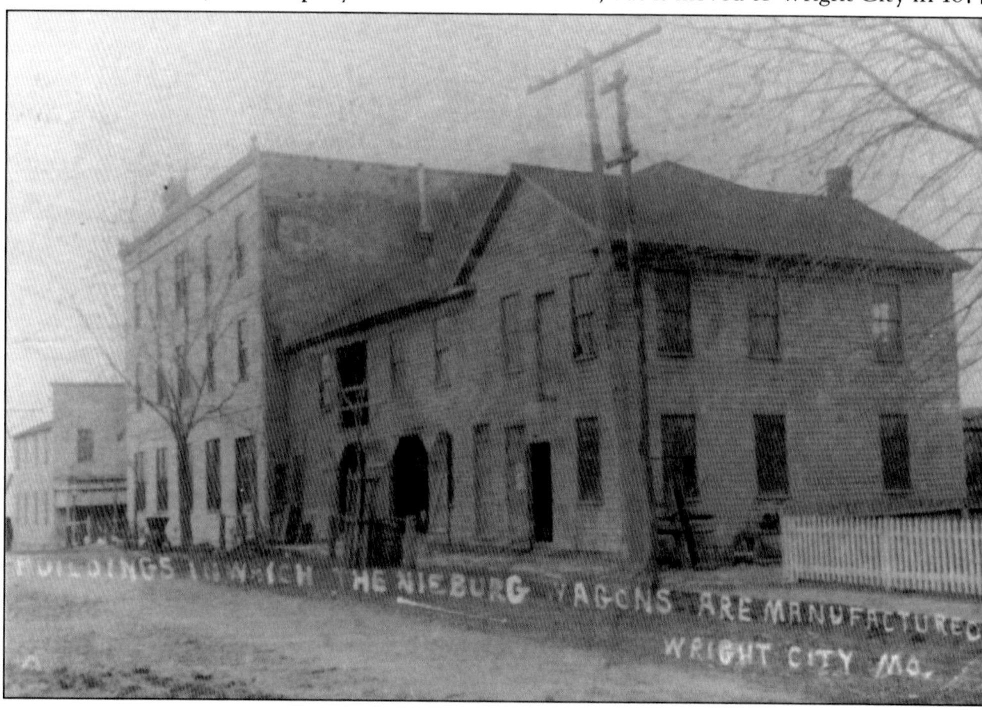

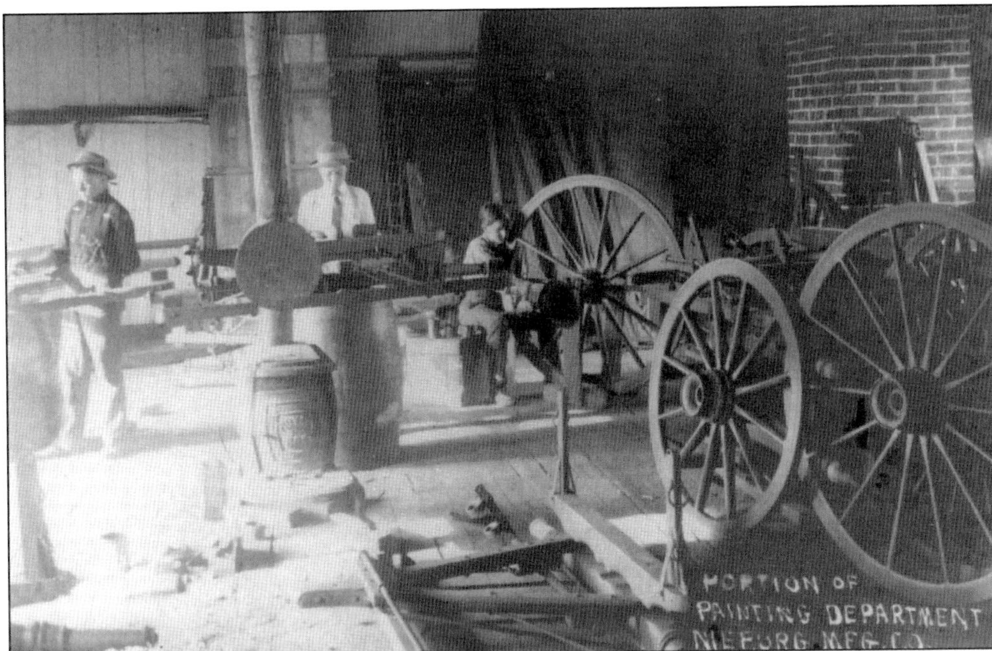

Friedrich Nieburg was born in Germany and immigrated to the United States through New Orleans at age 20 in 1855. After Nieburg moved his wagon factory to Wright City, he passed away in 1889. Three of his young sons, Charles, Otto, and William, continued his business on their mother's behalf until 1892, when it officially became the Nieburg Manufacturing Company. Charles became general manager and was trained in artistic carriage painting. Otto managed the iron works, and William managed all woodworking details

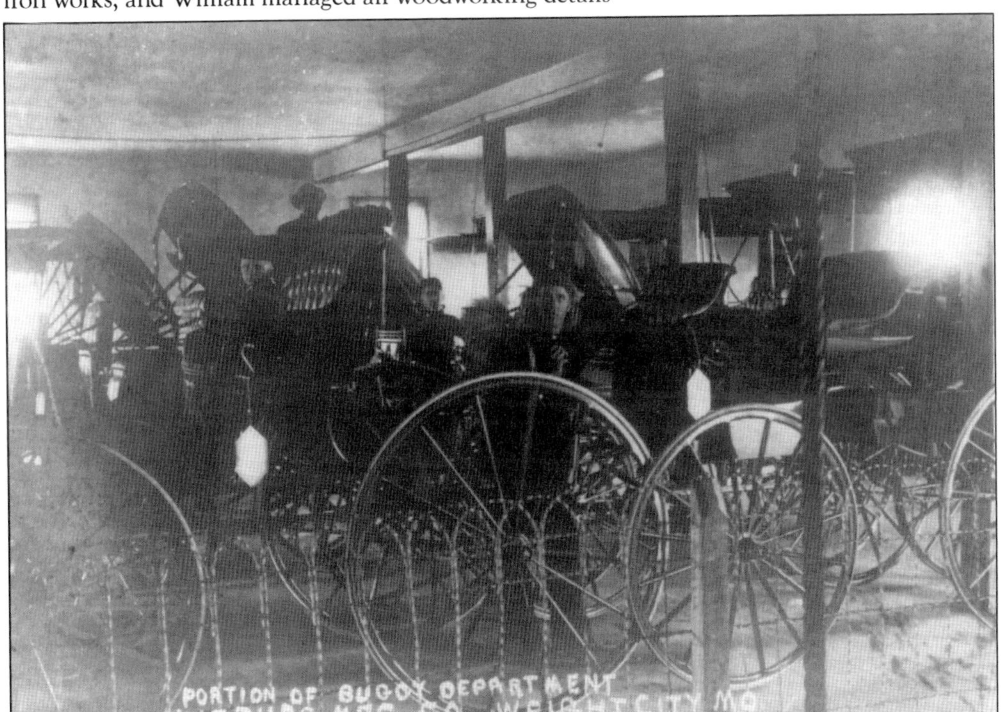

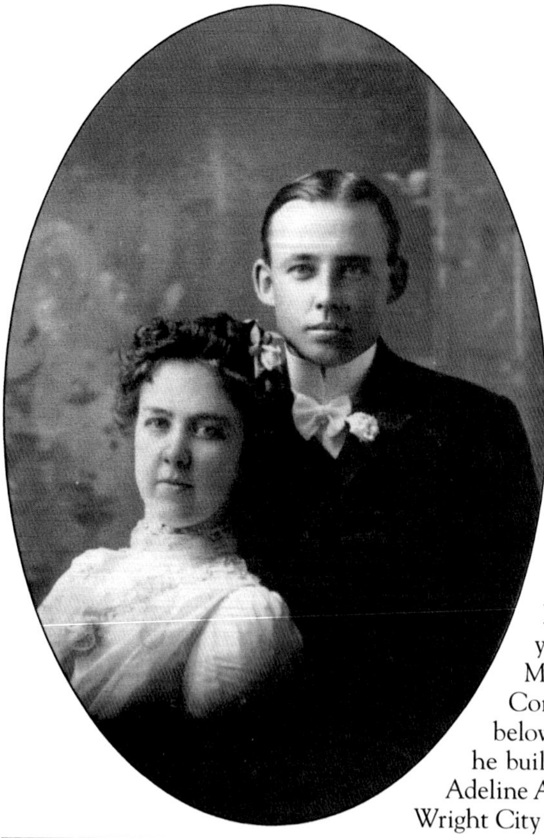

In the image at left is Friedrich Nieburg's youngest son, Florence, who married Anna Middlekamp and established a Nieburg Wagon Company at Warrenton. In the photograph below is the home of William Nieburg, which he built in 1897 in Wright City. He had married Adeline Althaus in 1896. Eventually, William ran the Wright City factory with his son Julius as his partner.

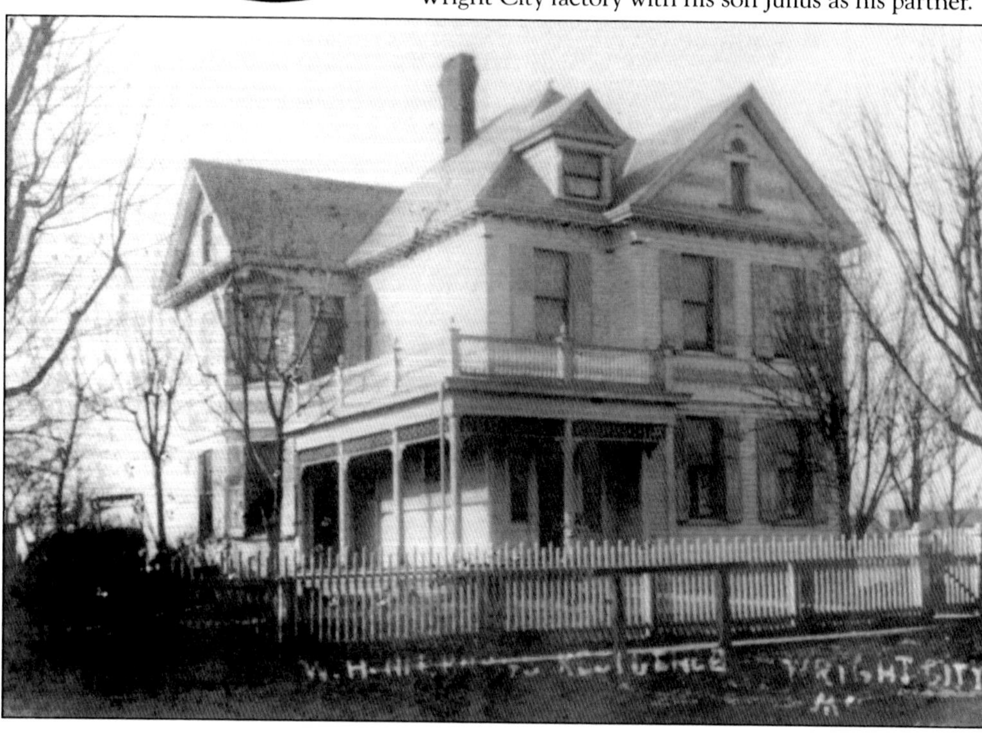

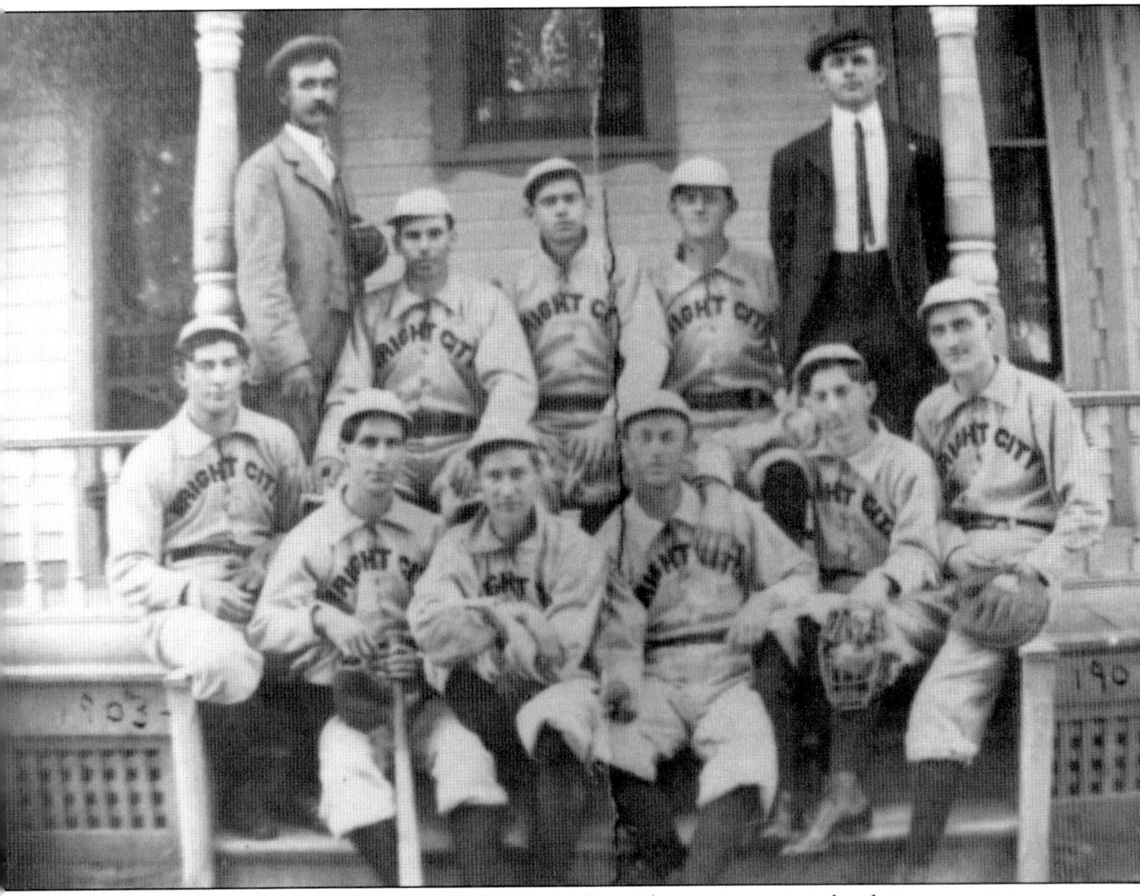

In 1909, the official Wright City Baseball League formed, as seen posing for their team picture above. This was a golden age—a time for summer picnics, ladies' teas, and dances for the young people. There were horse races at the county fair, which was held in Wright City. The city had grown up, and life was good.

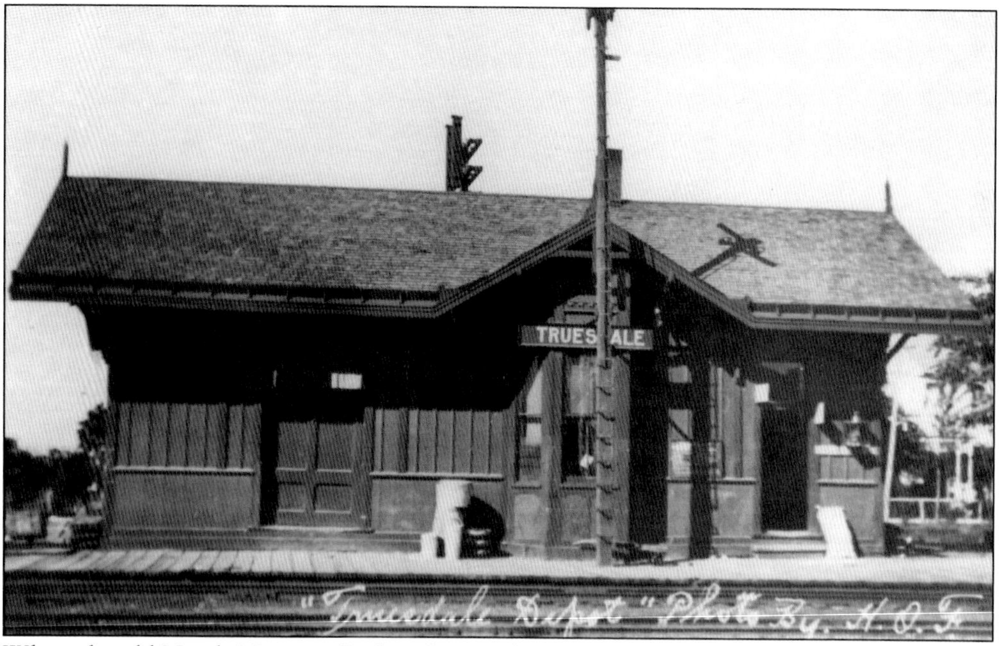

When the old North Missouri Railroad, now the Wabash Railroad, was moving westward, stockholders like William Truesdale purchased land up ahead and established the town and, thereby, the depot in 1857. The depot and freight station would be a thorn in Warrenton's side for 26 years, subjecting all merchandise and travelers to move through its location a mile and a half east of the much older town of Warrenton. Businesses in Truesdale sprung up, such as the Brockfeld Painting Company, just east of Central Wesleyan College and Orphanage. Truesdale and Warrenton were booming, and new homes needed the services of a good painter and wallpaper hanger. Johann Rudolph Brockfeld, who was born in Germany in 1854 and arrived in America in 1882, specialized in beautiful frescoes and grain painting.

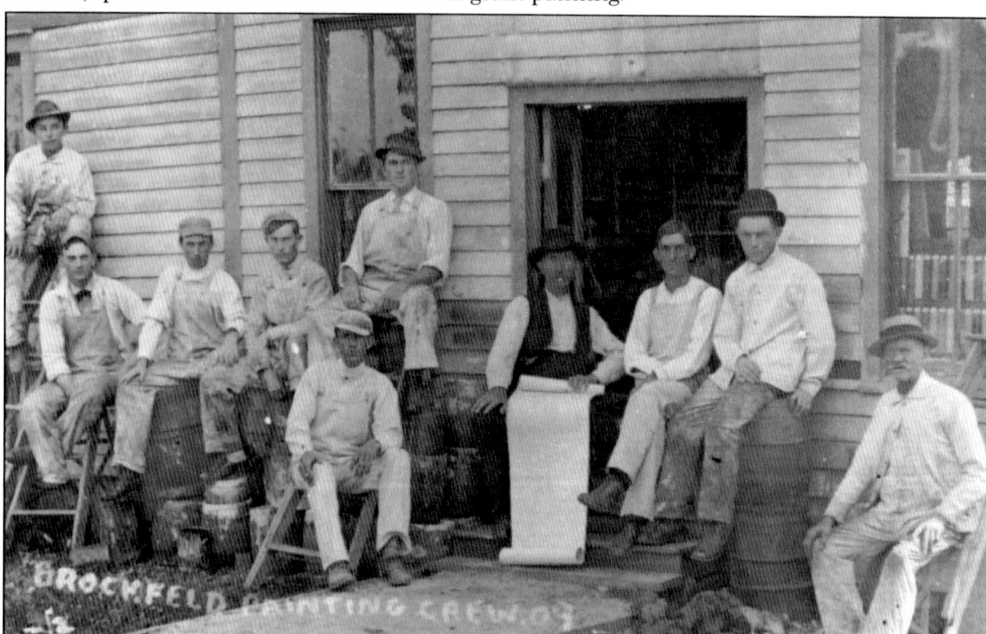

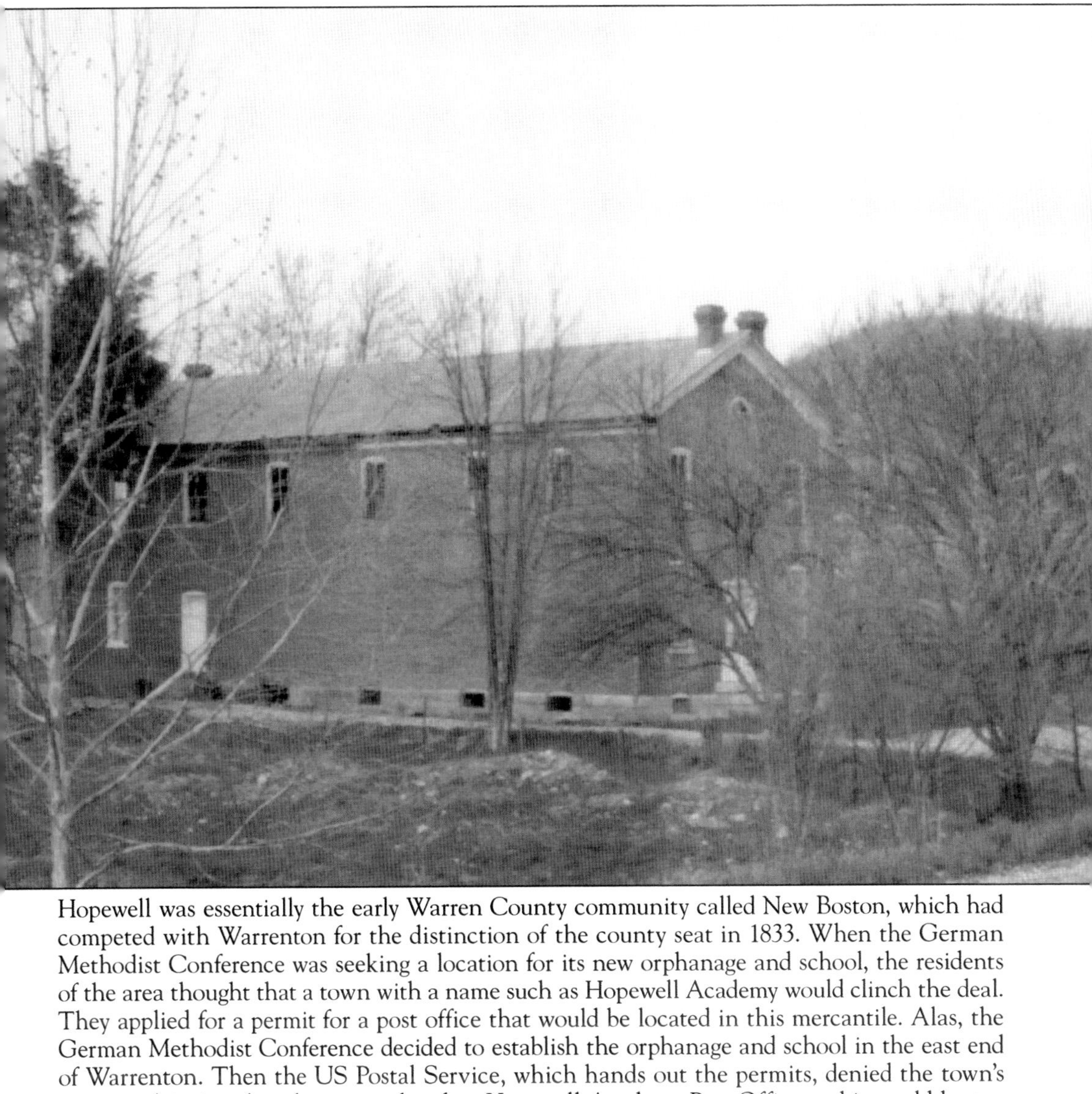

Hopewell was essentially the early Warren County community called New Boston, which had competed with Warrenton for the distinction of the county seat in 1833. When the German Methodist Conference was seeking a location for its new orphanage and school, the residents of the area thought that a town with a name such as Hopewell Academy would clinch the deal. They applied for a permit for a post office that would be located in this mercantile. Alas, the German Methodist Conference decided to establish the orphanage and school in the east end of Warrenton. Then the US Postal Service, which hands out the permits, denied the town's request, claiming that there was already a Hopewell Academy Post Office and it would be too confusing to have second one with the same name, so the community became Hopewell instead. This building is often referred to as the Hopewell Academy, leaving passersby with the impression that it was a large school at one time. In another confusing local story, this was where former slave William Kunze learned his trade of chair making from his former owner from Germany, whose identity is unknown.

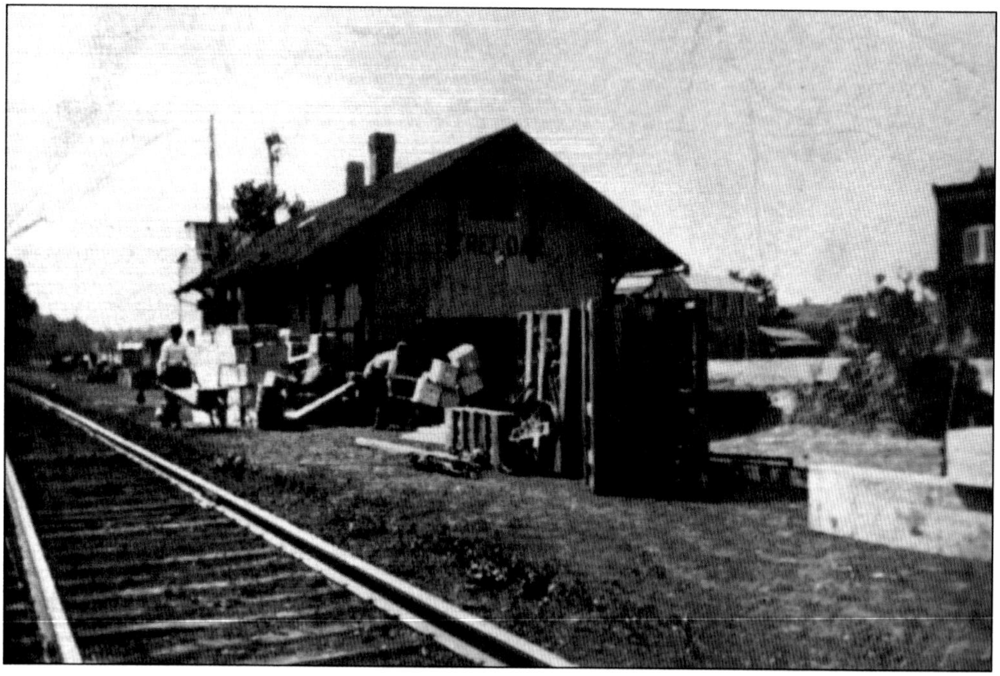

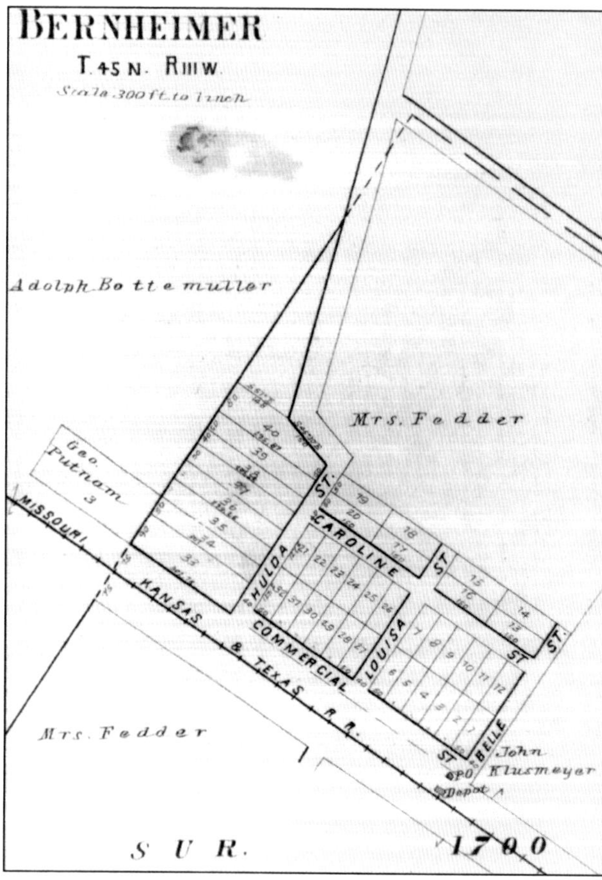

The Treloar Depot, seen above, was built when the Missouri, Kansas & Texas Railroad passed through in the 1890s when the town became established. Kruegerville began when Fritz Krueger took over as the area's postmaster. It was established near the earlier town of Pinckney, which was now located in Franklin County, and south of a newly established Pinckney, where the church had moved. Also seen in the image above is the depot of Missouri, Kansas & Texas Railroad, nicknamed the "Katy" Railroad. The Missouri River's constant flooding influenced life in the river bottoms a lot, filling it with uncertainty. The town of Bernheimer, as seen on the map from the 1901 atlas, was west of Treloar but before Gore and Case.

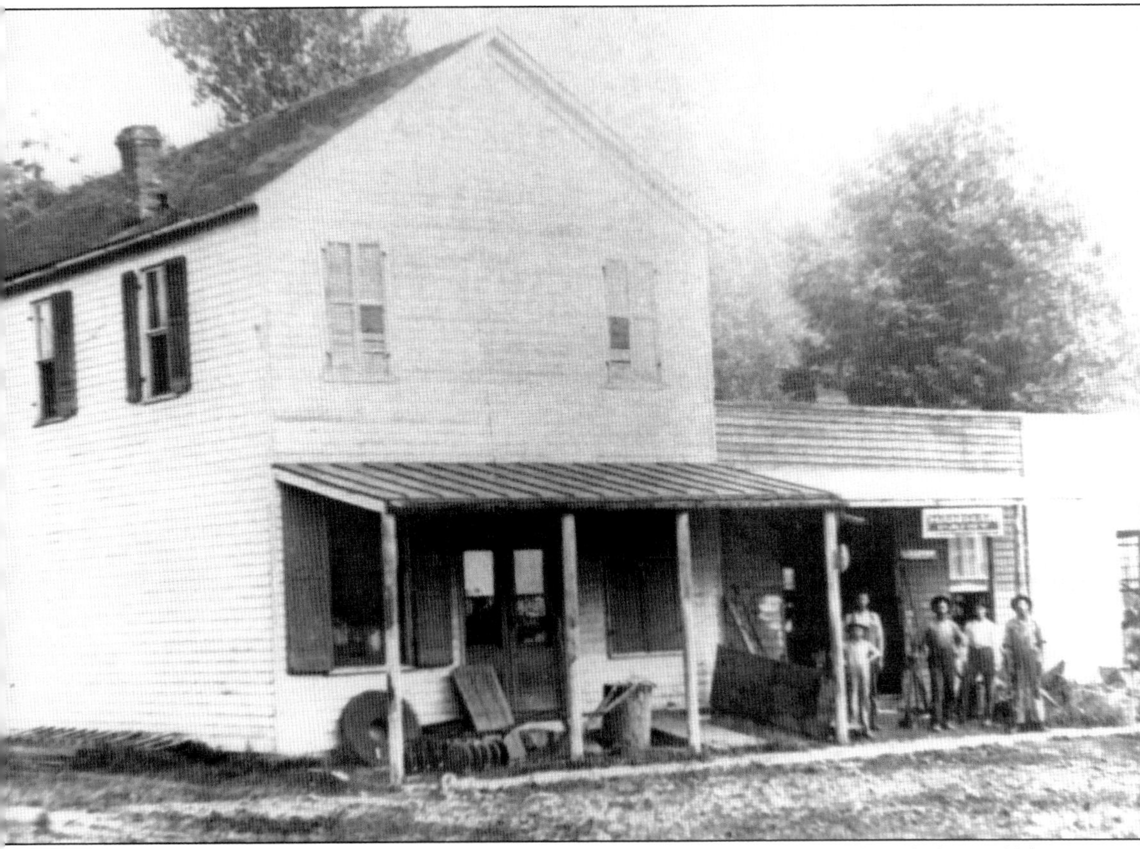

William Henry Gruebbel, the son of German emigrants William and Emilie (Schneider) Gruebble, was born in 1862. He is seen here at his blacksmith shop, a trade that he learned from his father. His general store also housed the post office. After floods ravaged the area, Gruebbel moved from Kruegerville to Treloar and worked at the Bank of Treloar. In 1881 and 1904, the Missouri River suffered the worst floods since the Great Flood of 1844.

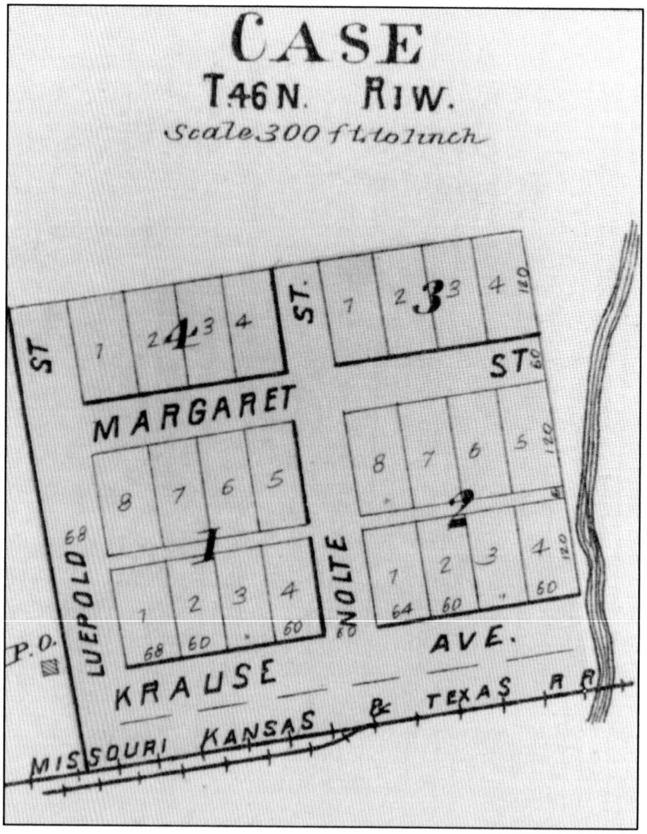

Further west in the Bridgeport Township, the towns of Case and Gore would be established when the Missouri, Kansas & Texas Railroad came through in the 1890s. Some of Warren County's earliest history had been recorded near here when Fort Clemison, the second fort to be built in the territory following Fort Osage, was constructed to protect area families from Indian raids. Early families like the Talbotts had moved here as some of the Boone families moved west to escape civilization over at Charrette Village. The Loutre Slough, which formed the Loutre Island where the fort was built, enters right where Case and the train station were later constructed.

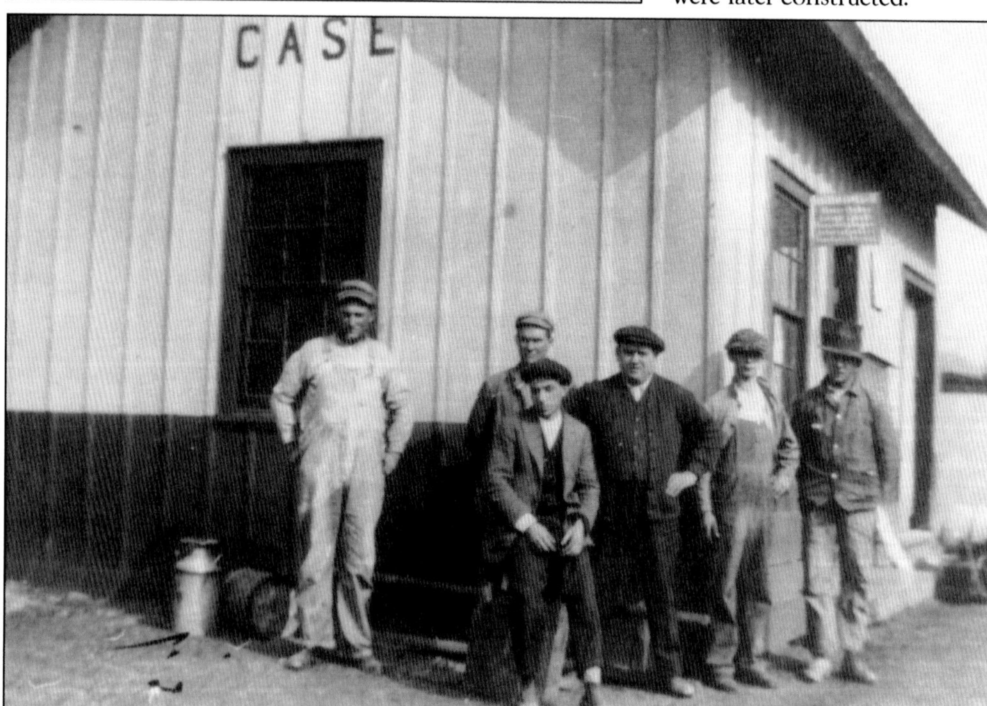

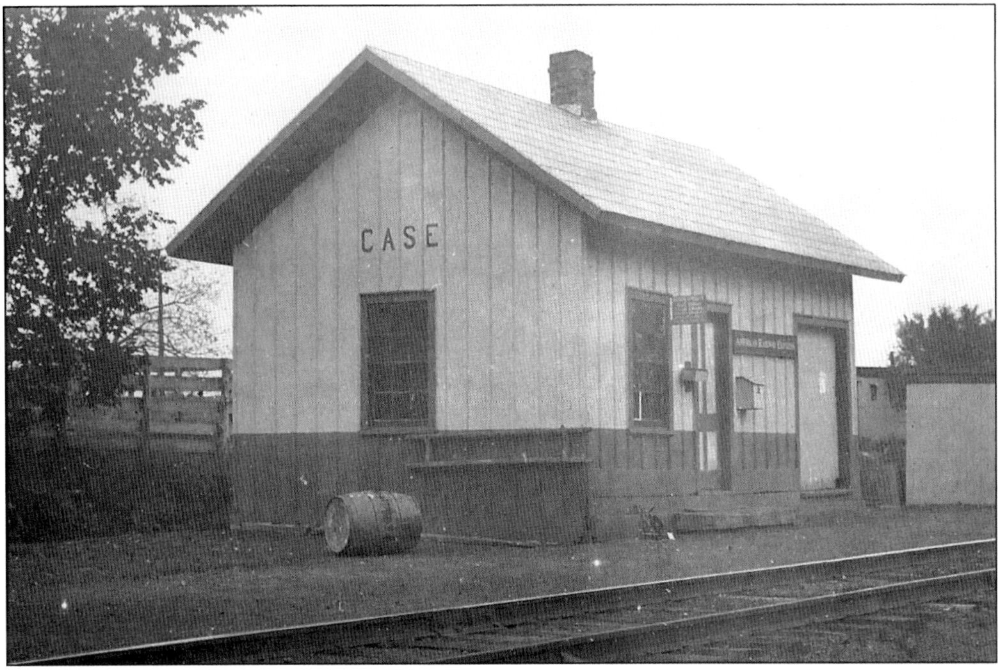

Mathias Luppold was born in Wurtenberg, Germany, in 1826 and had come to the United States in 1851. By 1870, he and his wife, Elizabeth (Held), had four children: William, born in 1859; George, born in 1865; Emilie, born in 1863; and Herman, born in 1869. Mathias Luppold established the store below at Bridgeport Landing, an important steamboat refueling stop, by 1870. Sometimes Bridgeport Landing was referred to as the town of Bud. The Case depot, seen above, was located across Luppold Street from where the Luppold store and Mathias Luppold's home stood, seen in the far left of the photograph. After Mathias died and the railroad came through, William continued to manage the store where the post office was located. Pictured below are sons William (left) and George (right) in front of the store. (Both, courtesy of Linda Locke Heck.)

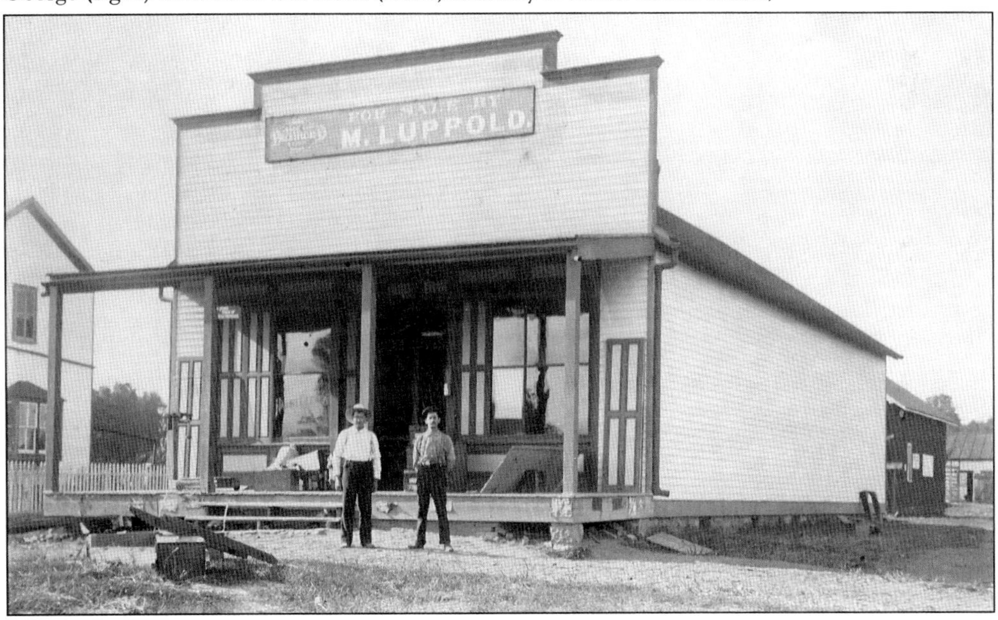

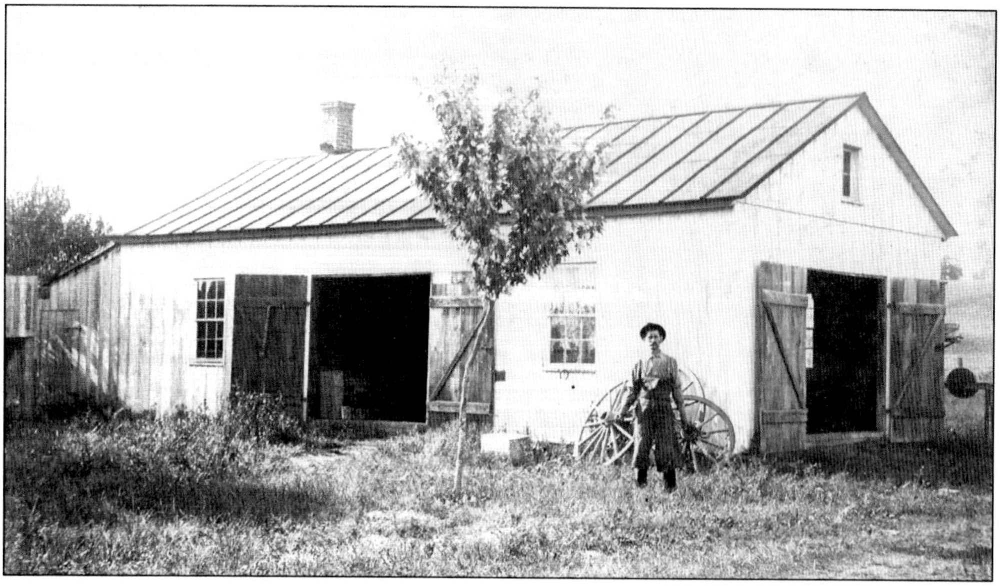

Mathias's second son, George, was a blacksmith, and his shop shown here was behind the general store. His brother Herman had also learned the blacksmith trade from their father and worked with him. George's wife, Mary Waller, was from the prominent Virginian family of Joseph Granville Waller, which had come to Warren County in 1822. George was the first to marry and lived next to his mother and siblings in a smaller house he had built. Mary taught school to the area children. The image below is an unusual photograph of the interior of George's blacksmith shop. (Both, courtesy of Linda Locke Heck.)

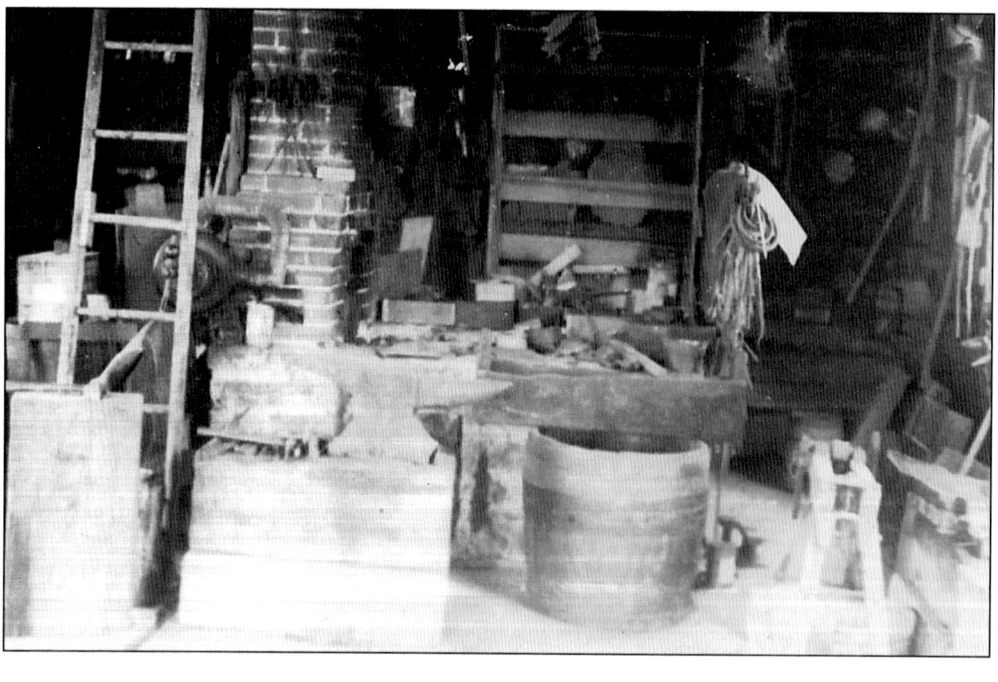

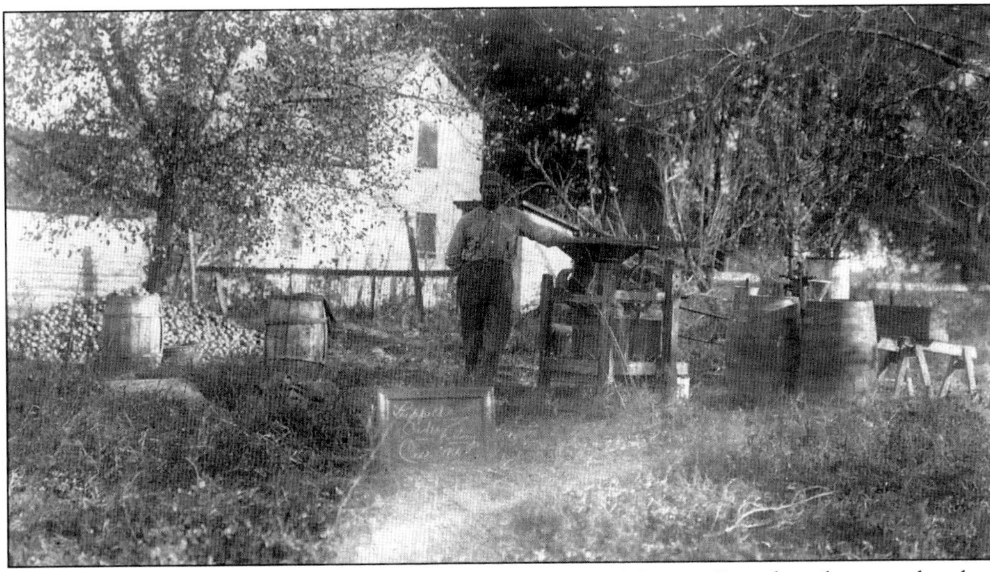

The sign in the grass reads "Luppold Cider Factory, Case Missouri," in this photograph taken behind the Luppold home. The giant apple press is about to be put to work squeezing all those apples seen piled under the tree behind an unidentified Luppold. If any juice was not used to make cider, it would have probably been ferried across the river to Hermann, where the juice would have been distilled at one of the area wineries to make apple brandy. In the image below, the young ladies appear more excited to show off their new baby lamb to the photographer than their friends who chose to visit them. (Both, courtesy of Linda Locke Heck.)

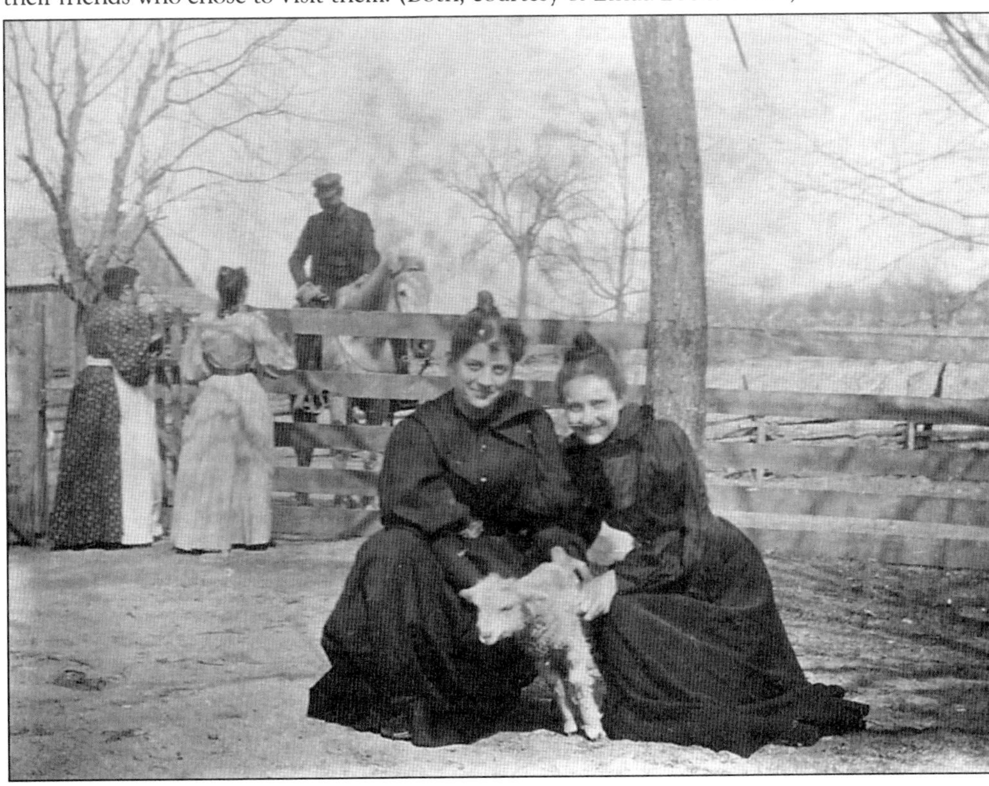

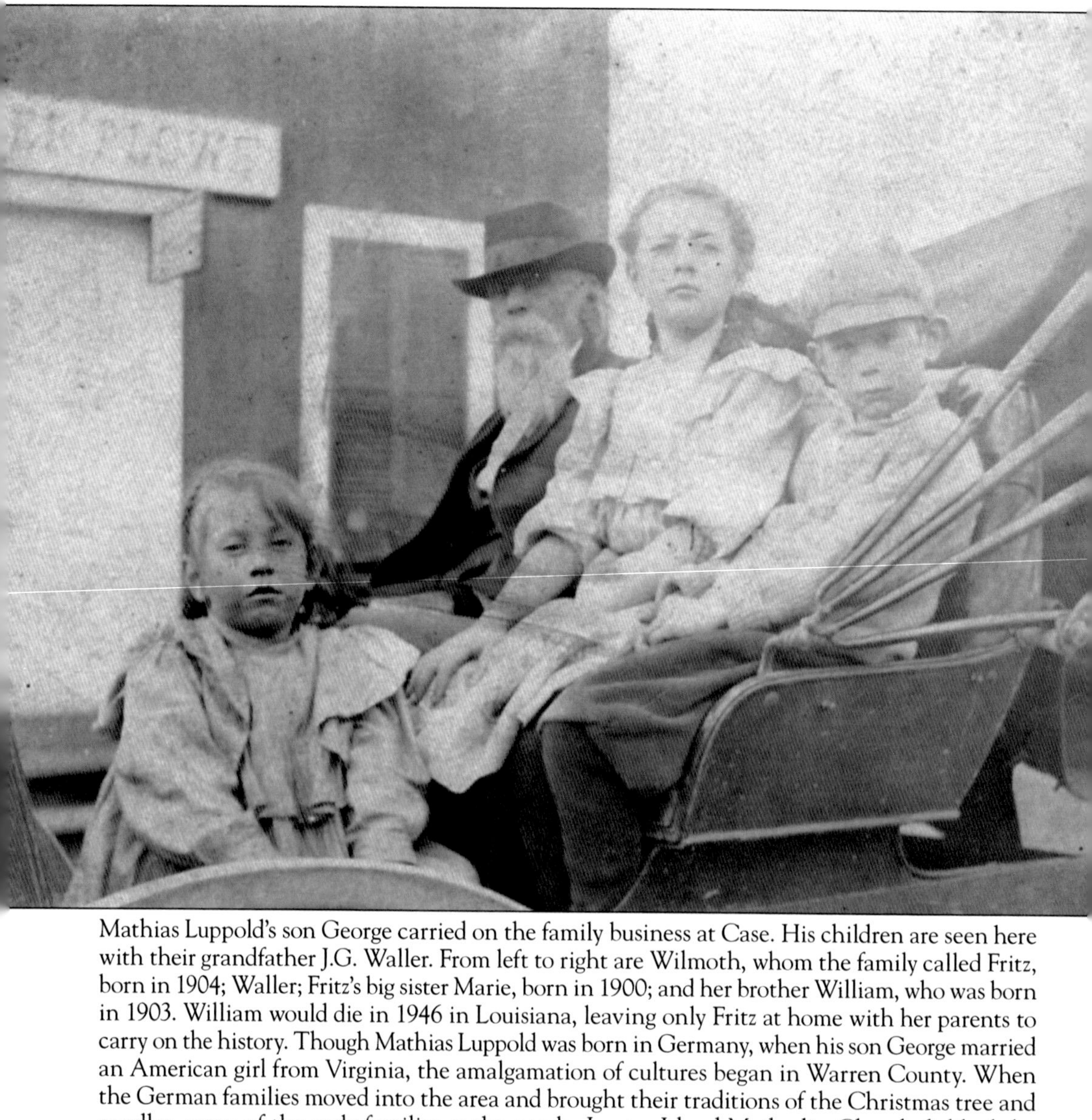

Mathias Luppold's son George carried on the family business at Case. His children are seen here with their grandfather J.G. Waller. From left to right are Wilmoth, whom the family called Fritz, born in 1904; Waller; Fritz's big sister Marie, born in 1900; and her brother William, who was born in 1903. William would die in 1946 in Louisiana, leaving only Fritz at home with her parents to carry on the history. Though Mathias Luppold was born in Germany, when his son George married an American girl from Virginia, the amalgamation of cultures began in Warren County. When the German families moved into the area and brought their traditions of the Christmas tree and candles, many of the early families at the nearby Loutre Island Methodist Church disliked the idea. When the cultures clashed, new churches were formed so that the traditions could continue. (Courtesy of Linda Locke Heck.)

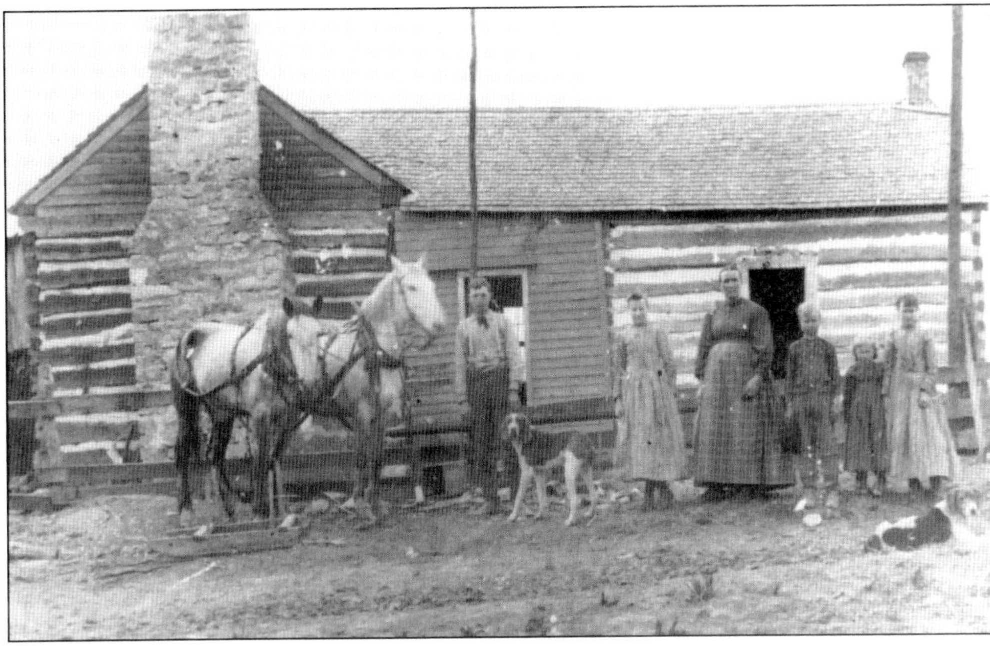

North of Case in Bridgeport Township lived the family of James R. and Ellen Wright. James had been born in Missouri, and his family had moved to Bridgeport Township from Virginia early on. In 1874, he married his wife, Ellen. In the early photograph above are, from left to right, James, Nannie, Ellen, Hade, Ida, and Francis. They may have used the general store at Pendleton, located northeast of their home. Below is the second store of Herman Gerdemann, whose father was a German emigrant; it was built north of the earlier building when the train came through the area in 1880.

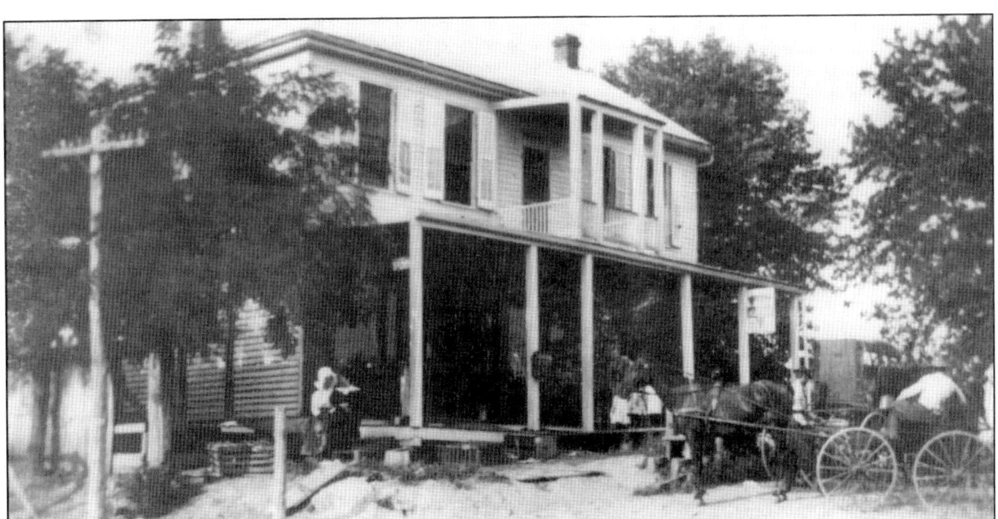

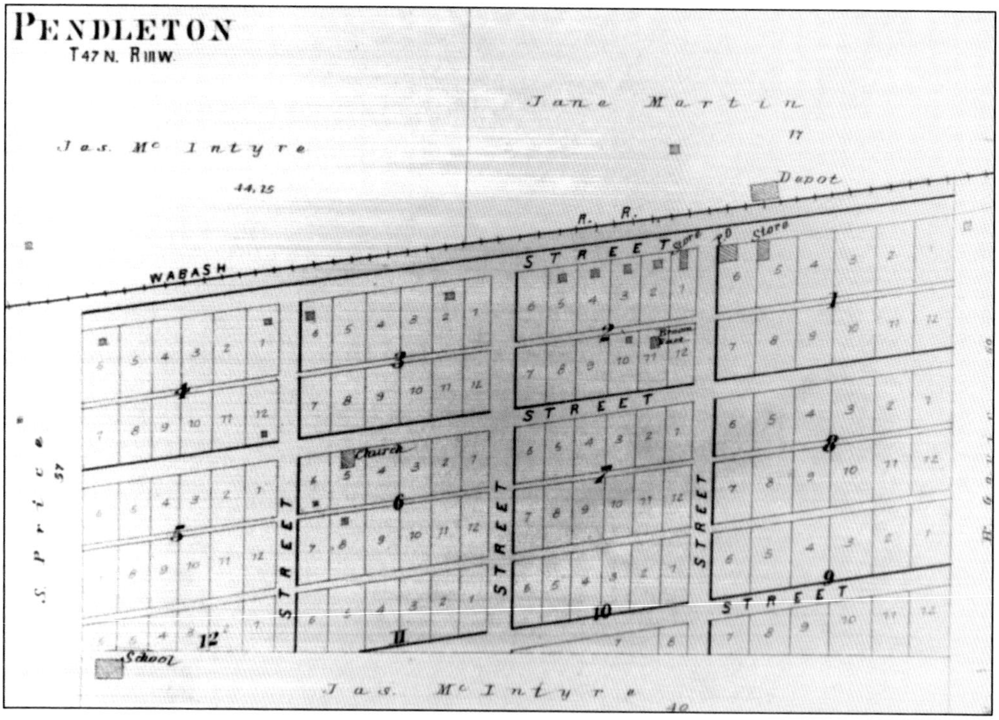

Seen on this 1901 map, the depot for the Wabash Railroad (previously the North Missouri Railroad) was located along the north side of Pendleton in 1883. Chiles served as the depot's station agent, making sure the large wooden water tank for fuelling the steam locomotives was kept full.

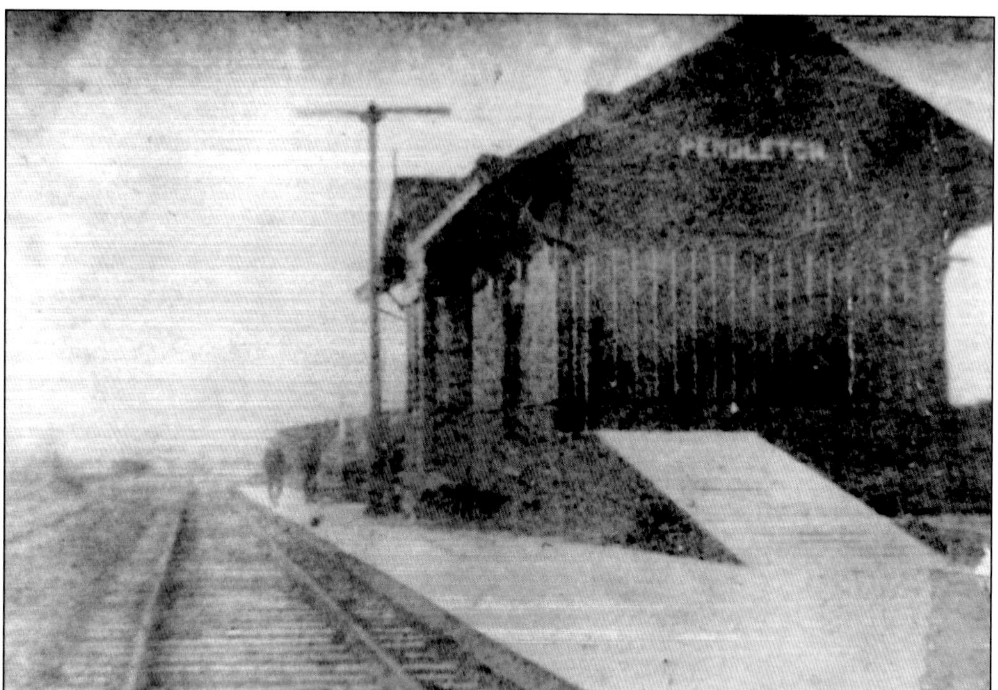

Six

Churches and Schools

As each city, town, or village was platted, two of the first buildings considered the most important were the churches and schools. Often built before any other, they served as community centers, a place for everyone to gather and meet. In early years, they was often one building constructed of logs and used for school when it was in session and for church on Sundays. Traveling ministers meant that services were sometimes held of one faith on some Sundays, alternating with other faiths on other Sundays. The structures were put in to use in times of crises, for gathering the community after a storm, or when celebrating a happy event such as a wedding or harvest. Ladies' quilt circles or ice cream socials made them the center of each community.

With the arrival of the first settlers from Kentucky and Virginia came Baptist meetings at Marthasville. Methodist ministers traveled to bring the word to communities like Pinckney and Loutre Island, among others. By 1830, Jesuit priests were visiting at Dutzow, and they soon brought Catholic churches to Concord Hill and Warrenton. With the German immigrants also came the Lutheran church and the Evangelical churches that would later become the United Church of Christ. Some churches adopted a minister only to find out later that he was too much of a Freethinker and discharge him, like at Holstein. Other communities were not against this and continued to come to meetings on various Sundays.

As soon as any community began to gather, the families' first thoughts turned to education. Early academies at Warrenton, Charrette, and Pinckney confirm this. In the early 1800s, such academies were only for the young men and were private, so only well-off families could afford the tuition. The young ladies would be taught more useful arts while learning their reading and writing in a private home. By the mid-1800s, Missouri passed laws establishing school lands, meaning that the sale of these lands would fund a one-room school for that township. However they were established, they were usually considered the most important buildings in every community.

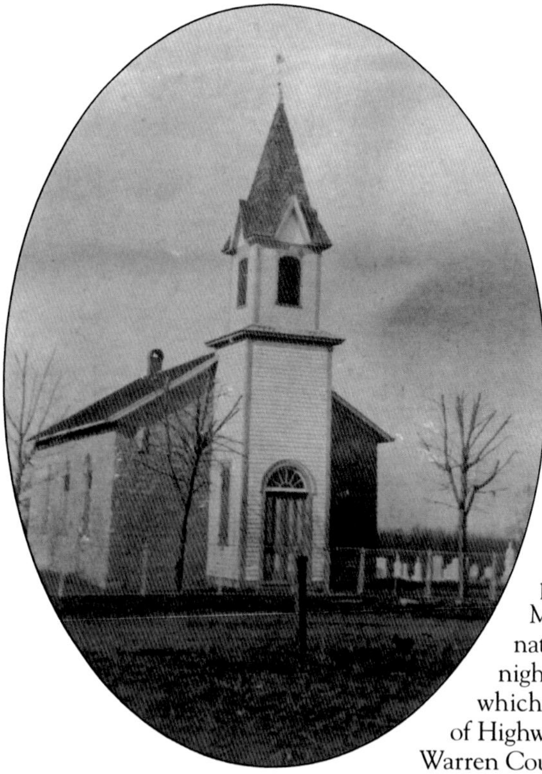

The St. Paul's United Church of Christ at Steinhagen, seen at left, was located four miles north of Warrenton on State Highway 47. It was established in 1865, and this stone church was built about 1875, though the steeple was added in 1895. Some years later, when the church needed a new roof, no one could be found willing to repair the steeple, so it was removed. Shown below is the Salem Methodist Church, built in 1859 on land purchased from Fredrick and Minna Bock Morsey. Originally, Brother John Swahlen, a native of Switzerland, held camp meetings every night in the first converts' homes. The church, which once stood north of Warrenton and east of Highway 47, had a bell that is now in front of the Warren County Historical Society.

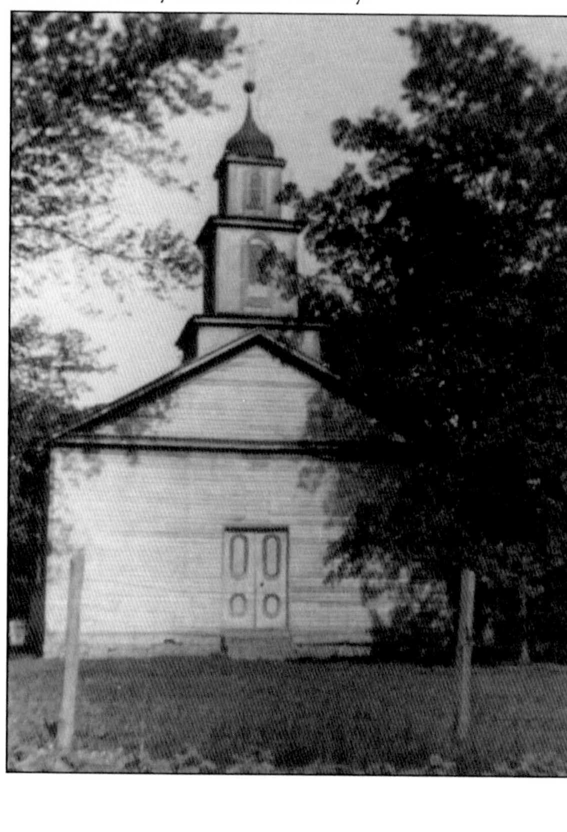

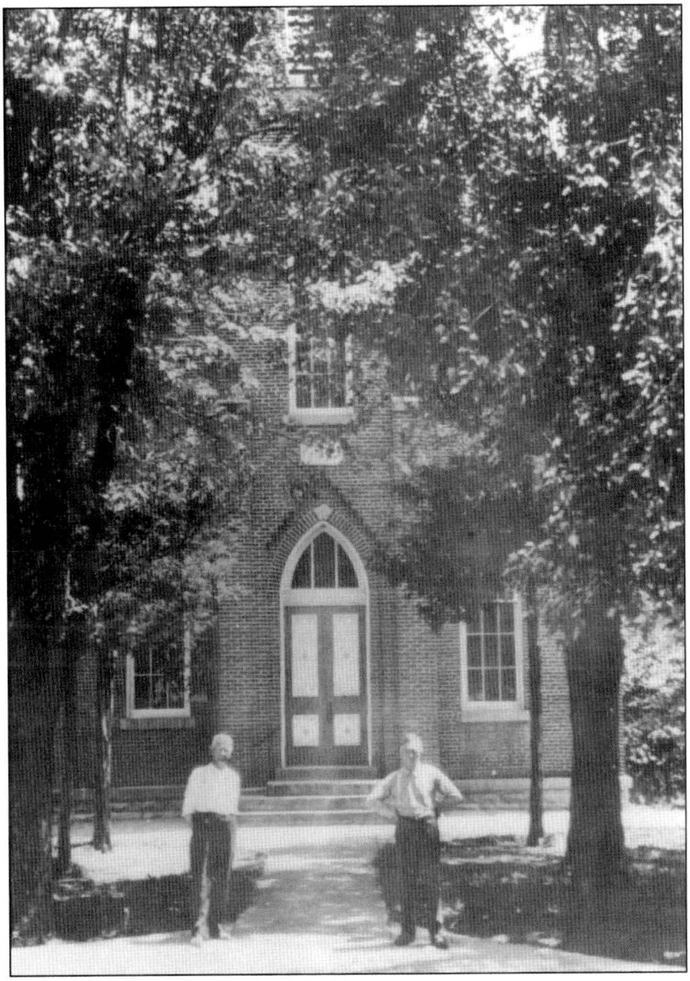

The German Lutheran church on Charrette was founded on land given by German immigrants Fredrick Niemann and Ernst Lehmberg. The first pastor was Herman Garlichs, who served not only this church but also what would become known as Stracks Church and the Evangelical church at Femme Osage, where the synod was founded. The first building was constructed of logs and was eventually replaced by today's brick Immanuel United Church of Christ in 1884. The image below of the Holstein School taken at the beginning of the school year in 1908 illustrates how much the community had prospered and grown.

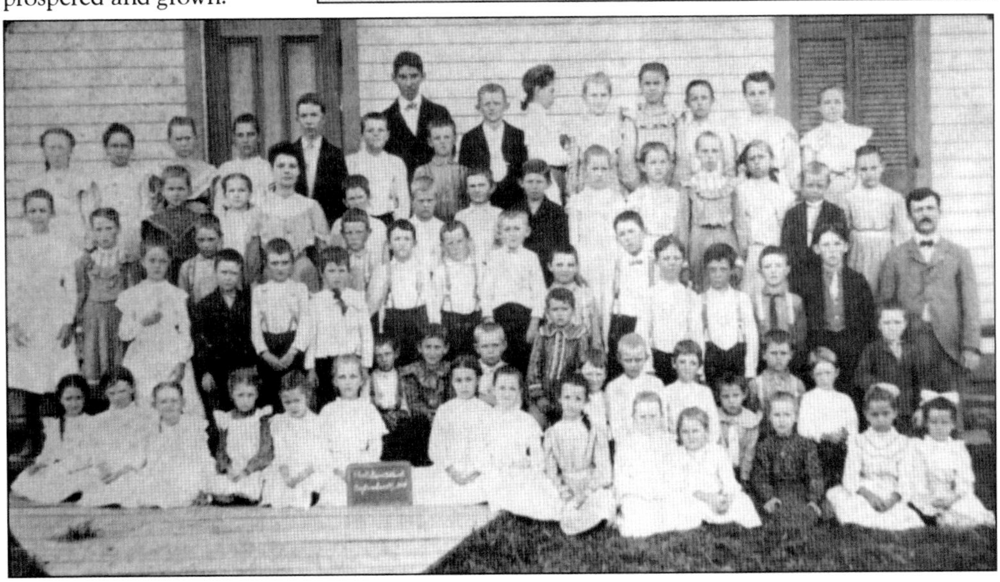

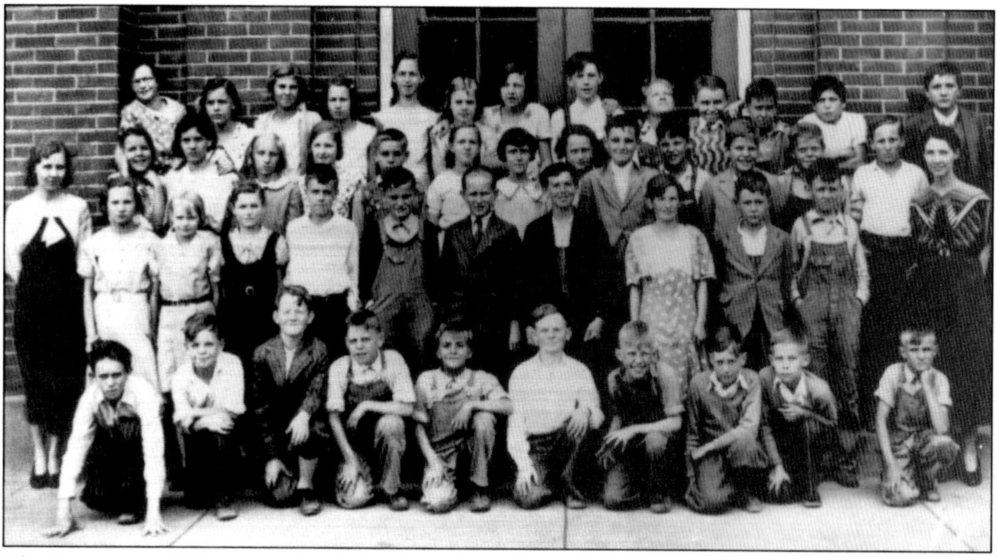

The large city of Warrenton had a brick building for its fifth and sixth grades, as shown here in 1932. From left to right are (first row) McGee, Frick, Grimes, Kuhl, Bell, Frick, Riley, Yocum, Luttman, and Wilkerson; (second row) teacher Jewell Luttman, Baxley, Backs, Coil, Cook, Gaulding, Isenman, Williams, Riley, Schaper, Beard, and Lantham; (third row) Lovell, Jaspering, Fischer, Harter, Vieth, McCracken, Ordelheide, Alderson, Farmer, Comer, Jaspering, Moore, and teacher Louise Bordeaux; (fourth row) unidentified, Sullivan, Grant, Goodman, Zielmann, Windman, Lamy, Requat, Myers, Lohman, Fensler, unidentified, and Belker. In the photograph below is the Warrenton School building, located on Oak Street just east of Market Street.

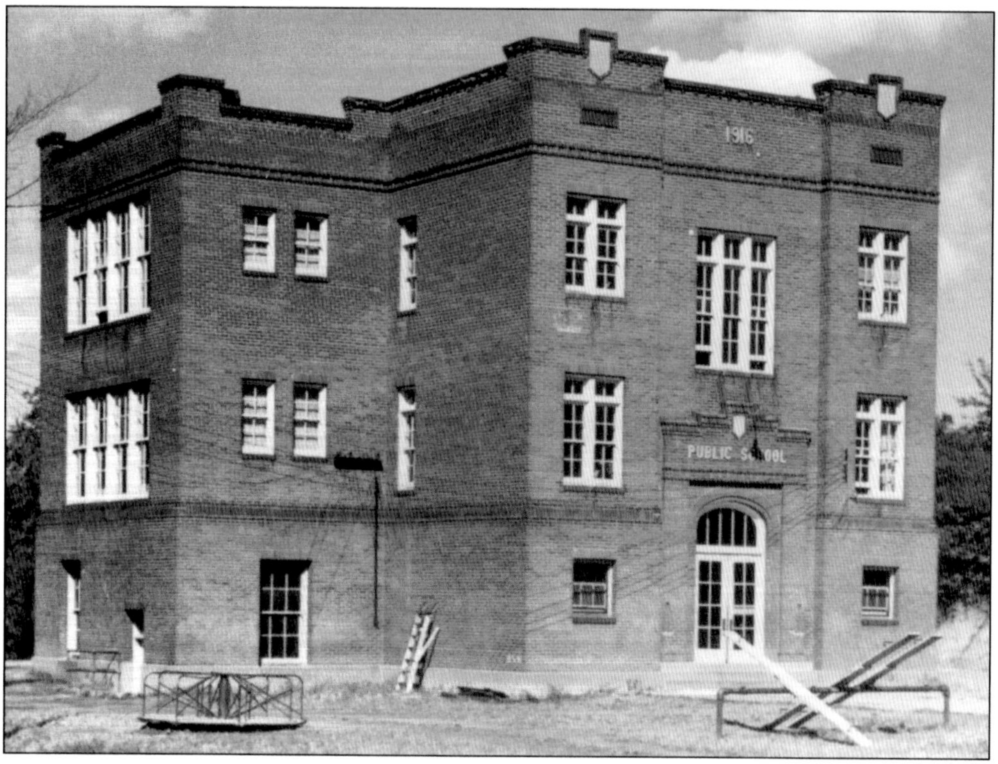

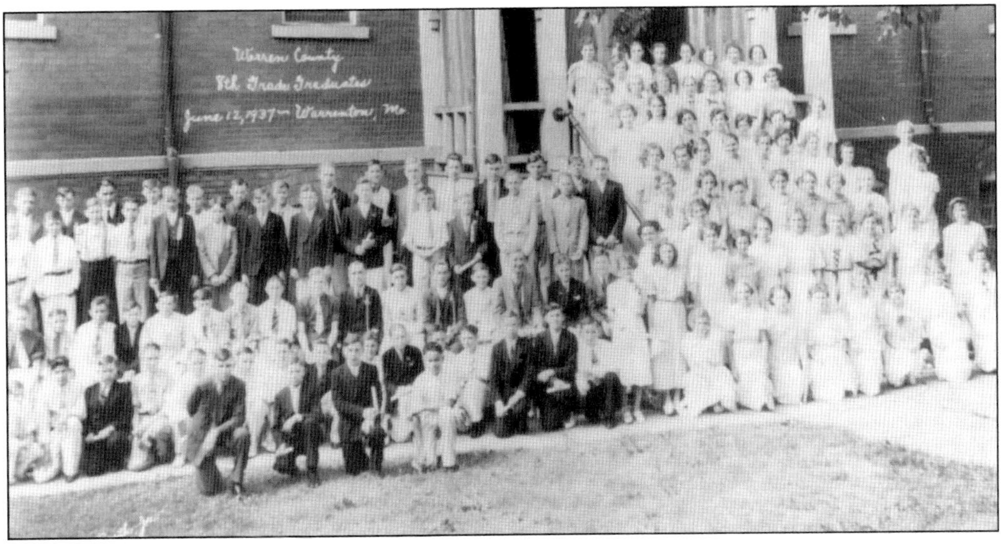

In 1937, the eighth-grade graduation of all county schools was held in the Niedringhaus Gym on Central Wesleyan College's campus. This was the custom; instead of just the formalities for a couple of students, they partook in the large event attended by all of their families. In the photograph below is the German Evangelical church in Wright City. In 1880, Rev. H. Feix was called to Wright City to organize 40 men and their families into the Friedens Evangelical Church. For years before that, the pastor of the Lippstadt Evangelical Church made frequent trips to Wright City to conduct services. A much larger brick church replaced the early frame church in 1923, and in 1955, the name became the Immanuel Evangelical and Reformed Church.

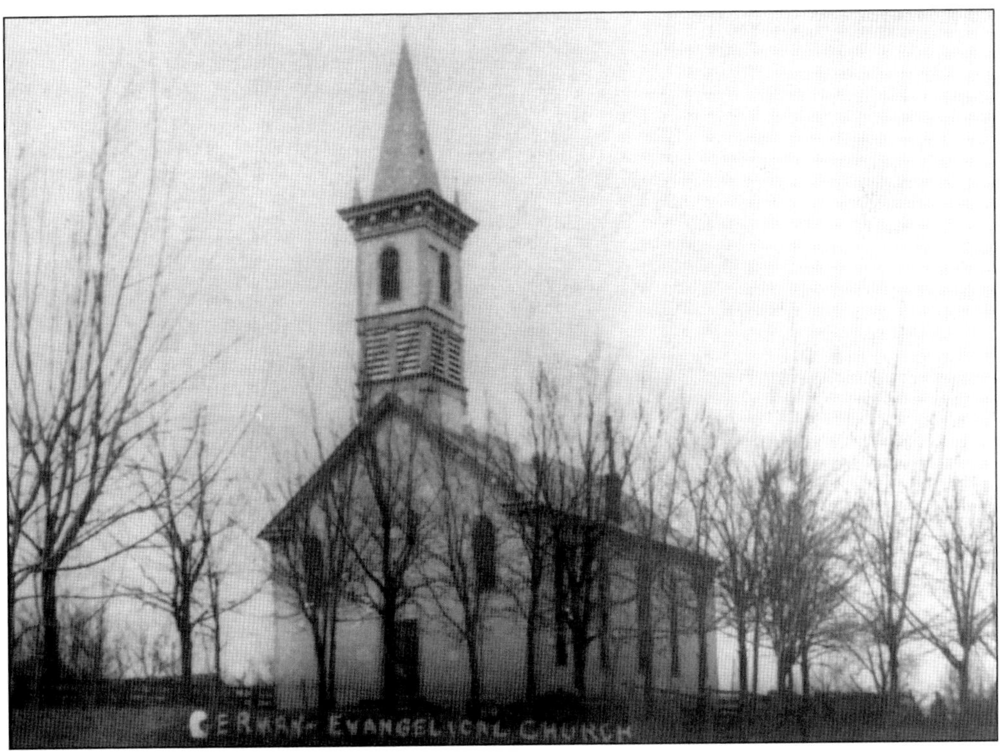

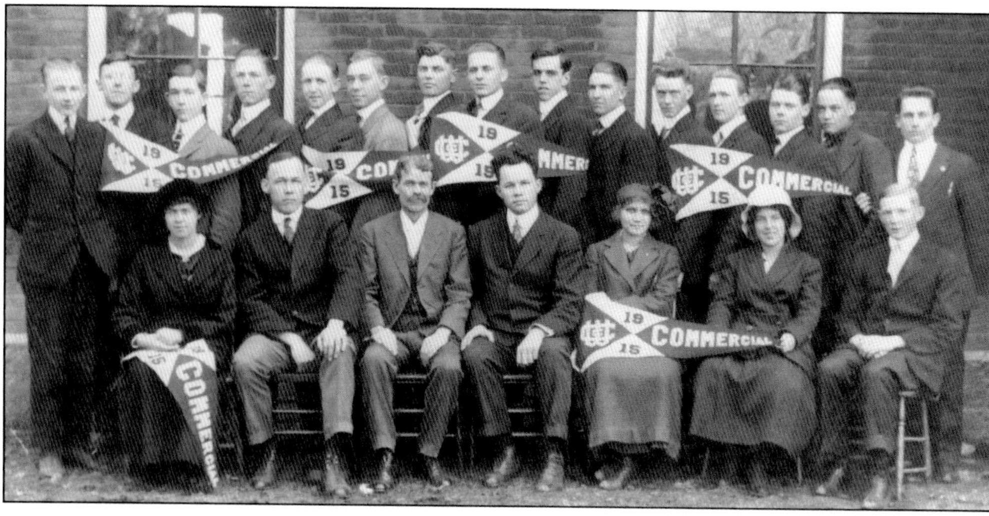

Above is the 1915 graduation class of the Commercial School at the Central Wesleyan College. Below is the confirmation class of the College Methodist Church of 1930. In the photograph are, from left to right, (first row) Katie Scheer, Corine Farmer, Elsie Klingle, Orylan Miltenberger, Ralph Bothe, Edwin Gaulding, George Kuhl, Clyde Cox, William Lanham, and Harold Hoecker; (second row) Lucille Landwehr, Dorothy Jennings, Donald Witte, William Gomer, Clarence Bole, Victor Walker, Alberta Lanham, Mina Hess, Opal Walling, Ruth Alice Linnert, Melna Landwehr, and Marie Lanham; (third row) George Bolm, Robert Hess, and Rev. F.S. Eitelgeorge.

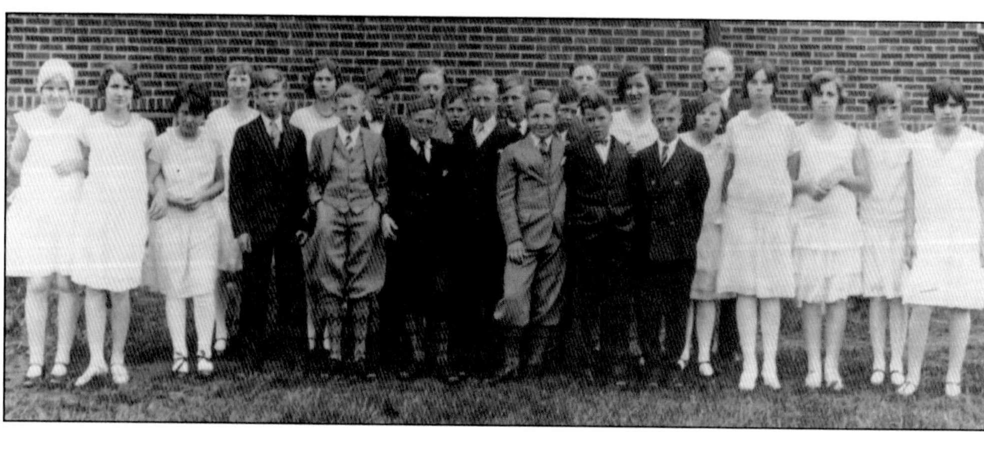

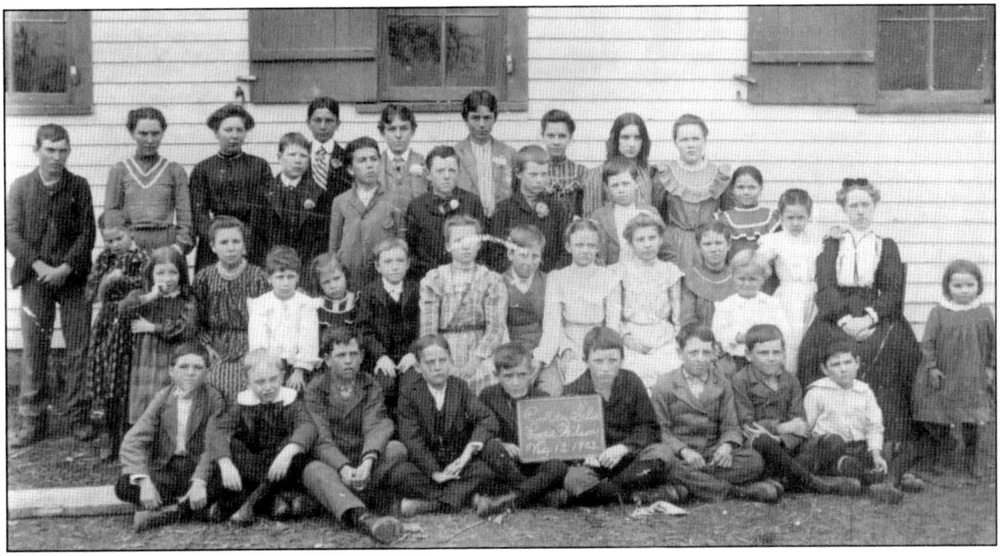

In 1902, Rosa Wilson, seen above seated in the second row, second from right, was the teacher of the Pendleton School. The Shelton School, which sat north of Pendleton, was once also used for church meetings. A large cemetery lies nearby.

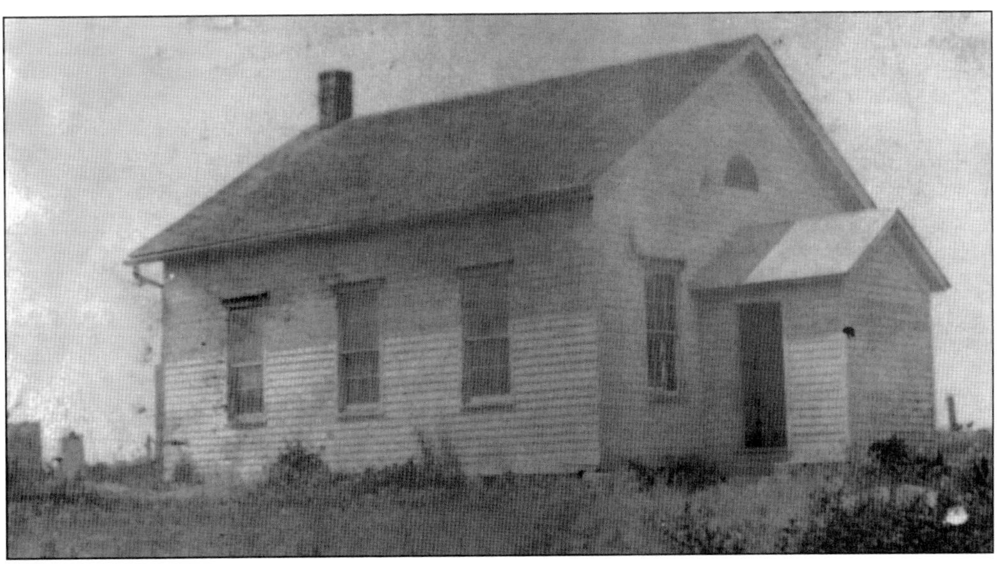

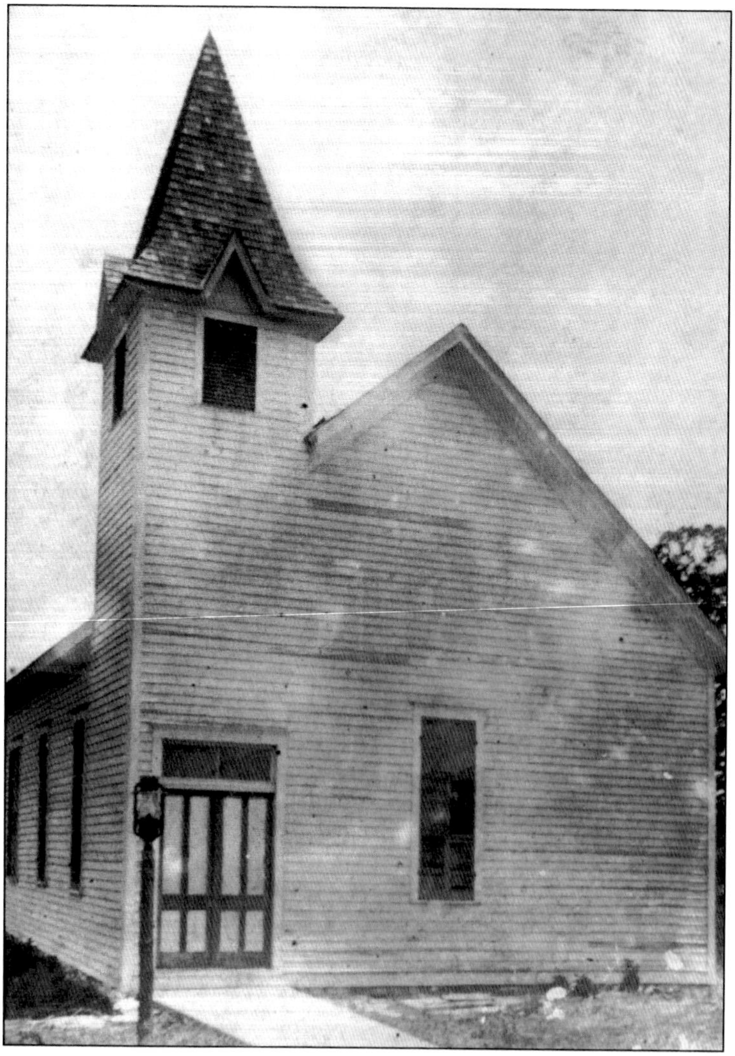

At Pendleton, the Methodists built this church in 1902 after a terrible fire destroyed an earlier church. The earlier church, the Camp Branch Church, was a Methodist Episcopal (South) church located west of Warrenton. Camp Branch was a stagecoach stop on what began as the Boone's Lick Trail, the road that led from the Boone home to the family's salt lick business near Arrow Rock. Shown below is the early Wright City School in 1908.

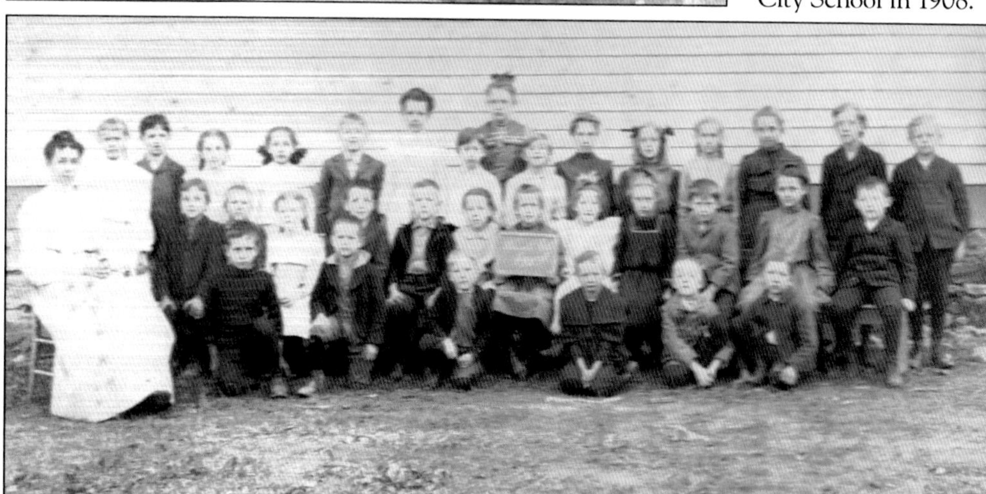

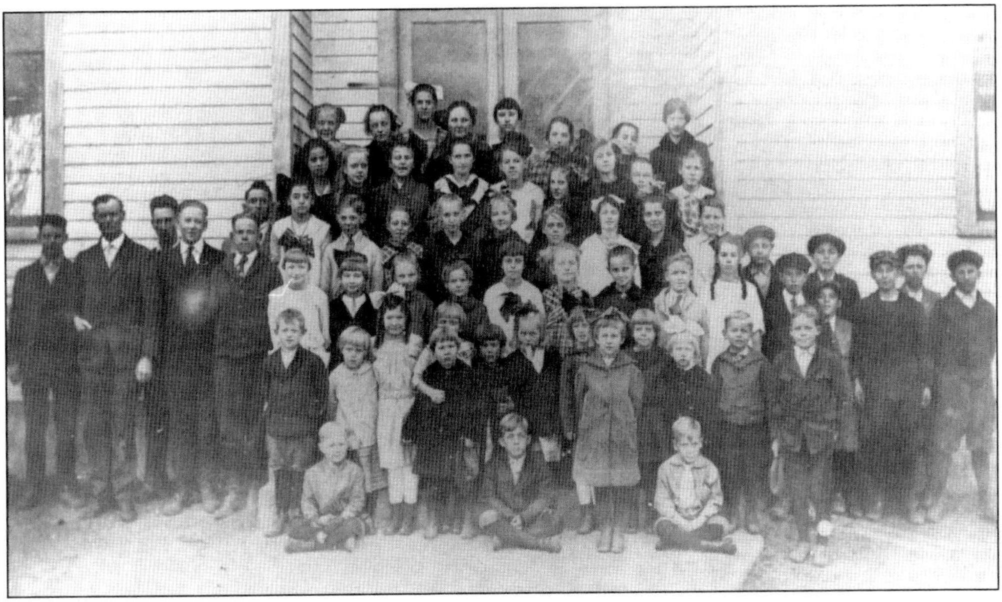

Wright City's frame school had been built in 1905. Excited about their new building, many students showed up an hour early the day it opened. Wright City's public schools were established in 1865, when the residents hired Landon Rummons as a teacher. Many of the earliest residents of Wright City were Southern Methodists, whose church was torched when Union troops attacked the town during the Civil War; Capt. Joseph L. Fant applied the torch that did the deed. This Methodist Episcopal (South) church, built by David Blast, replaced that former building in 1870.

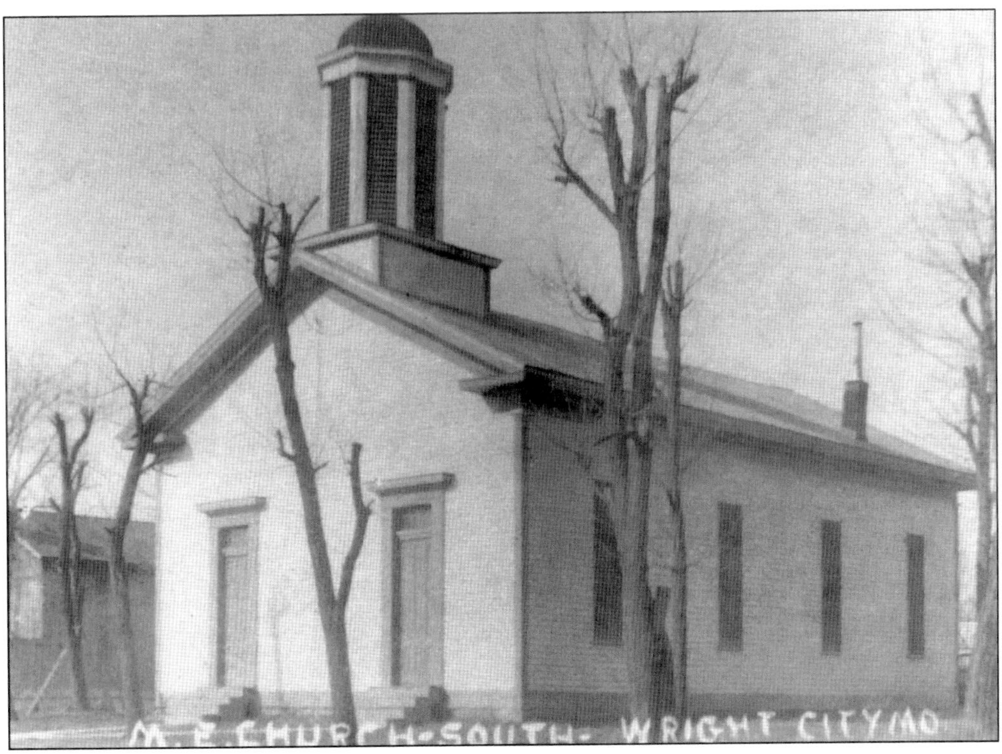

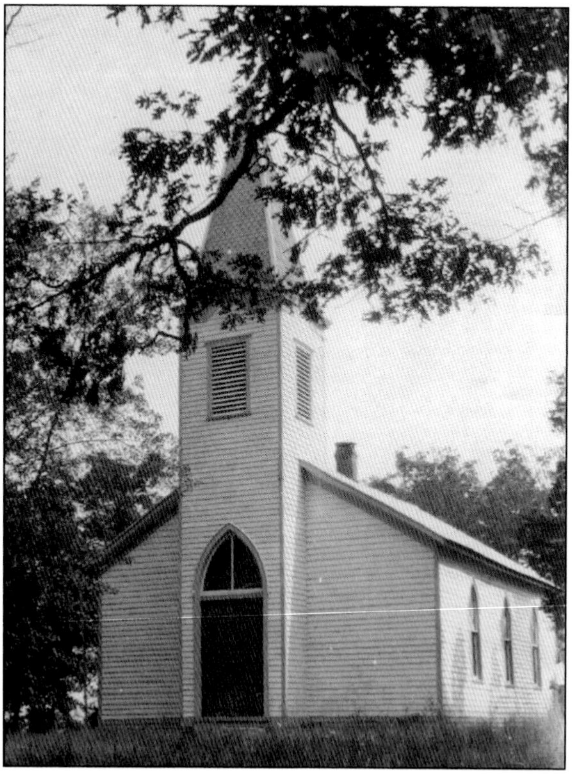

The German Lutheran Evangelical church of Harmony was established in 1842, when Reverend Garlichs traveled there to preach. Later, Charles Strack arrived and preached there for many years, so the church became known simply as Stracks Church. In 1941, the Charrette Memorial Association took up its care, even rebuilding after a fire in the 1980s. Many of Warren County's earliest German settlers lay buried in the Stracks Church Cemetery. Charles's sister Charlotte, an emigrant from Giessen, Germany, married George Muench, the miller and brother of state senator Friedrich Muench, at Lake Creek. The community that Stracks Church served, located west of Wright City and east of Warrenton, was referred to as Pitts. Although Pitts did have a post office and school, the town didn't ever become much larger than a few businesses. Below is a 1936 class picture from a Pitts school.

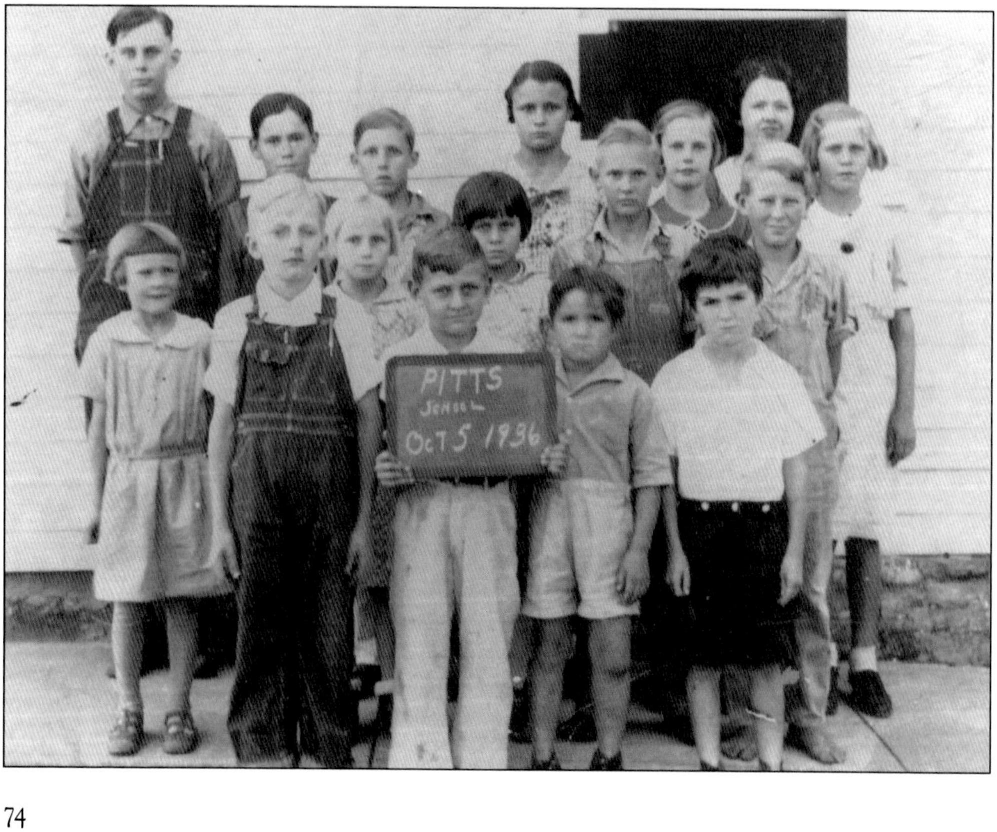

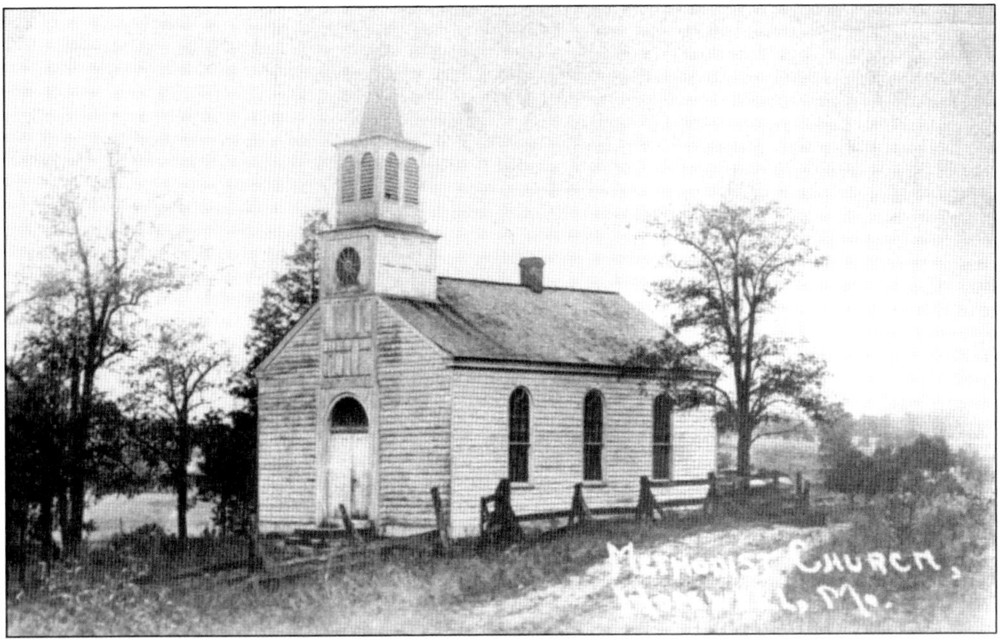

This log Methodist church in the New Boston–Hopewell community was built in 1831. This may be the Ebenezer Church or one that replaced that earlier church. Organized by the Methodist Episcopal Church North, it was a mission church with a minister visiting this and several others church on alternating weeks. The church sat on a knoll near where Highway 47 passes today, with its cemetery on a nearby hillside. The school below replaced an earlier schoolhouse which lay north of the church and was built on land deeded by German emigrant Gerhard Hackmann in about 1880. Built south of the church, it was along Highway 47 at the intersection of Heggemann Road.

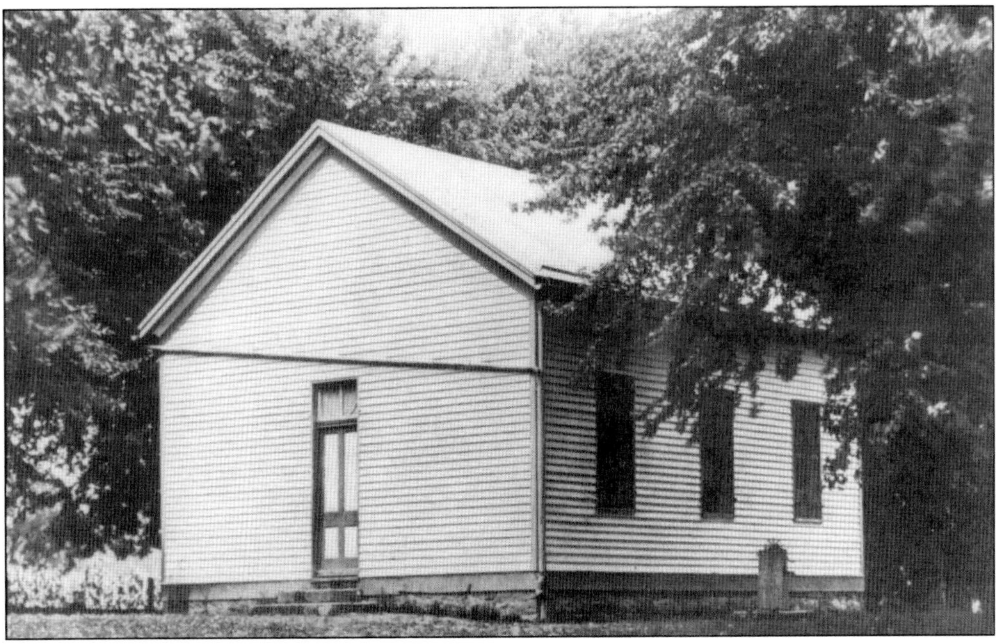

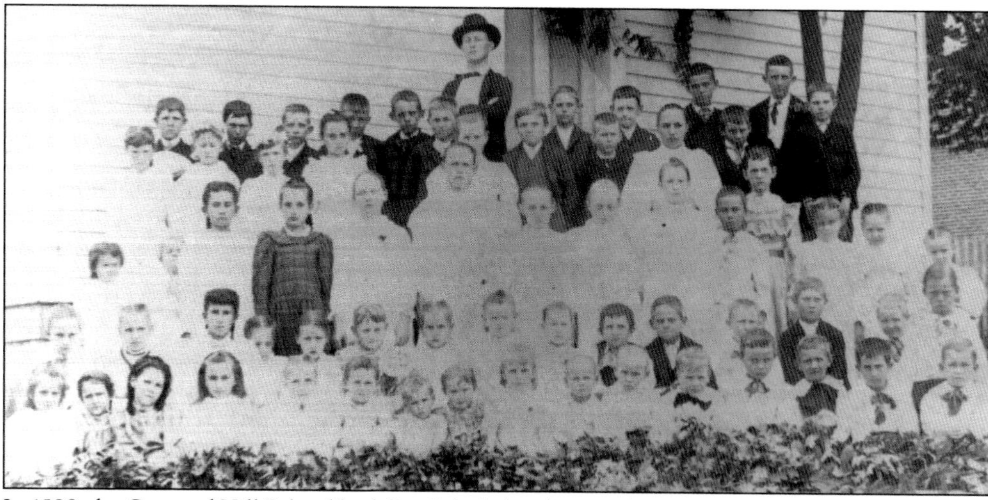

In 1898, the Concord Hill School had Gus Scholz (rear) as teacher, as well as the following students, from left to right: (first row) Emma Vogelsang, Minnie Zilgelt, Anna Zilgelt, Rose Bocklage, Anna Lefarth, Louise Barringhaus, Cecilia Liermann, Agnes Hellebusch, Roxie Liermann, Gus Liermann, Jake Lierman, Larence Liermann, Frank Barringhaus, Leo Glosemeyer, Ben Mebauer, and George Borges; (second row) Josephine Barringhaus, Frace Lefarth, Emma Mebruer, Mathilda Scholz, Lizzie Liermann, Martha Hellebusch, Regina Macke, Addie Eckelkamp, Addie Borges, Clemence Mebruer, Robert Glosemayer, Henry Liermann, Ben Hasenkamp, Henry Hagedorn, and Frank Heggemann; (third row) Regina Mebrer, Anna Schultz, Frances Mebruer, Laura Vogelsang, Katie Haskamp, Addie Bocklage, Anna Nieder, Cecelia Bocklage, Louise Liermann, Josephine Barringhaus, Rosie Zillgitt, Frances Meyer, Anna Lefarth, and Frances Sickmann; (fourth row) Lizzie Liermann, Katy Hennekin, Josephine Liermann, Alice Vogelsang, Mary Eckelkamp, Henry Sickmann, Frank Liermann, Mary Nieder, Albert Liermann, and Joe Kruse; (fifth row) Frank Schulze, Ben Borges, Leo Hellebusch, Edward Hennecke, Ben Glosemeyer, Robert Borges, Albert Schafer, Joe Eckelkamp, Gus Zillgitt, Ben Hellebusch. Below is the Oak Grove Baptist Church, built in 1897.

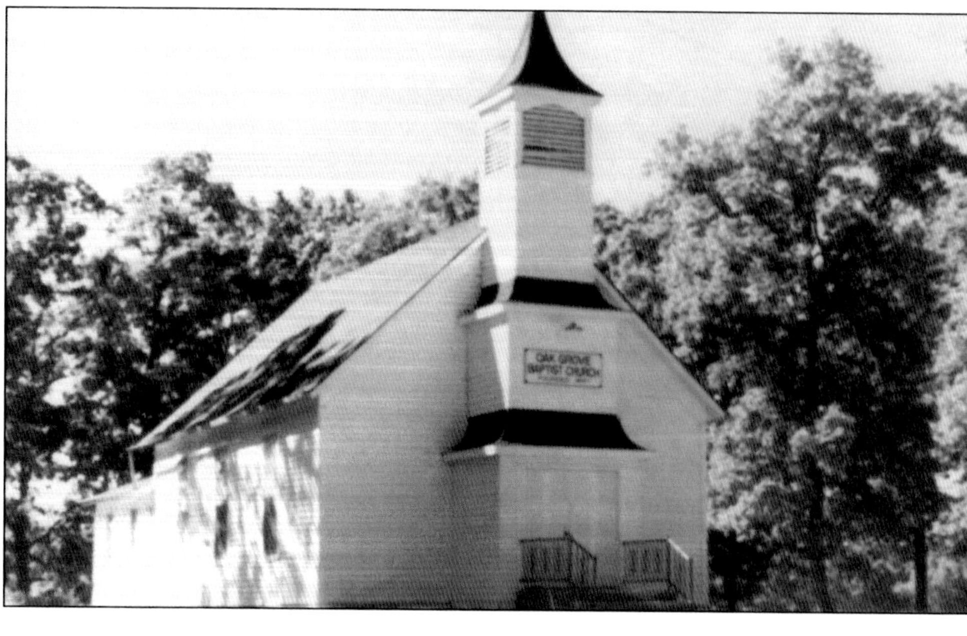

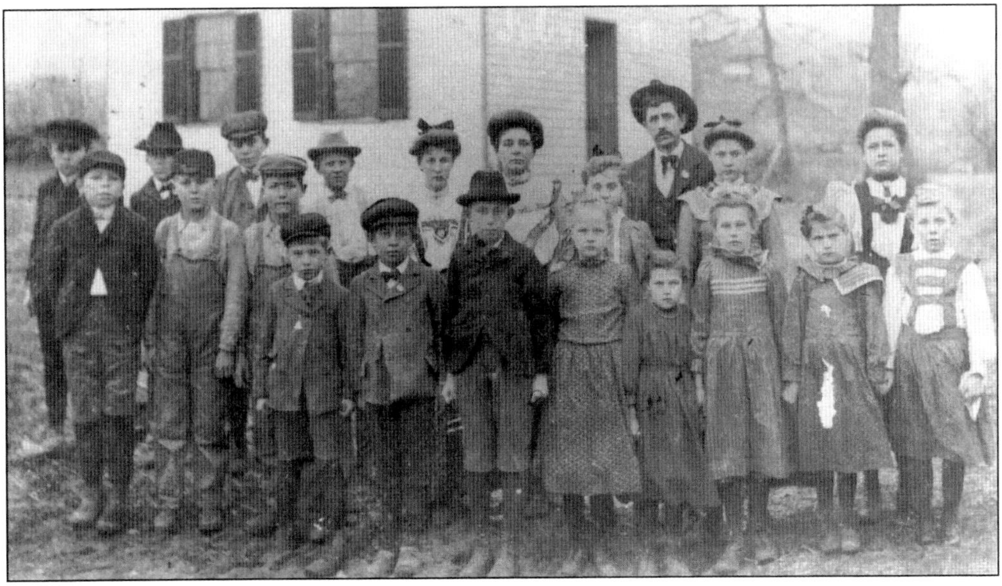

The Bethlehem School No. 44 was located north of the Smith Creek School. Students were, from left to right, (first row) two unidentified Wehmeyer brothers, Louis Schwerdt, M. Ottensmeyer, Edna Meyer, Alma Ackman, Olga Ackman, and Clara Schwerdt; (second row) Hugo Ackman, Florence Ackman, unidentified, and Maggie Jaeger; (third row) George Ellerbruch, unidentified, Herman Swerdt, Freddie Wehmeyer, unidentified, Clara Ackman, teacher Charles Thee, Hulda Ackman, and Elda Ellerbruch. Below is the Sunnyside School, for which Sunnyside Road was named.

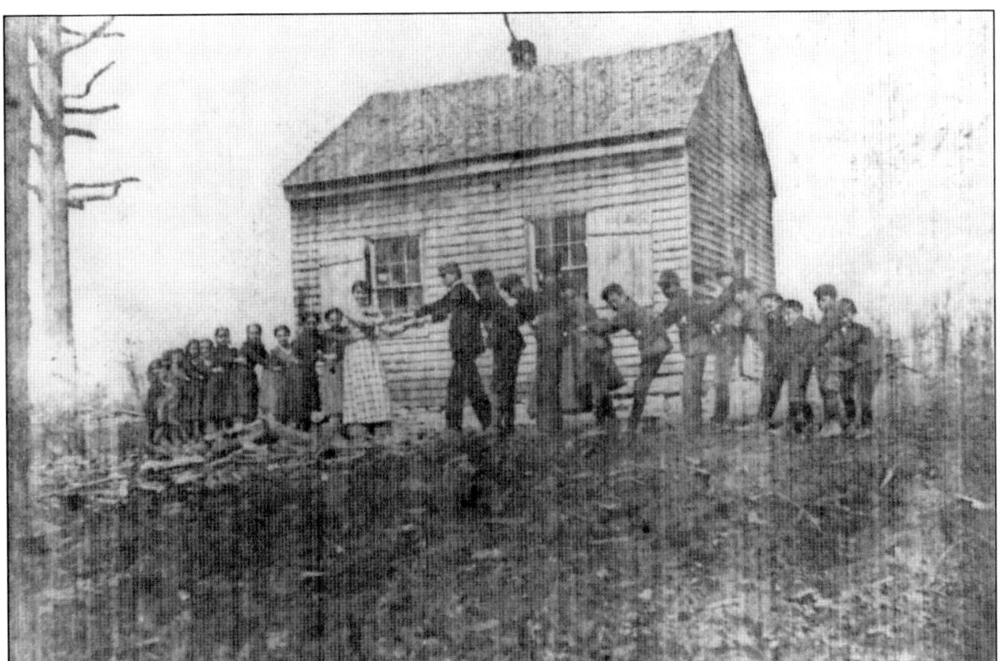

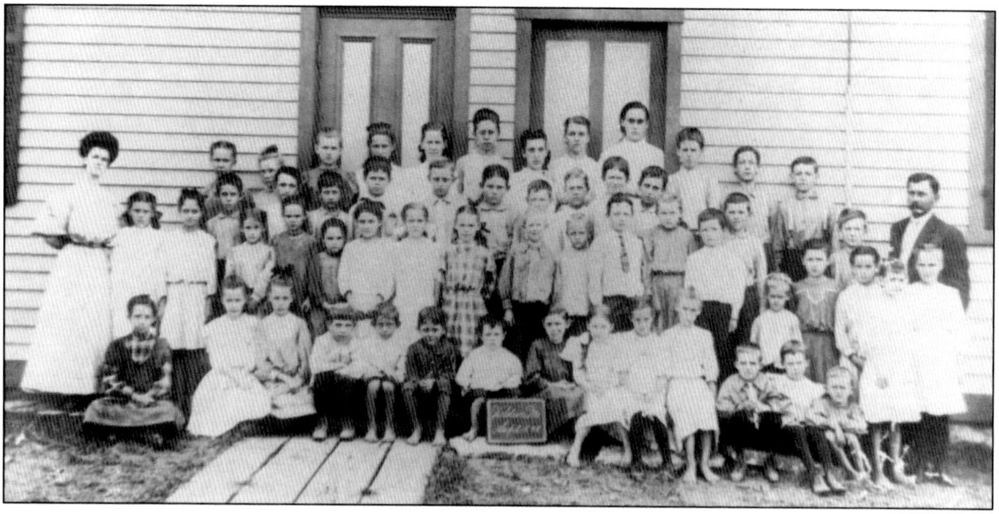

Seen above in 1908 is the Holstein School, which had grown so large that it required two teachers with two separate classrooms. Below is probably the smallest school, most likely Rush Island's school, which was built for the families who lived on the island south of the Bernheimer area.

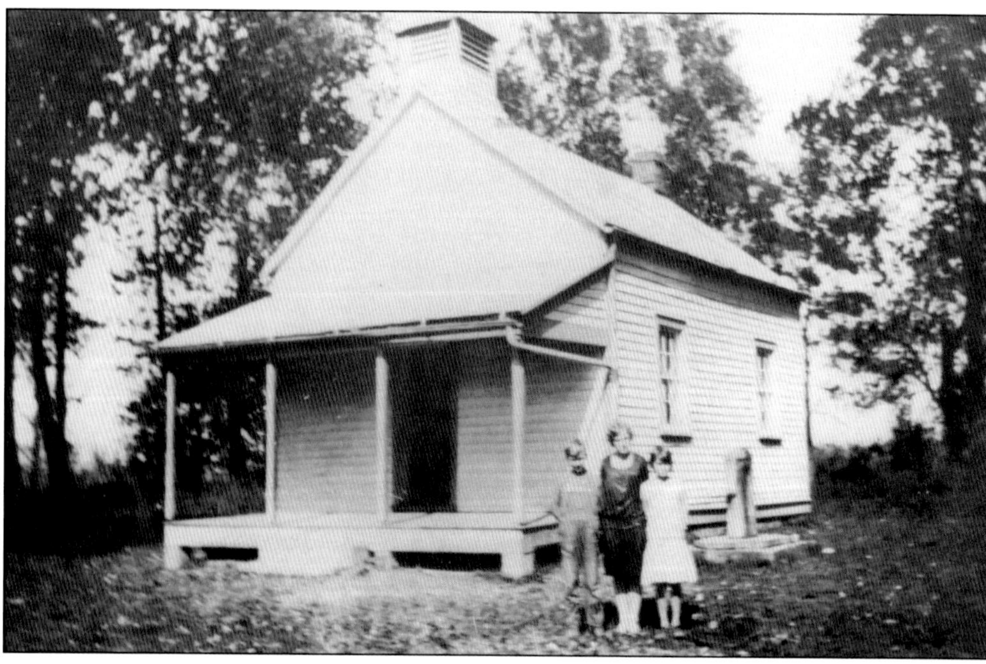

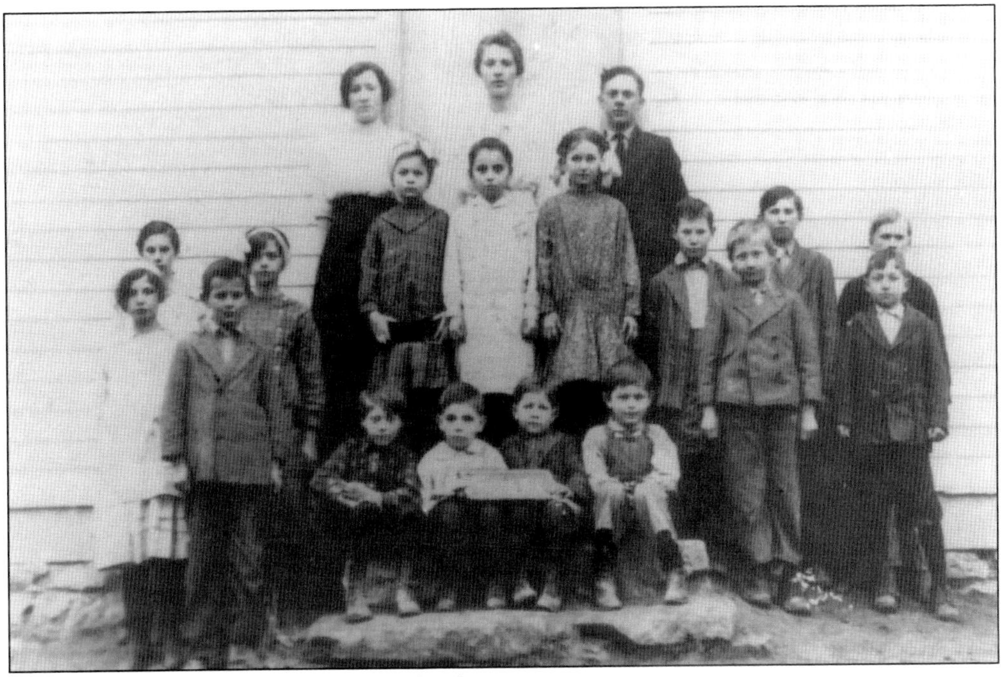

These students are at the Lime Kiln School in District 12, three and a half miles northwest of Warrenton, in 1914. Students included in the picture are Tille Wilson, Annie Determan, Edith Ocum, Gladys Voss, Elenora Sprick, John Morris, Gilbert Nordwald, Floyd Durham, Clarence Oberhellman, Allen Bryan, Nellie Froderman, Carl Determan, Edna Morris, Flayus Durham, Wesley Sprick, Arthur Determan, Emmet Driemeyer, and Leroy Yocum. At right is a souvenir card that would have been presented to the student at the close of the school year from the Kruegerville School in District 2. It was given to the students by teacher Fred Luetkemeyer and directors H.H. Wessel, Louis Hoelscher, and Fritz Niemeyer.

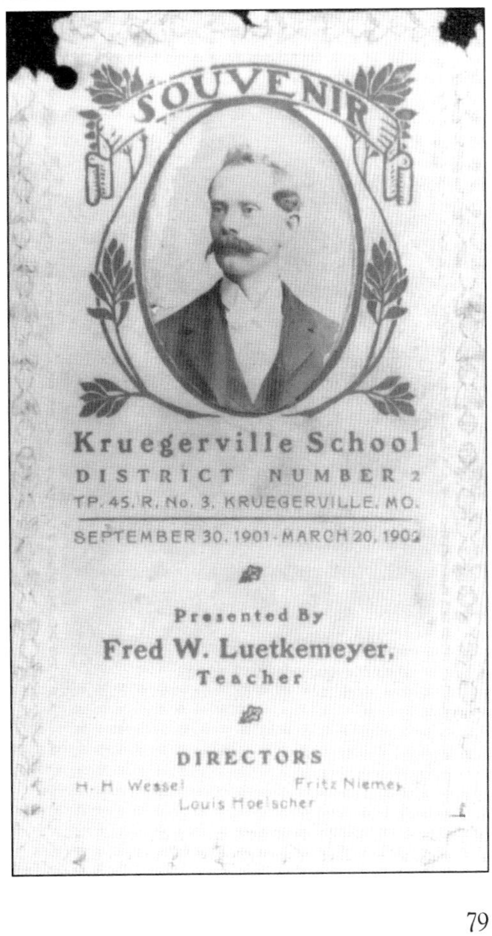

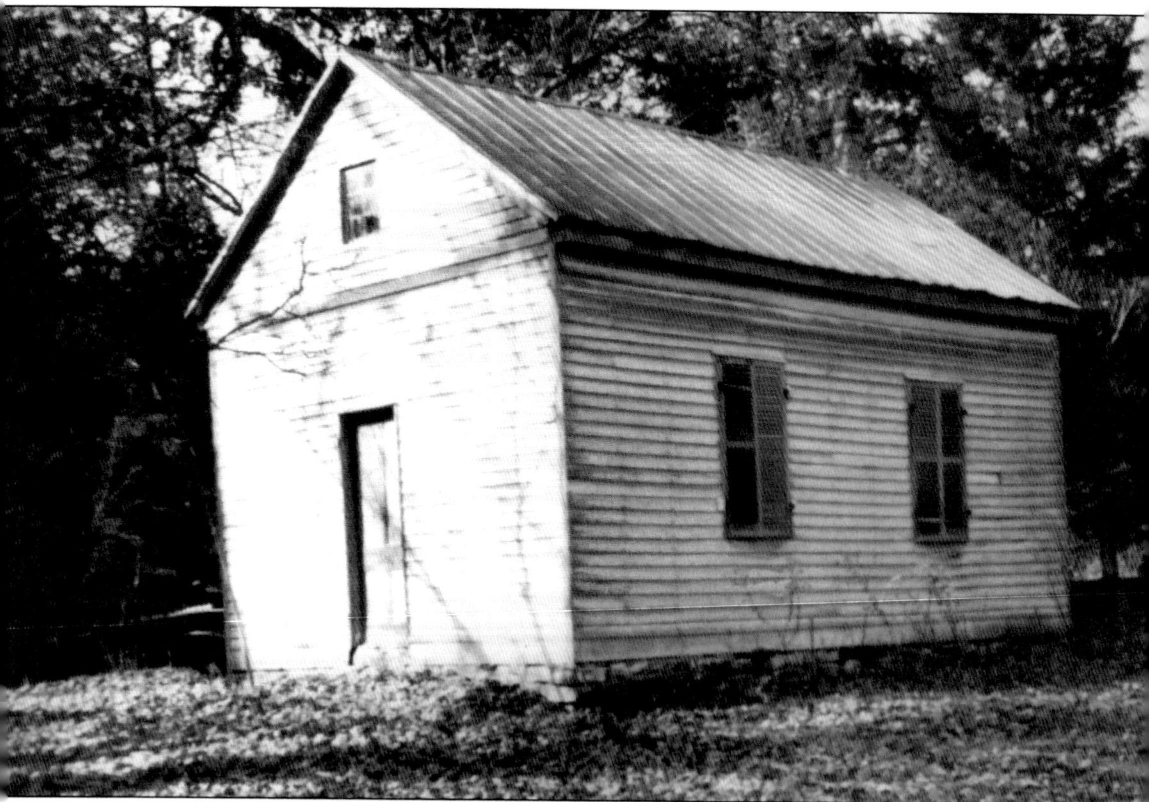

The days of one-room schools grew to a close in the 1950s, when new laws mandated costly procedures that small country districts could not afford. The only option was to reorganize into larger districts by combining the smaller area schools. This was the Cedar Valley School, where John Luetkemeyer first attended school north of Hopewell after arriving from Germany at age 12. Years later, he returned as a schoolteacher. His own son followed the same pattern.

Seven

THE COUNTY SEAT

Mordecai Morgan settled in 1818 on the Boone's Lick Trail just east of the creek. When Warren County was first established in January 1833 and named in honor of Joseph G. Warren, a hero of the Revolutionary War, a panel of three commissioners was appointed by the legislature to name the location of a county seat. Jacob Groom of Montgomery County, Felix Scott of St. Charles County, and Jesse McDaniel of Franklin County were assigned that difficult task. In May, a temporary court began in the home of Mordecai Morgan, causing great agitation. When two of the three commissioners reported in favor of the town of New Boston, a town about 16 miles south on the road to Marthasville, the battle began. John Owings, Samual Ward, John Northcutt, and Jesse Cain wanted to each donate land at the intersection of Sections 11, 12, 14, and 15 in Township 45 North Range 2 West to establish a town. Jesse Harrison was named the town commissioner; the town, with 100 lots and 16 reserved for the county, was advertised in the *Missouri Republican*; and lots were sold. A mercantile, mill, school, and church were established, but the debate raged on when the commissioners announced that they did not feel the location was appropriate.

The legislature appointed a new set of commissioners: James Finley of Lincoln County, Benjamin Emmons of St. Charles County, and John H. Smith, who replaced Thomas Mosley of Montgomery County. Dr. John Jones of Charrette Creek demanded that Carty Wells explain why he should not be compelled to move the records to John Wyatt's house near New Boston. The issue wasn't resolved, even on June 11, 1835, when the commissioners reported they had accepted the donation of 55 acres from Henry Walton of St. Louis and five acres from Mordecai Morgan.

So the issue was put to the voters on January 15 and 16, 1836, and the seat of justice was finally officially set at Warrenton.

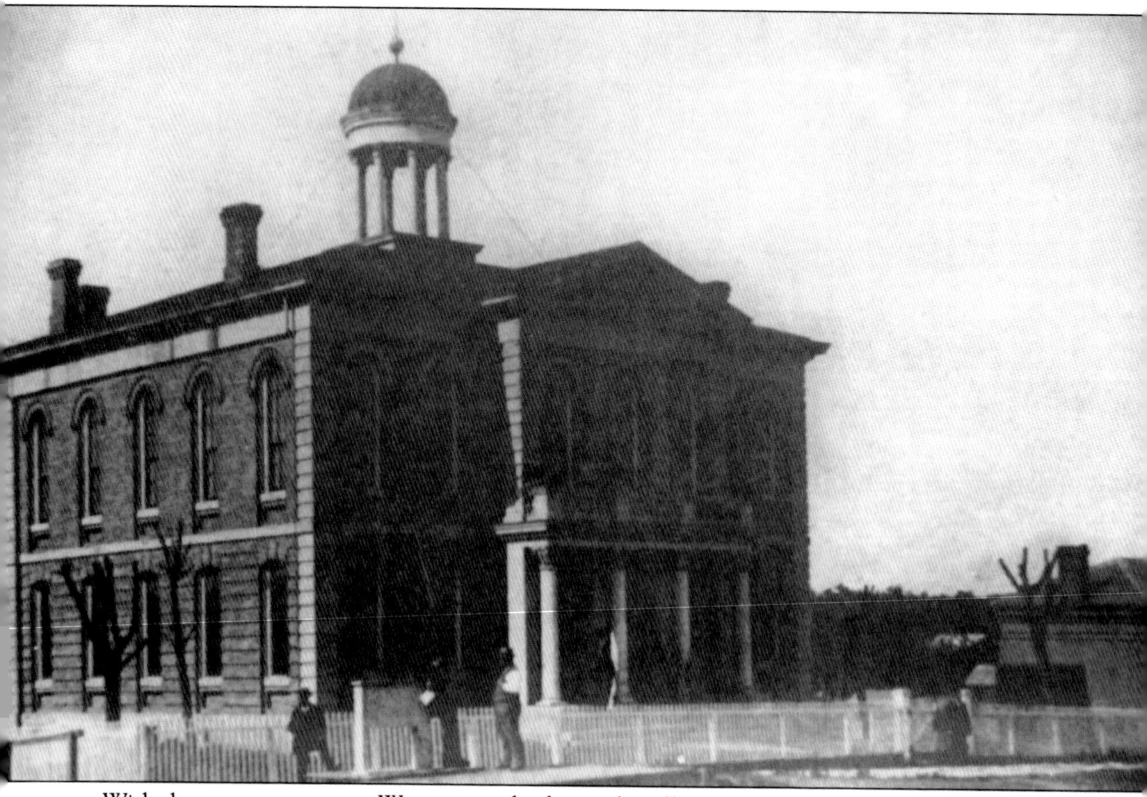

With the county seat set at Warrenton, the first order of business was to accept Solomon Jenkins's bid of $2,600 to build a courthouse. While that work was in progress, the first sessions of court were held in Joseph B. Wells's home, which later became Middlekamp's hardware store. The first plat of the town, drawn up by Henry Walton, had only three primary streets, Oak, Main and Walton, which were 40 feet wide. A second plat was discarded because it only included four blocks, which were called sections. The final plat, which had sections and additional smaller outlots or fractional sections was finally adopted. The first of the town's building lots were sold at Harvey Ford's mercantile, called Ford & Munson, in a building that still stands today at the northwest corner of Main and Market Streets. The first courthouse, built in 1838, was replaced with the courthouse above, which was completed in 1871.

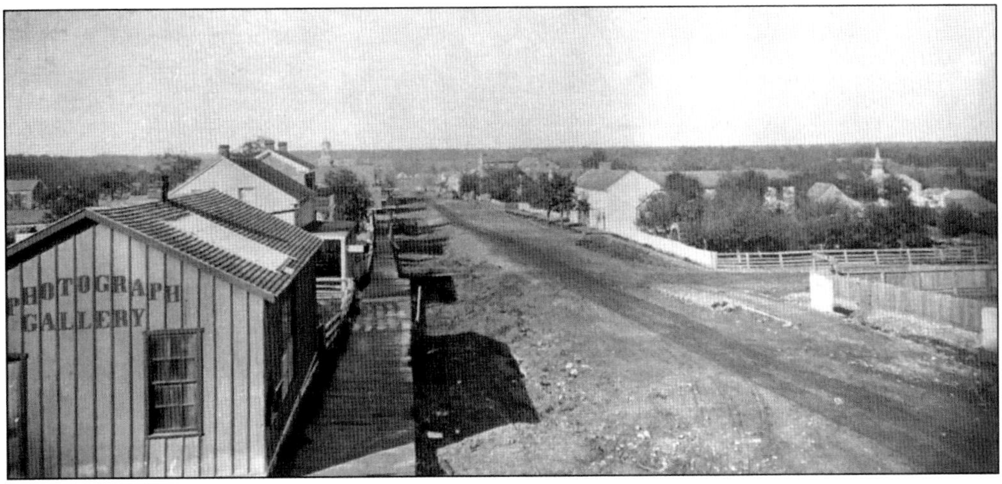

Both of these images were captured by photographer Rudolph Goebel, whose shop sat on the side of Boone's Lick Road, as seen in the top left of the photograph above. The late-1800s panorama, taken facing northwest, includes the Olive House, the large building in the center that served as a local inn. Just past that building is the home of John A. Pulliam, a wealthy owner of several tobacco factories and slaves before the Civil War. The southeast corner in front of his home is where the local slave auctions were held before the practice was abolished. In the image below, taken facing east, is Warrenton's Main Street, also known as Boone's Lick Road, with the Schowengerdt's Mercantile building on the right.

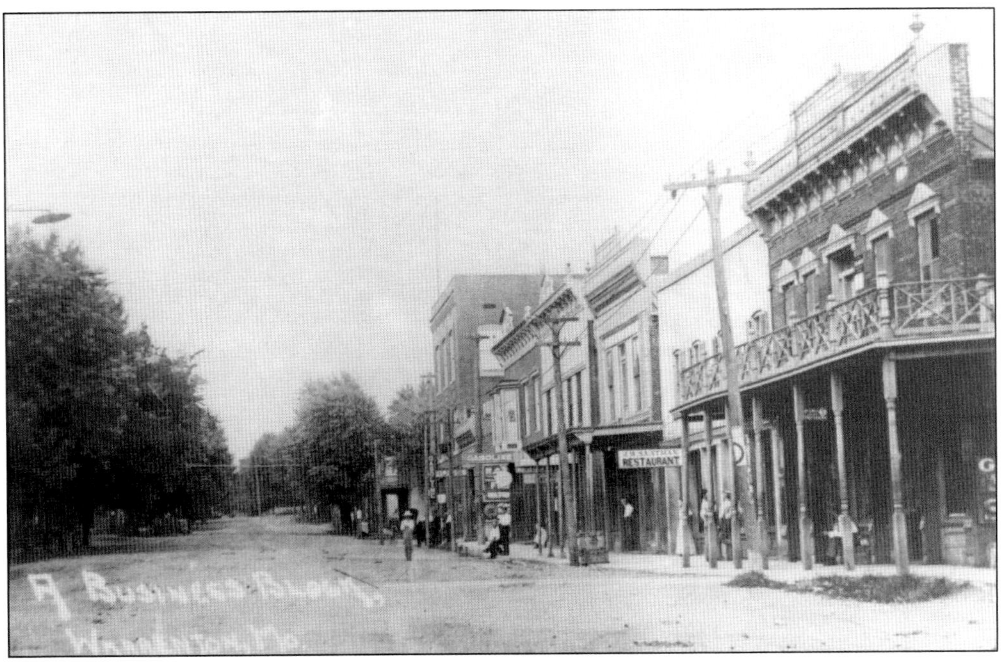

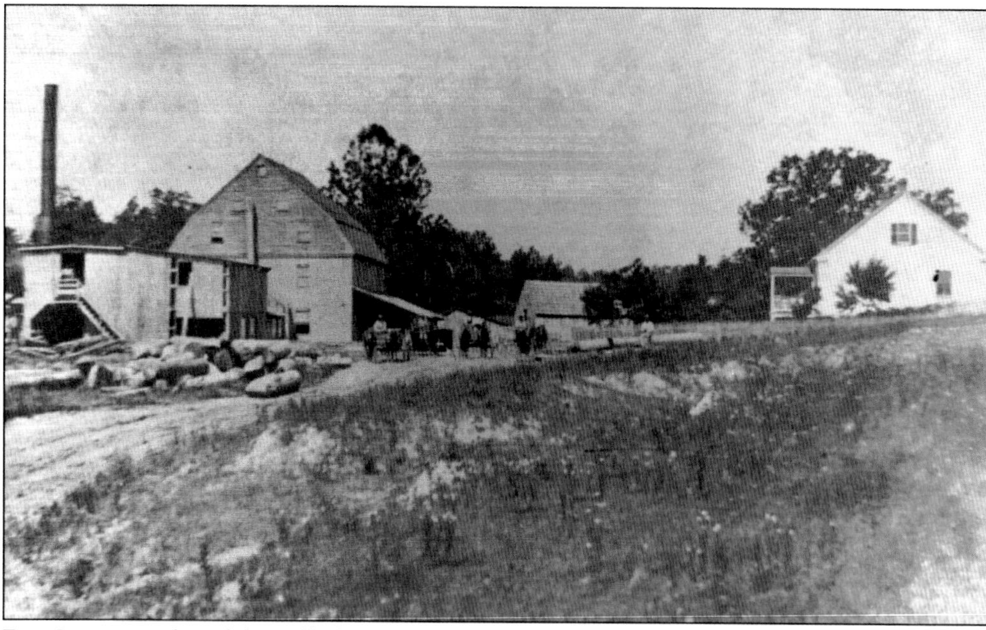

Fritz Sievert purchased the mill of Grief Stewart in 1873. The steam-powered mill ground corn and wheat, sawed lumber, and carded wool for spinning. Sievert also built a carousel that was powered by live horses, had a music box, and revolved; it was used each year for the Old Settlers Reunion. Fritz's son August went on to build the town's first electric-powered ice and electric light plant. This was just down the street, not far from the courthouse. Famous architect Thomas W. Brady of St. Louis designed this courthouse, built in 1870 by S. Conrad and Company. Just past the courthouse is the circuit clerk and recorder's office, which was designed to be completely fireproof.

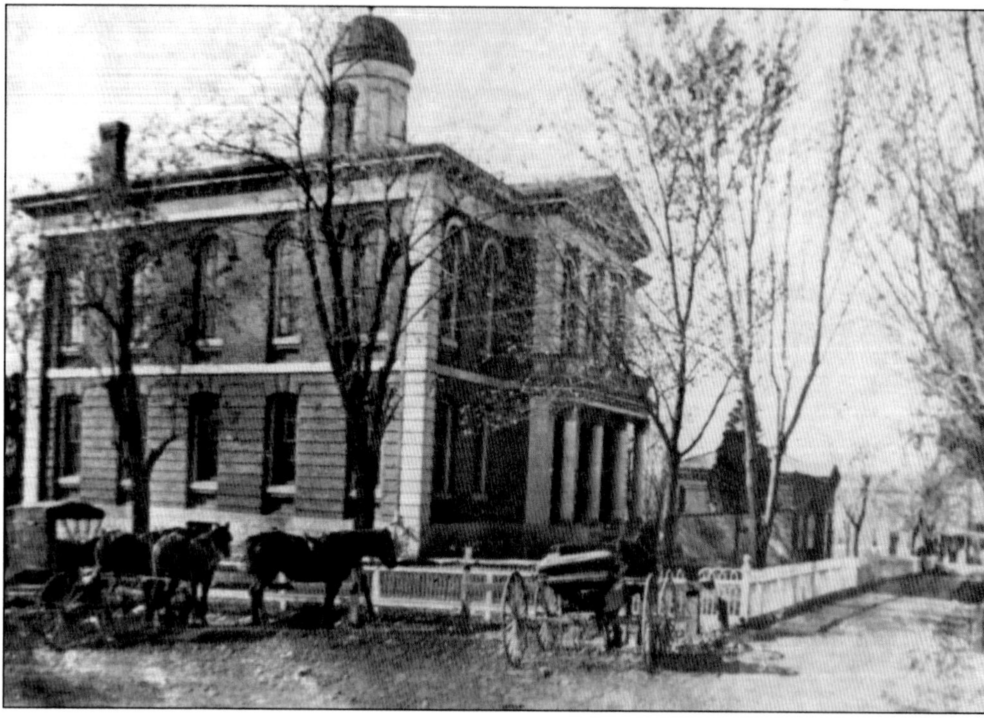

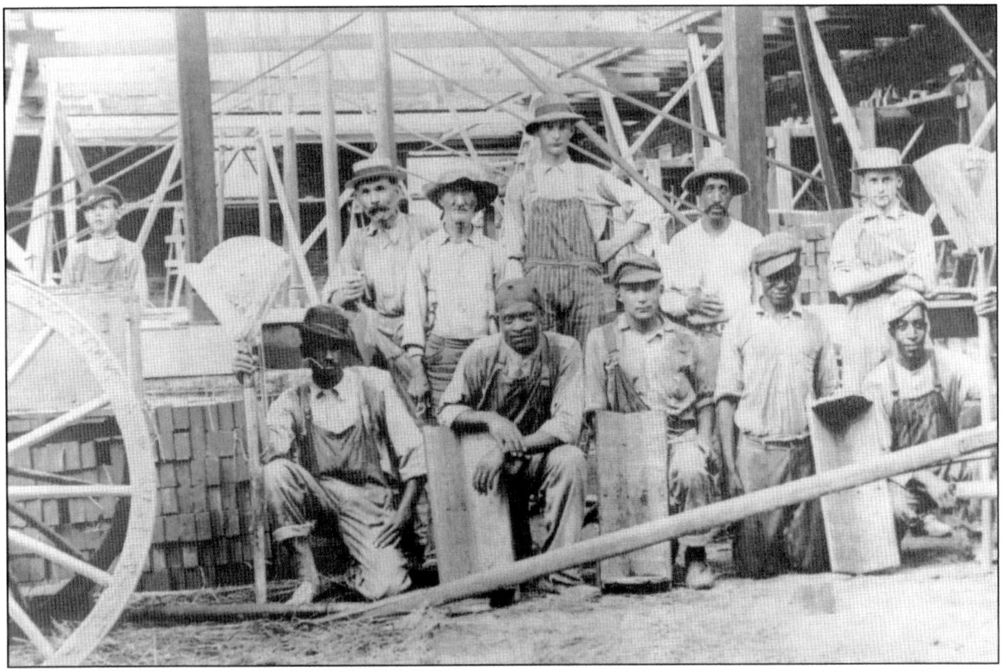

Herman Peitzmeyer operated a brick factory at the foot of the hill in about 1890. His factory, with his crewmembers shown here, made the majority of the bricks that built the courthouse and the fine homes and businesses of Warrenton and Warren County. They were even used to build the Hopewell Academy, nearly 20 miles away and down several hills. In 1883, Warrenton finally became a railroad town. For many years, the depot had been located in Truesdale, forcing all business to go through there. Five trains stopped there daily. Used as a passenger depot, it was filled with activity as traveling salesmen alighted, the postmaster hauled his sack, or news was picked up to be distributed.

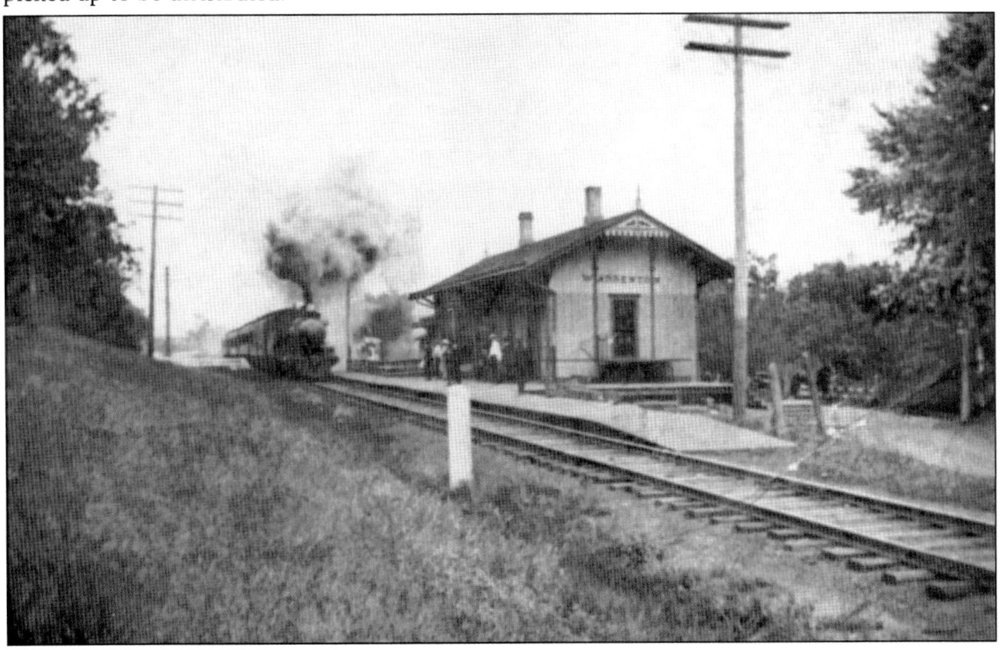

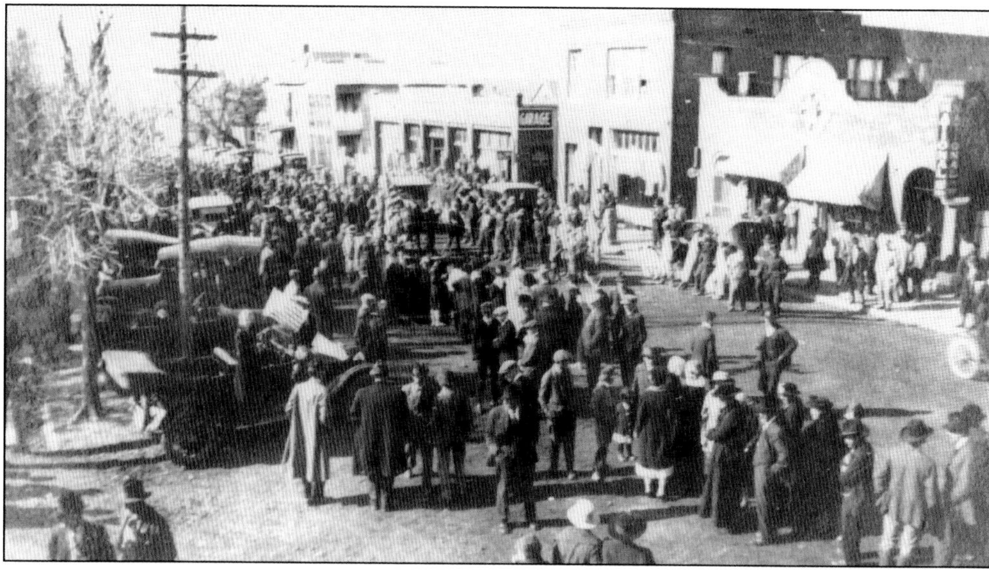

The courthouse was always the center of the city's busiest activity. In the image above, someone is making an important speech as hundreds of men look on during a cold winter's day. The last hanging in Warren County took place at the courthouse when 22-year-old William E. Church was hanged on January 10, 1907. The young man had brutally murdered his adoptive parents on August 30, 1903, and the crime had rocked the community. Flags are unfurled for the summertime patriotic parade down Boone's Lick Road, where local veterans are making their way to the city cemetery. Notice how the cars parked in the center of the 40-foot-wide street, keeping traffic on each side in the right direction. In the center of the street is a traffic pole that the city's community Christmas tree was wired to, a sight that only old-timers could recall.

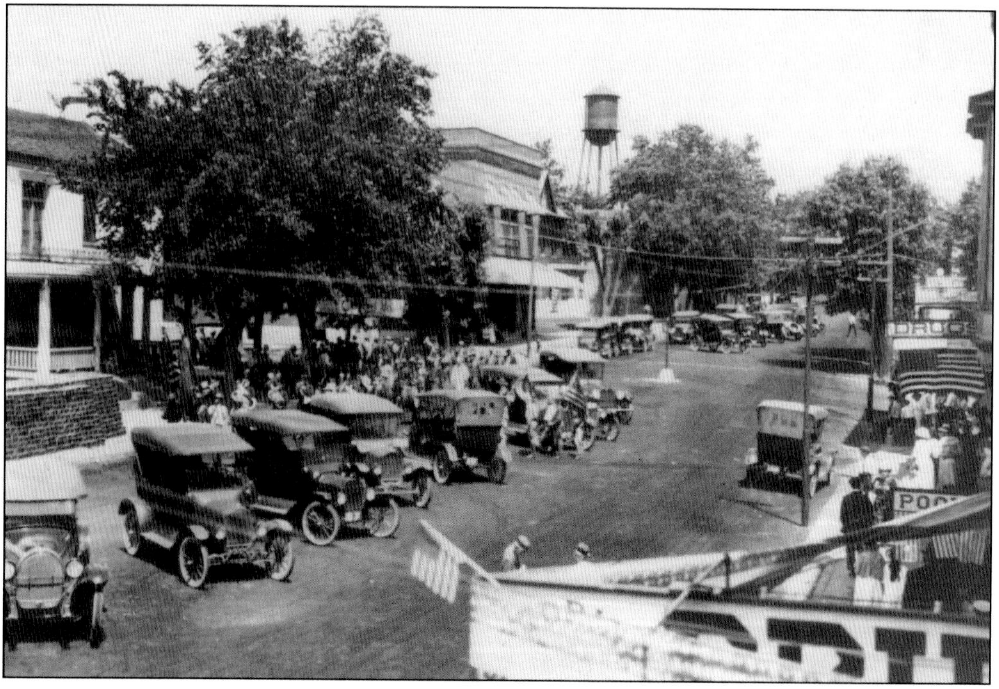

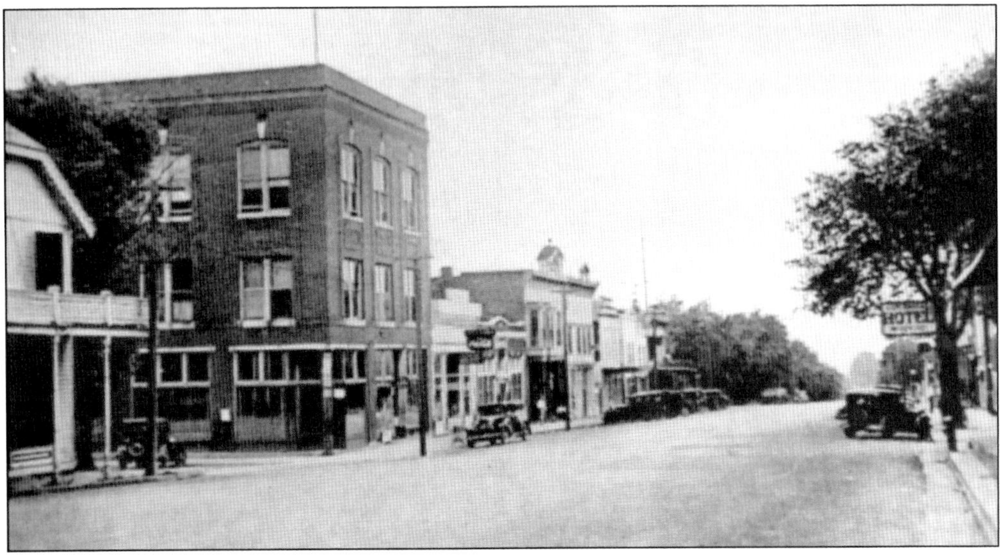

Warrenton's Main Street is part of the original east-west Boone's Lick Trail that travelers used to connect up to the Sante Fe and Oregon Trails further west. One hundred years later, the wagons were gone and replaced by the more modern mode of transportation, the automobile. Missouri State Highway 47 traverses Boone's Lick Trail as it heads from Interstate 70 to Marthasville and further south. Once a tree-lined avenue with some of the city's finest homes, it provided a memorable entrance to the city of Warrenton.

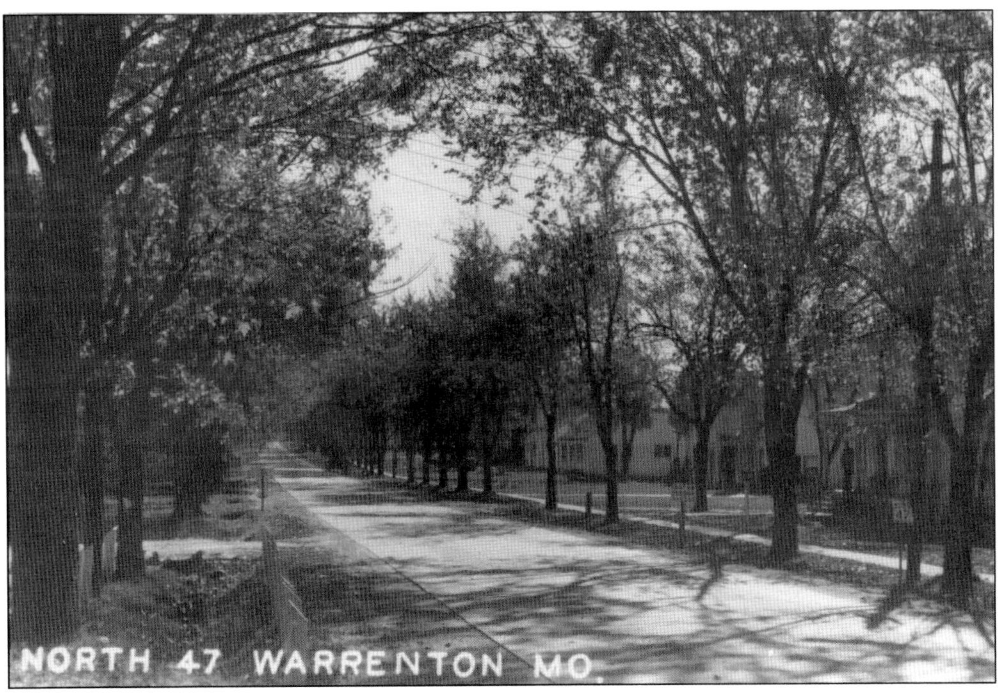

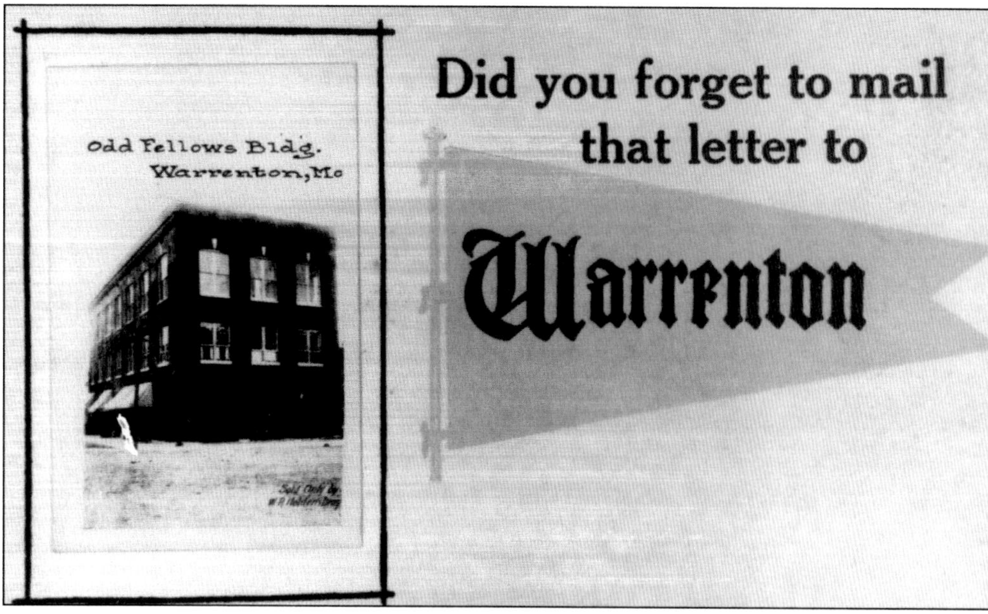

The large Odd Fellows building was one of the tallest and largest buildings in town. One could stop off for an ice-cold Coca-Cola at the soda fountain in W.R. Holden's Drug Store after mailing a postcard from Warrenton to friends far away. Main Street's traffic flow was changed again by moving the parking to the outside. To the right in the photograph below is the old Nieburg Furniture store, and just past that is the Modern-Colonial Hotel in the former Pulliam home.

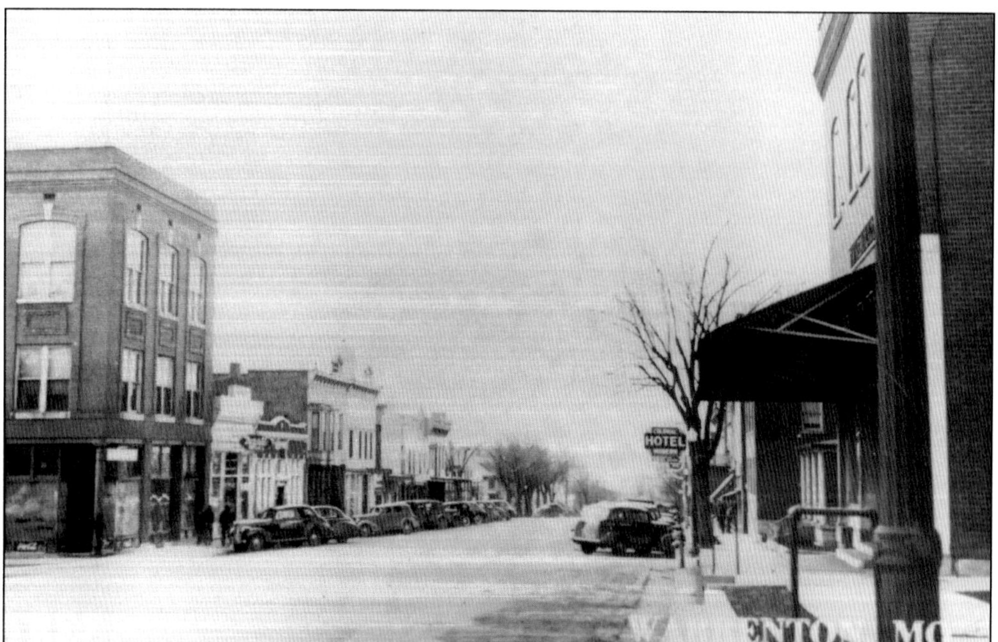

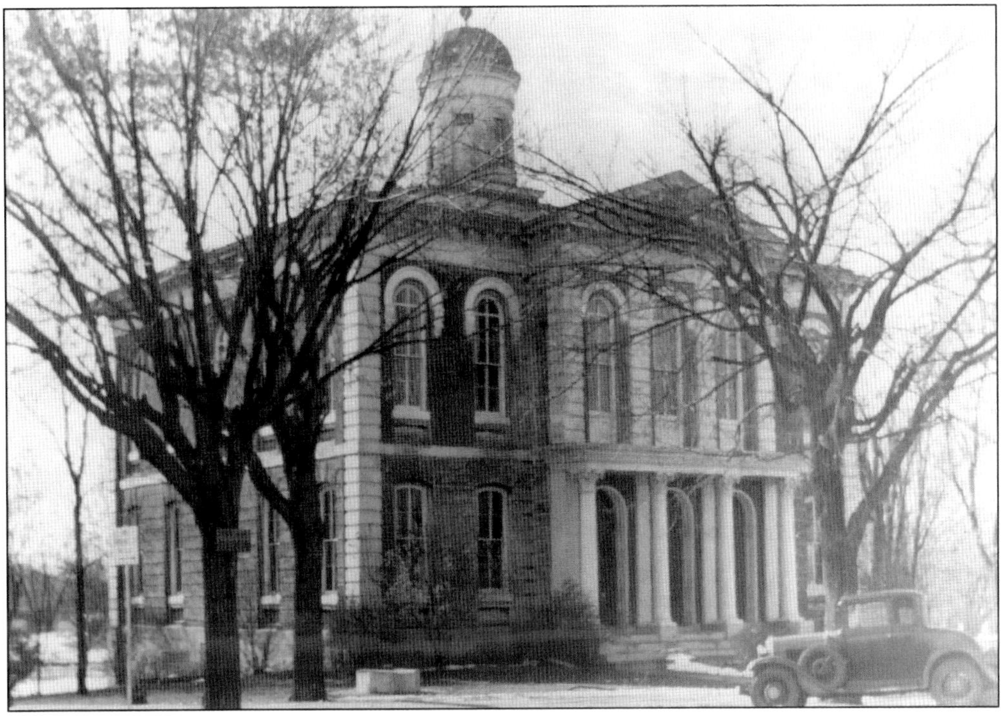

Above is one of the most substantial and elegant courthouses in Missouri. It was of Italianate design and contained a walnut staircase that curved its way to the second-floor courtroom. Beautiful metal ceilings graced its interior. The dome that sat on top was enclosed in the late 19th century. By the 1950s, as seen below, some of the original old buildings on Main Street were starting to disappear, but the old Odd Fellow building remained.

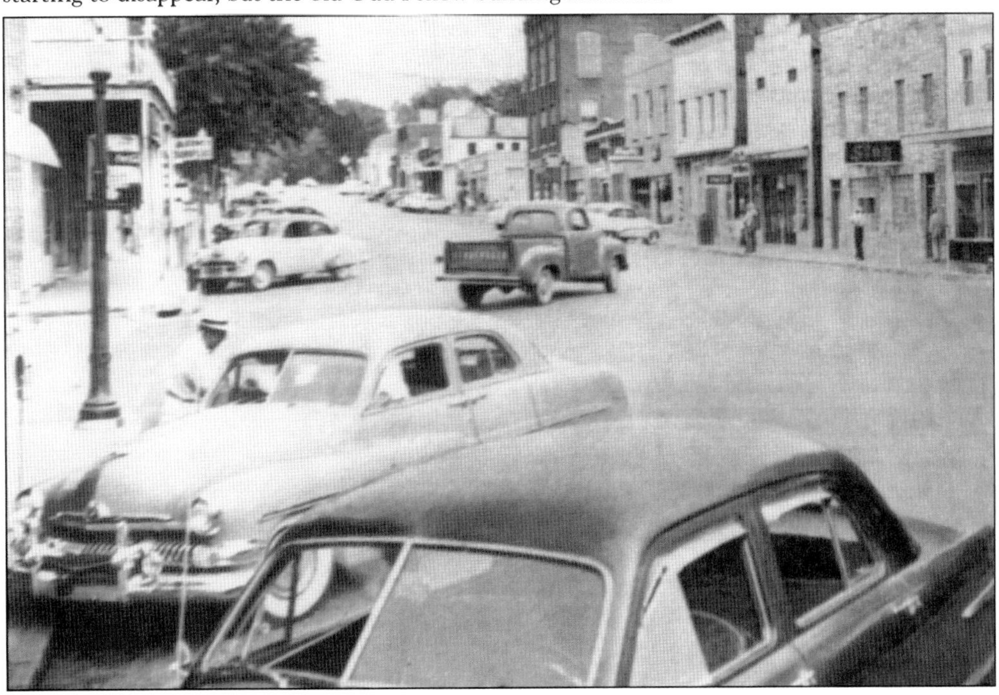

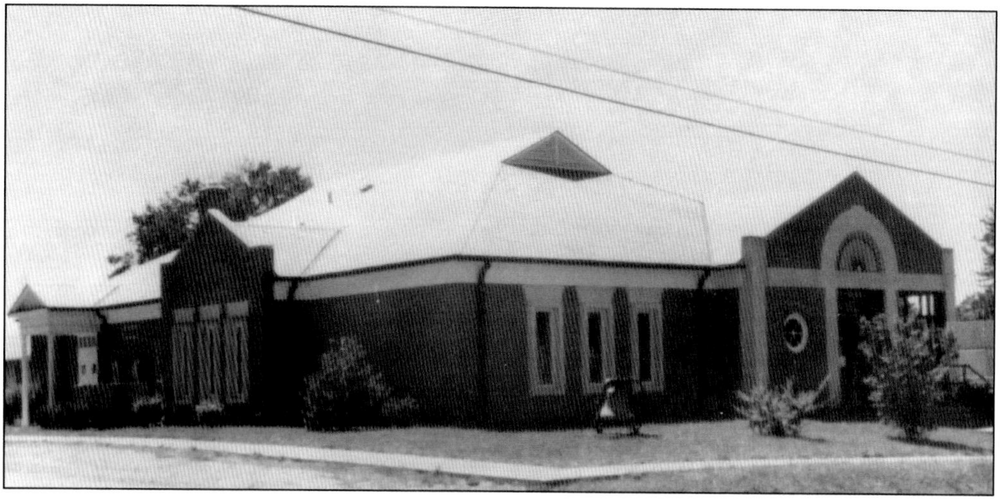

On December 16, 1981, the museum building committee for the Warren County Historical Society met and accepted bids from various contracting companies to construct the Warren County Museum (above) at the southwest corner of Market and Walton Streets. The building is in the process of receiving a new addition in 2011 thanks to the generosity of the Hummel family. The historic Warren County Courthouse (below) served the county for well over 100 years but had declined by the close of the 20th century. It was replaced in the mid-1990s with a more modern and state-of-the-art building necessary for the 21st century. New county administration buildings are being built in 2011 in a new location.

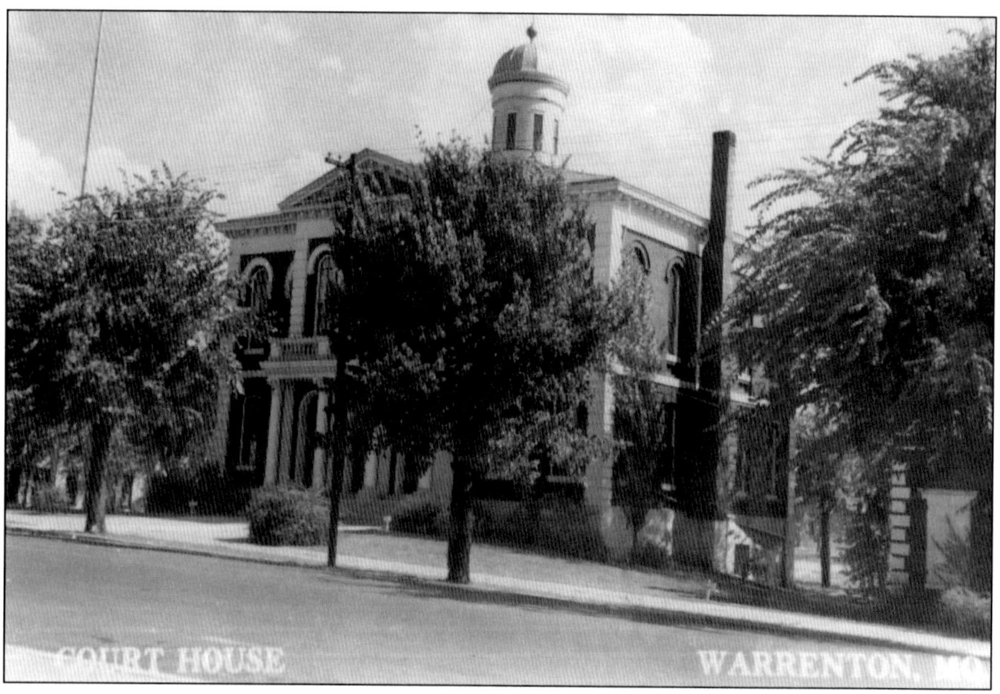

Eight

Life in Warren County

For over 150 years, life in Warren County has been filled with events, both joyous and sad, as well as people, both good and bad, that share a story of communities proud of their heritage and culture. From trailblazing pioneers like Daniel Boone to German immigrant authors, Warren County's story is filled with determined and amazing heroes.

While Warren County residents have built homes and carved lives out the wilderness, they have maintained a place for worship and an eye on the future with the education of their children. More importantly, they have always remembered to celebrate their heritage and traditions and enjoy their culture.

Assuring that their young were instructed with good moral codes, they have given them Scouting and 4-H activities. Music and sports have enriched everyone's lives. Countywide activities like the county fair and the centennial and sesquicentennial celebrations have enriched everyone's memories.

They have honored those less fortunate with the founding of the Central Wesleyan Orphanage and assured the welfare of others that are challenged through the good work done at Emmaus.

Life in Warren County has been filled with many of the triumphs and tragedies that faced the entire nation. The early emigrants from Germany who filled the county prior to the Civil War definitely contributed to the success of the Union army.

Those first German immigrants brought many of the traditions and celebrations still found in Warren County today, whether it is relaxing at the local winery, enjoying the local shooting contest, or attending the local church sausage dinner. The German culture still prevails in Warren County today, portrayed by the determination and strong pride in their community. Those first German immigrants followed Duden to Warren County with hopes and dreams of a better life for their families. Although sometimes criticized by those early immigrants, one who followed Duden did state, "While all is not exactly as Duden explained, in some ways it is even better."

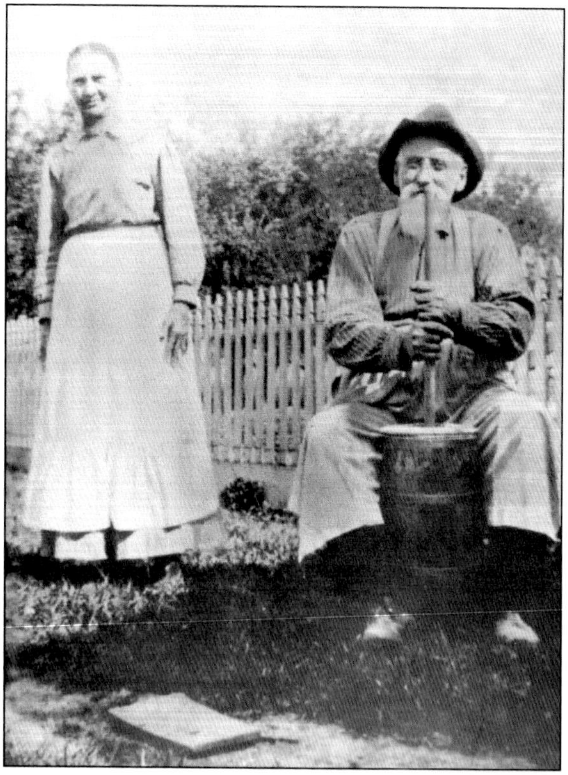

Henry Hasenjager and his wife, who lived at Treloar in the Missouri River bottomland, had a clear understanding of each other's roles at home. Henry knew his place was at the butter churn. In the photograph below are Dr. Sylvanus Griswold and his family in their home in Marthasville. The Griswolds were a wealthy and well-respected family that owned the cemetery Daniel Boone was buried in and fought to see the gravesite remain there when Kentucky came to reclaim its hero.

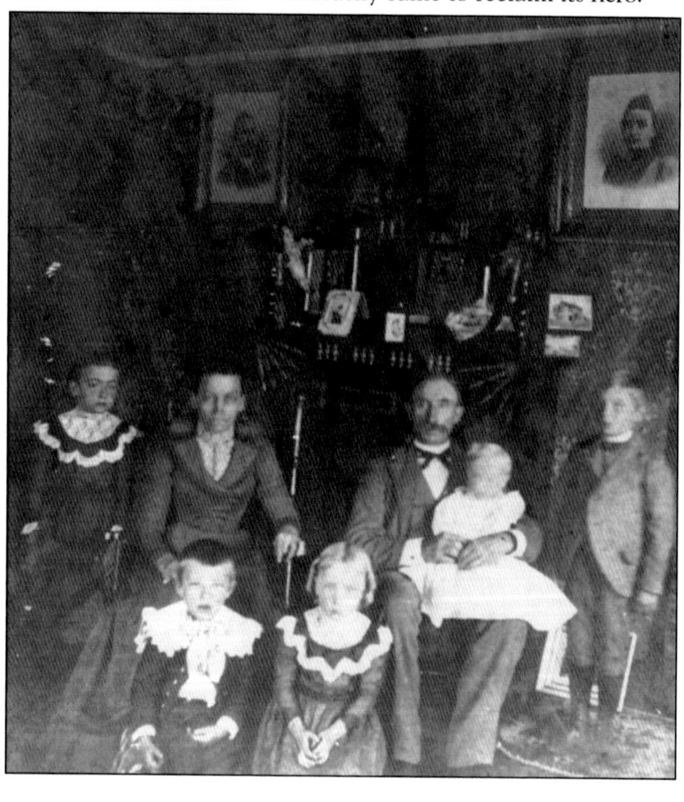

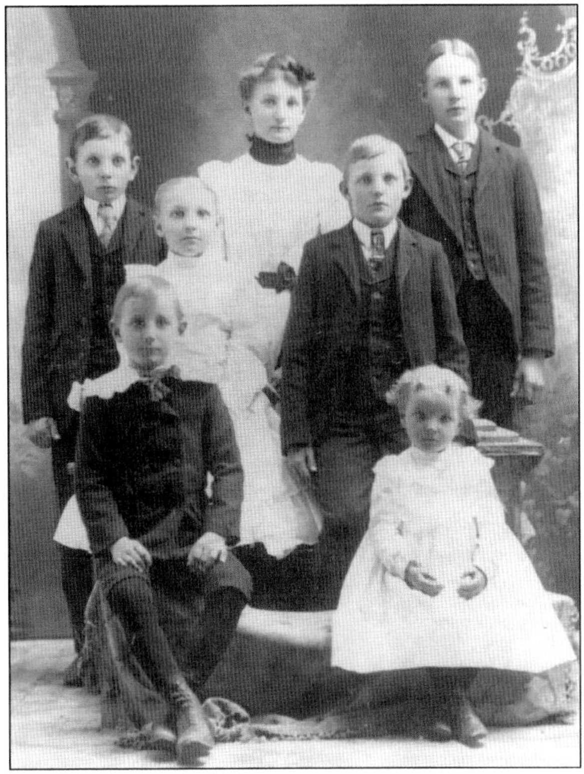

The children of Henry and Johanna Graue are, from left to right, (front row) Frank and Olinda; (second row) Clara and George; (third row) Clarence, Maggie, and Charles.

By the 1850s, Warren County was one of the most predominately German counties in the state, with a majority of its families being either German-born or of German descent, and they were spread out across Warren County. The early-1900s photograph below was taken at the Lefholz farm in the Smith Creek area. From left to right are Arthur Lefholz, Ted Lefholz, Laura Lefholz Peyton, Hulda Lefholz Gruebbel, their father Rudolph Lefholz, his wife Elizabeth Rekate Lefholz, her father William Rekate, and Rudolph's son Alonzo Lefholz. The beautiful gingerbread trim on the house was made by William Rekate.

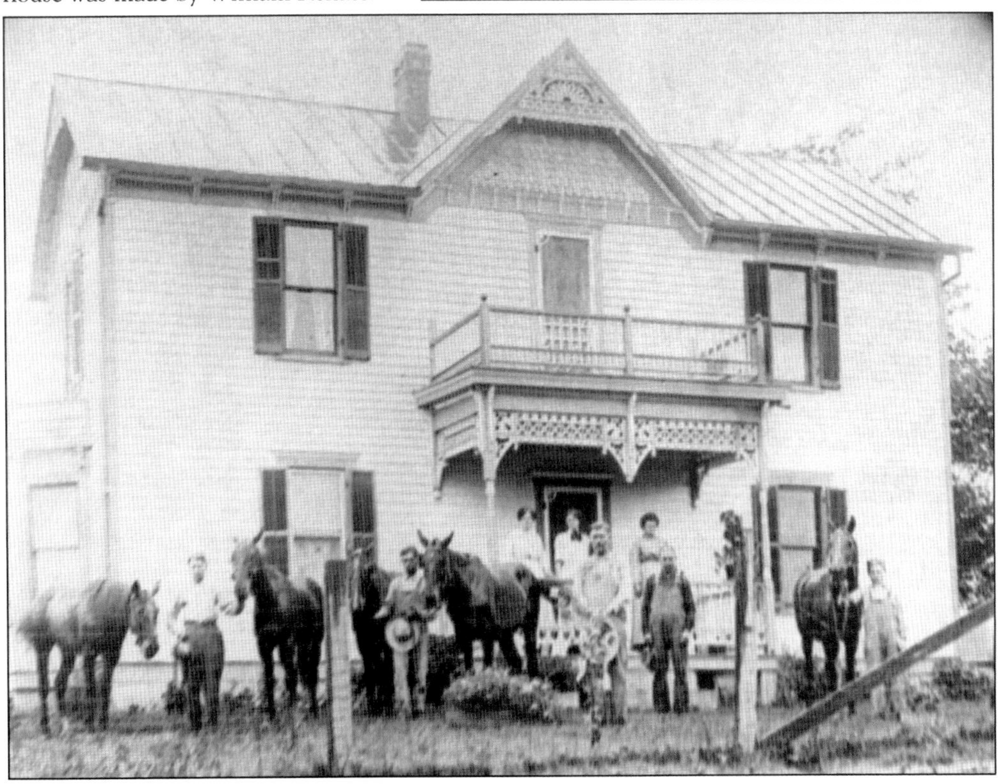

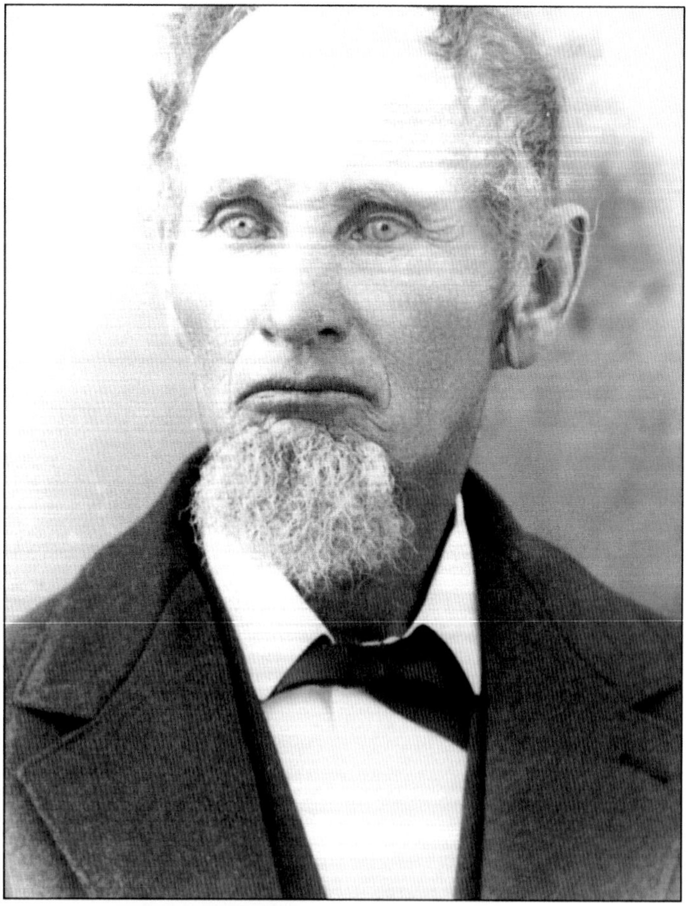

Seen left is Walter William Wehrman, born on February 5, 1825, in Hanover, Germany. Below is the Krauschner family from Silesia, Germany: (from left to right) Clara, Herman Henry, Lottie, and Frank. Gottfried Duden's book, published in 1828, had inspired thousands of Germans to believe that a better life with greater opportunity awaited them in America. Without fear of starvation or military oppression, they could carve out a new life on the frontier. It was this determination to create a better life for their families that makes Missouri the great state to live in that it is today.

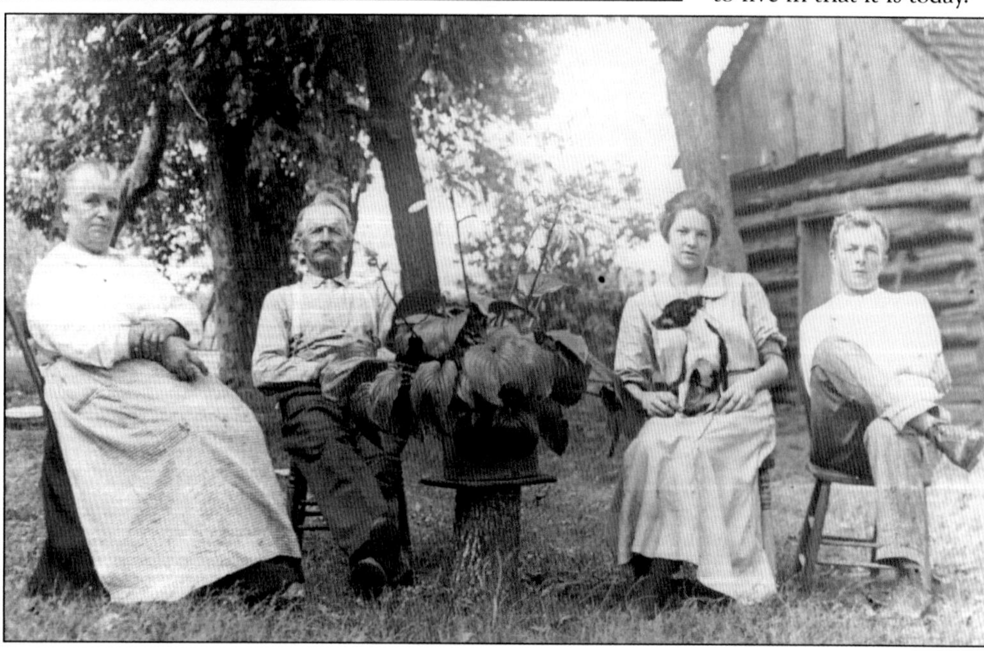

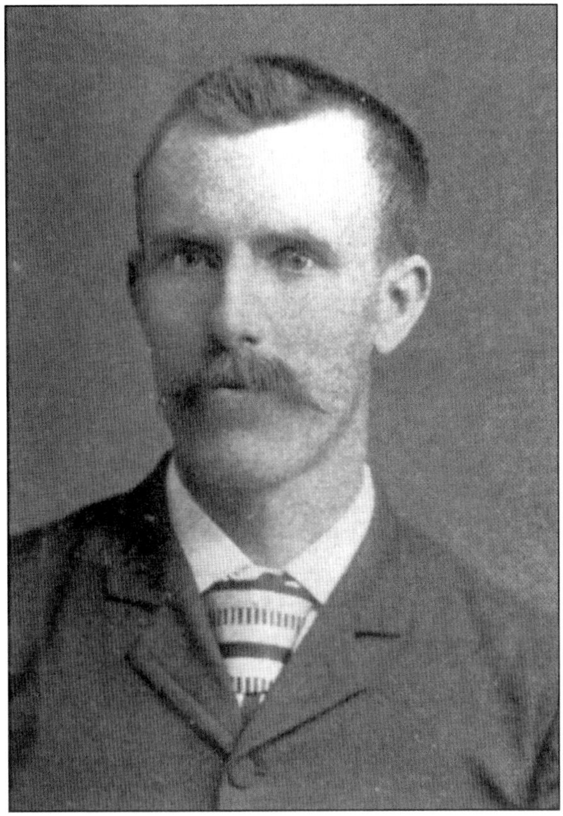

According to Gottfried Duden, there was opportunity for everyone in America. His book inspired H.H. Wessell, at right, to bring his family from Germany with the Giessen Emigration Society in 1834. In 1914, all of the Warren County officials were of German ancestry. In the photograph below, the ones identified are county assessor Henry Hagemann (first row, far left); F.W. Kehr, who was superintendent of schools (first row, third from left); presiding judge Henry Schowe (standing, far left); and Bejamin Frick, the county surveyor (standing, third from left).

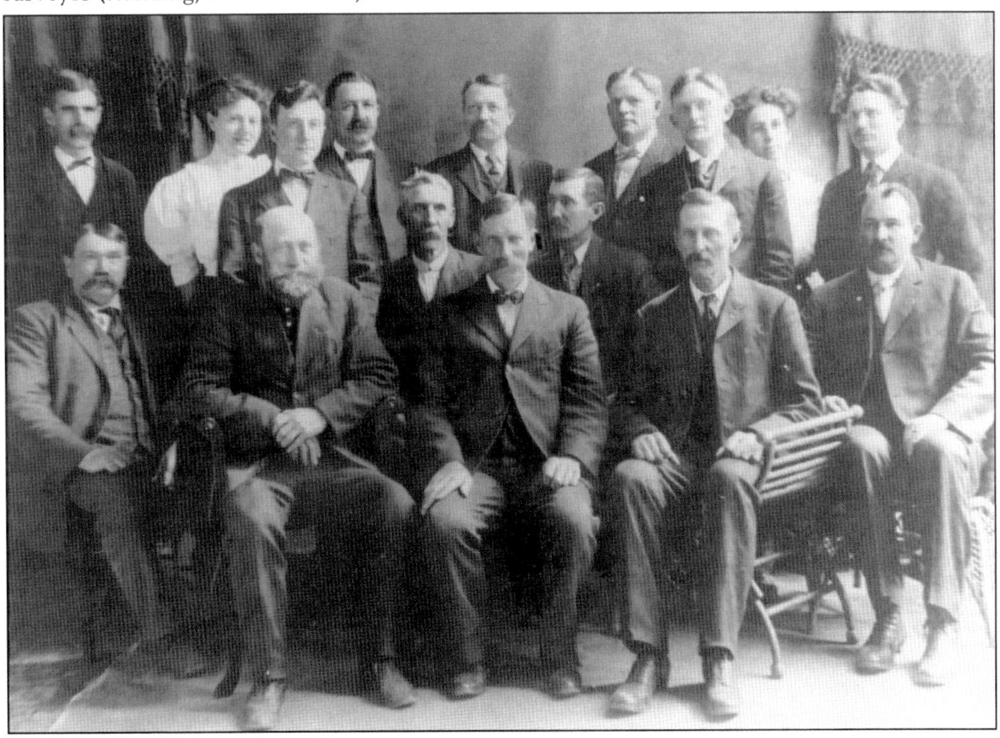

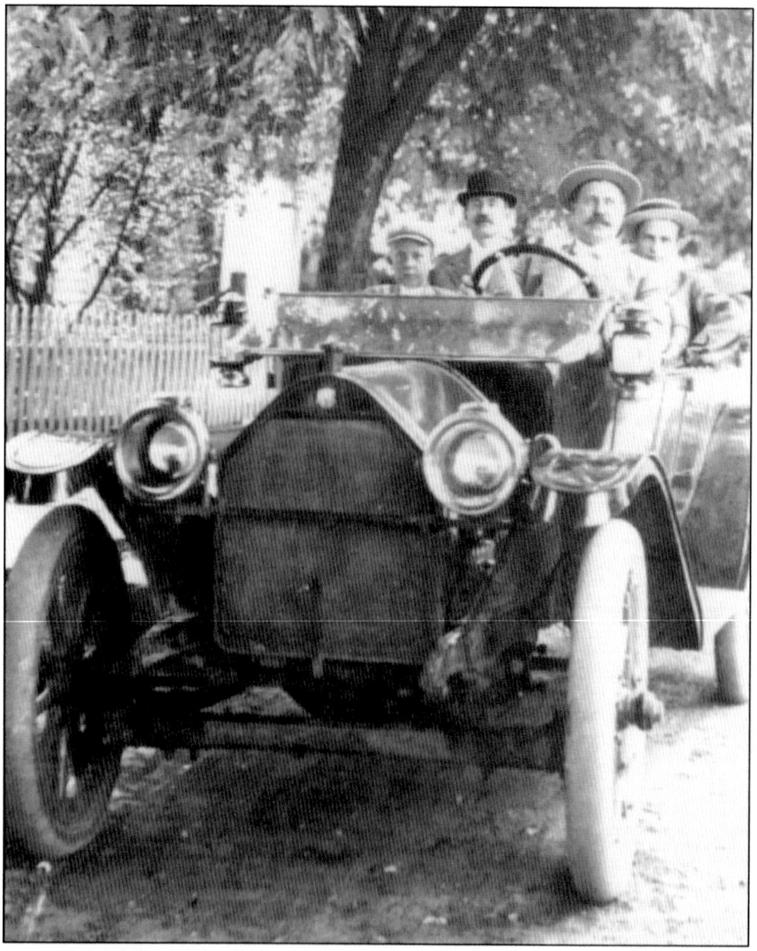

George Blattner (at left, in the driver's seat) was born in Pitts in 1850 and began his career in merchandising. He switched to cashier at the Wright City Bank and was quite a successful businessman. Below, George Block, in the back row, was one of the youngest in his family but definitely the tallest, known as the "giant on Sunnyside Road." He never married. His home had some special amenities, such as the extra-tall door in the front.

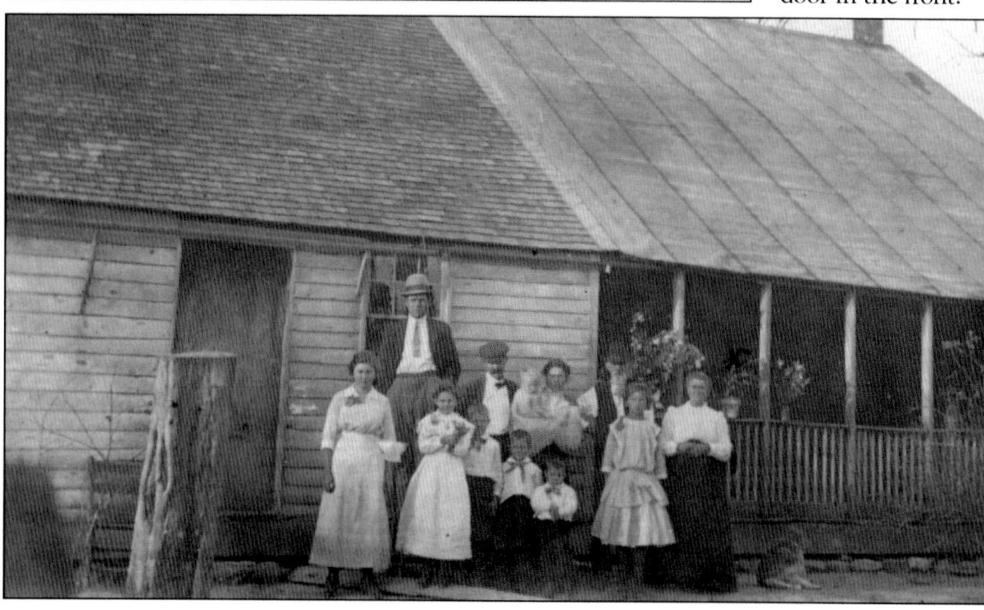

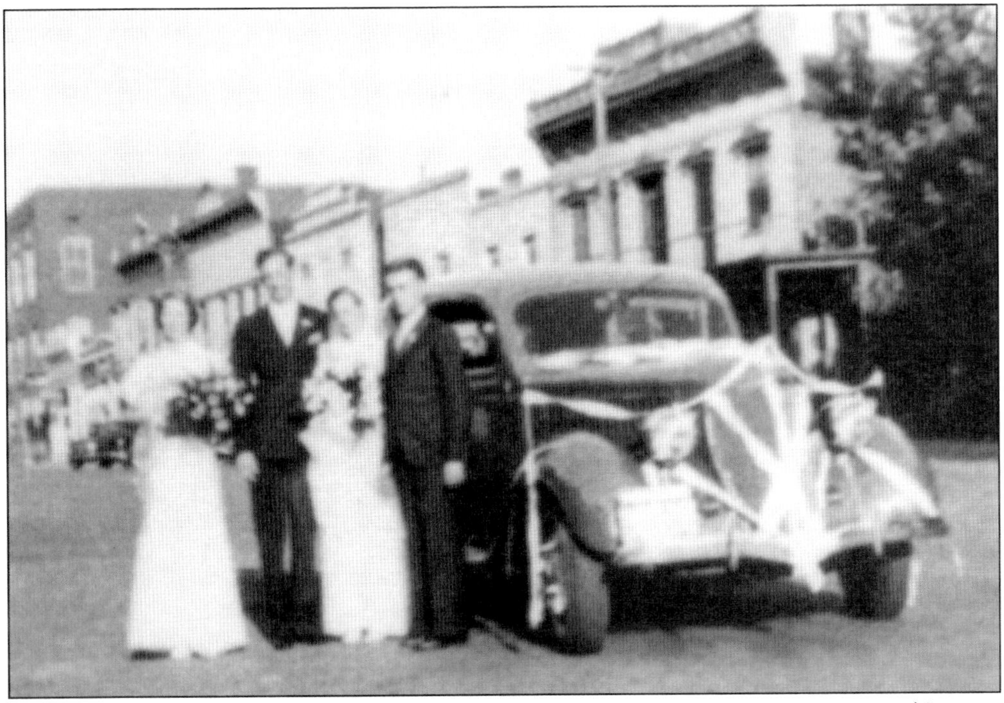

When Friedrich Hermann "Otto" Krueger, son of Fritz and Minnie Krueger, married Lenora Wilhelmine Louise Hanke on August 26, 1923, they stopped and posed as soon as they came out of the courthouse. Seen below, the Central Wesleyan College's basketball team won 22 games and only lost two in their 1928–1929 season under Coach Polster's excellent management.

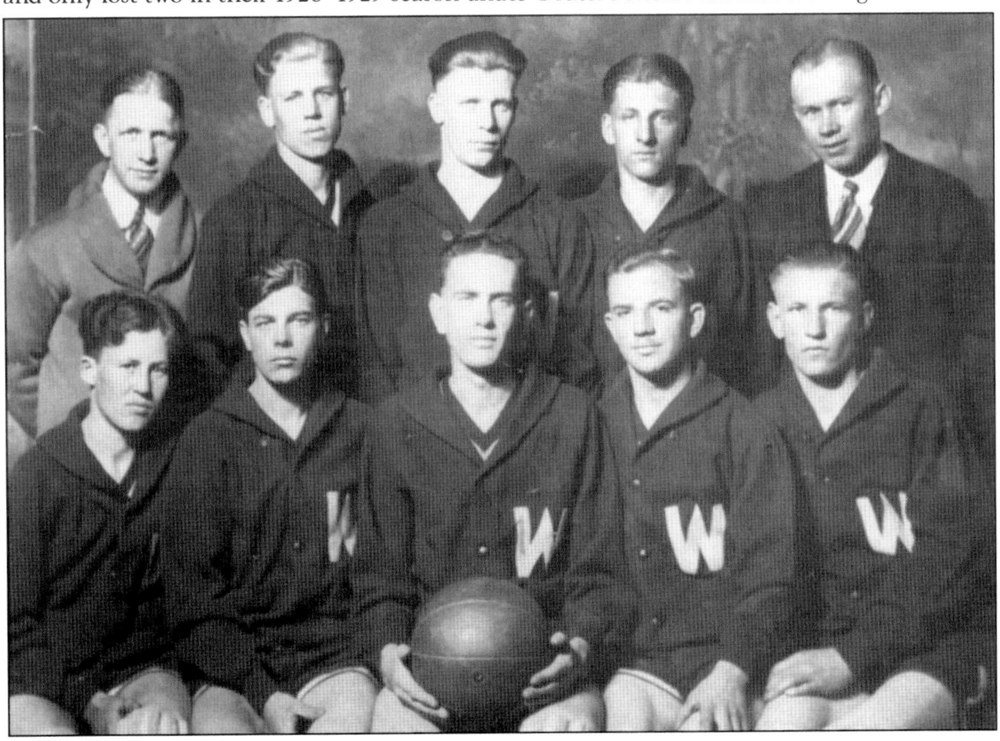

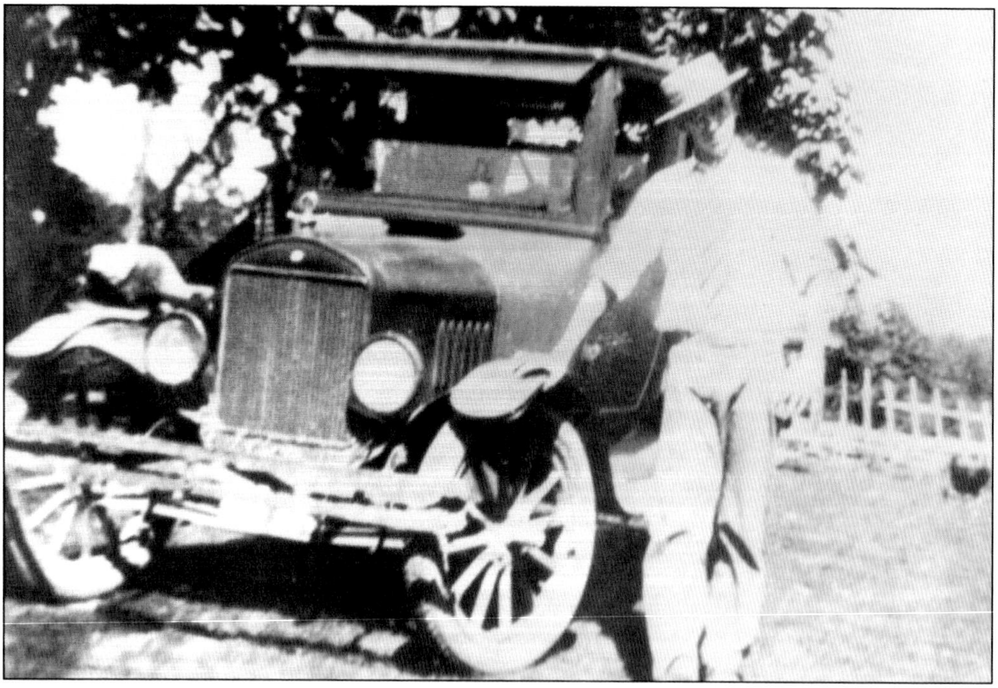

This dapper young man from the Pendleton area is Elmer Gerding, posing with pride in front of his new car in 1932. Below is Paul Brockfeld enjoying his Cub Scout hike. Cub Scouts, a division of the Boy Scouts of America, came to Warren County in 1951 when Pack 370 was formed.

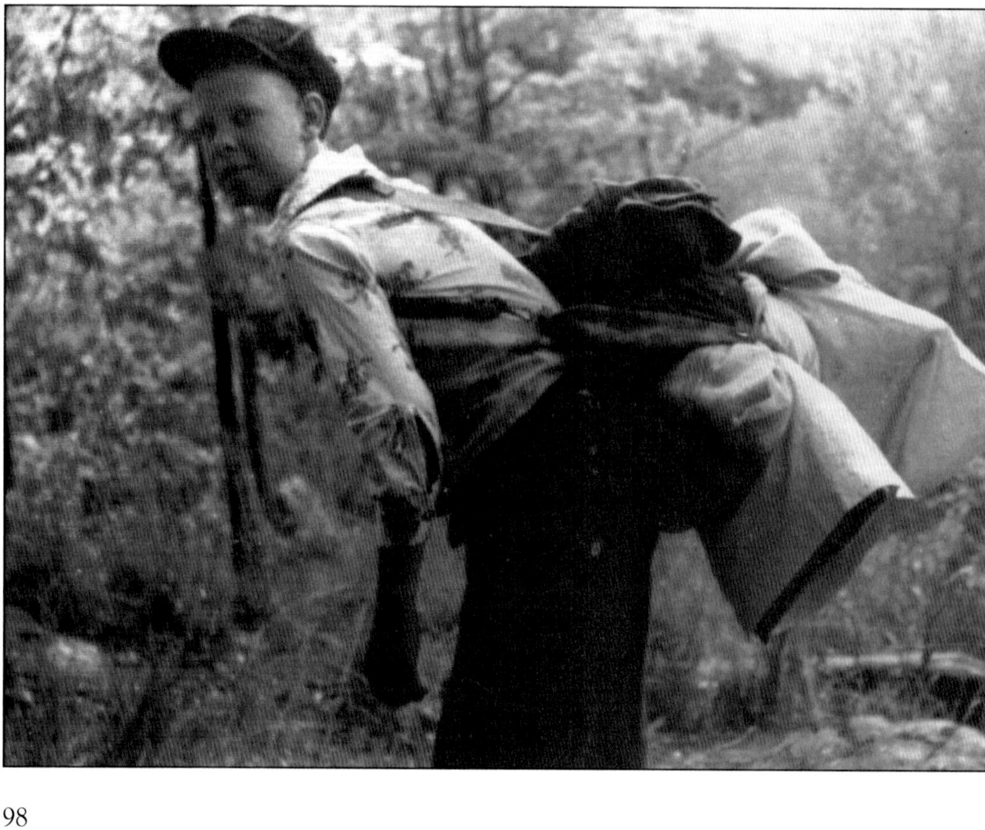

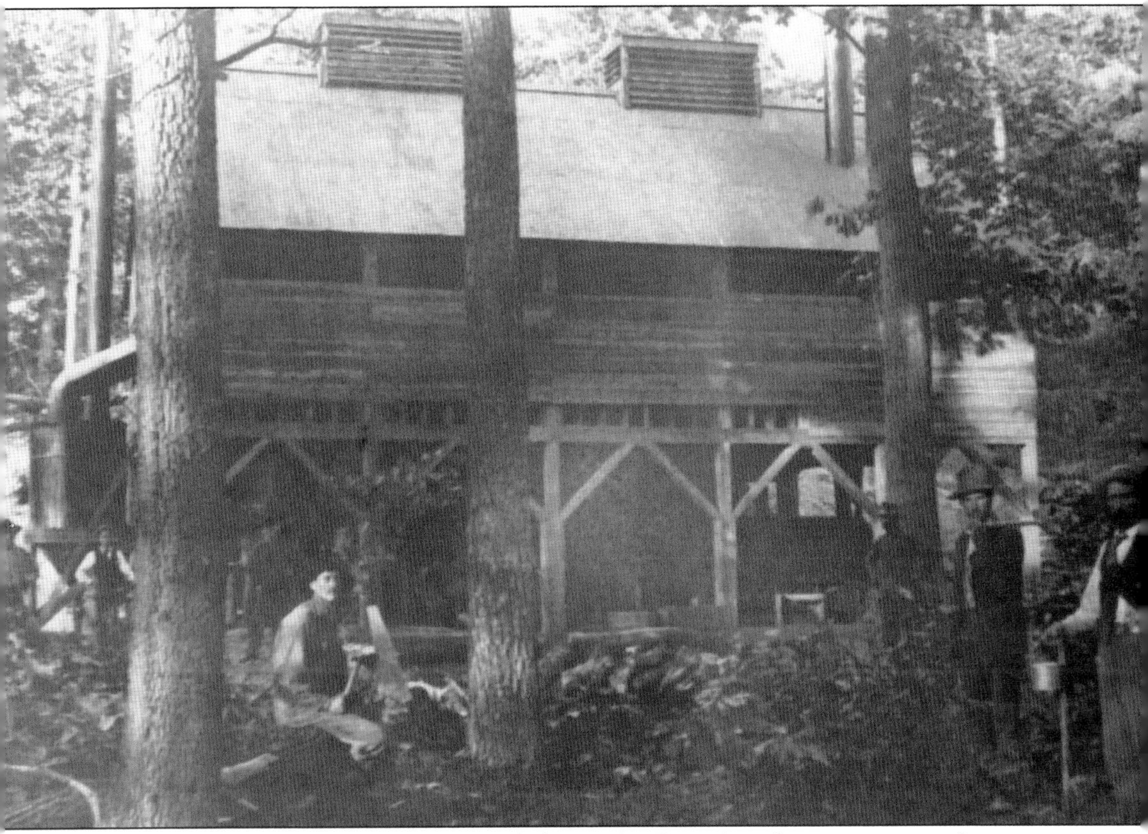

This image of a tobacco factory was captured about 1870. First, the tobacco was put in the steam box, which held about 200 pounds of tobacco, 20 to 25 times each day. From the steam box, it was taken to the stemmers, who removed the midribs and stems of the tobacco leaves. After it was dipped in a solution of salt, sugar, and licorice, the tobacco went through the wringer and was placed on racks in the dry room. From the dry room, it went back to the steam room, where it was put in bulk, moved to the plug machine, and weighed. From the plug machine, it was taken to the wrappers and then the tagging room. There, it was pressed, made in to cakes, and packed. Finally, the tobacco was ready to be stamped and sold.

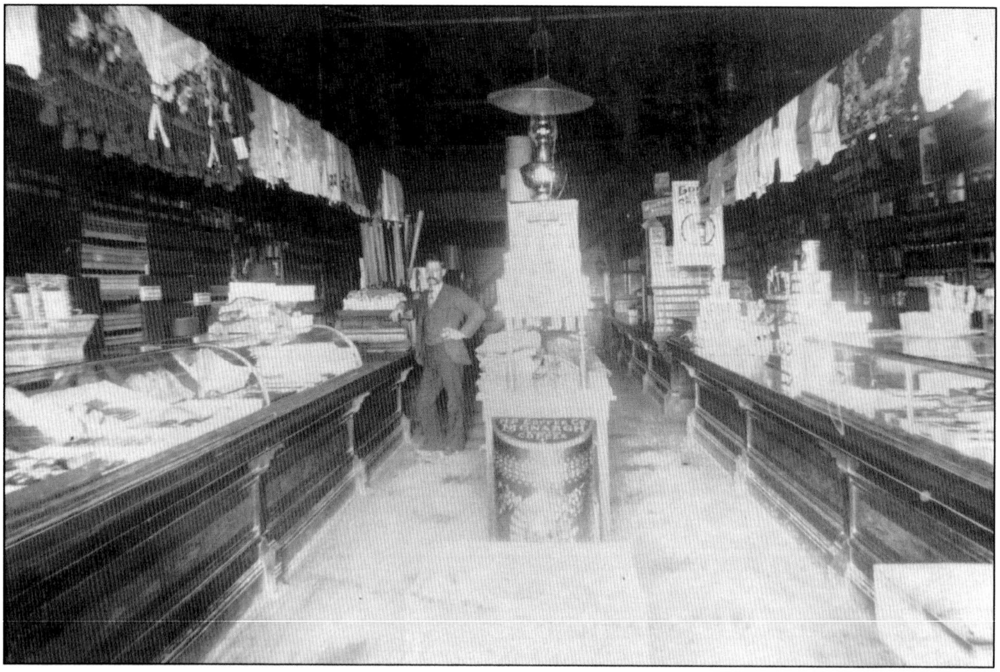

Above is a view of the interior of the Schaper Mercantile in Wright City, with Gus Schaper proudly displaying his wares. The forerunner to today's department store, general stores had a little of everything for everyone. The mercantile was in business until 1919. In the image below, the Reese & Meyers Store was located in the Opera House building on the corner of Boone's Lick Road and West Street. There, one could buy real Buster Brown shoes, a Keen Kutter, Standard Patterns, or even gasoline sold by the gallon jar.

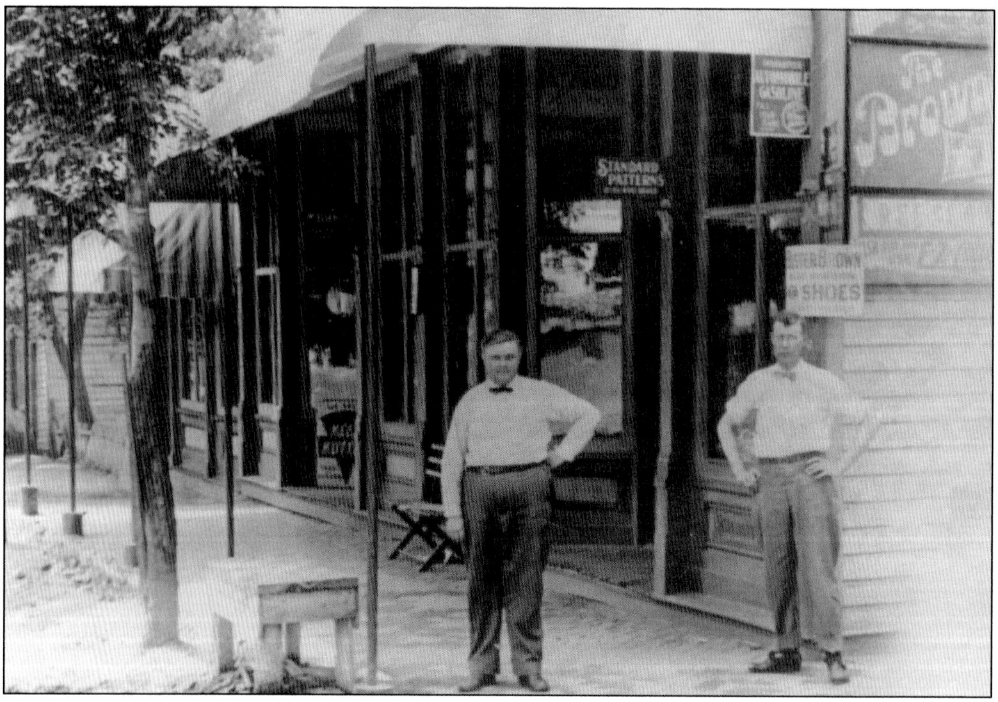

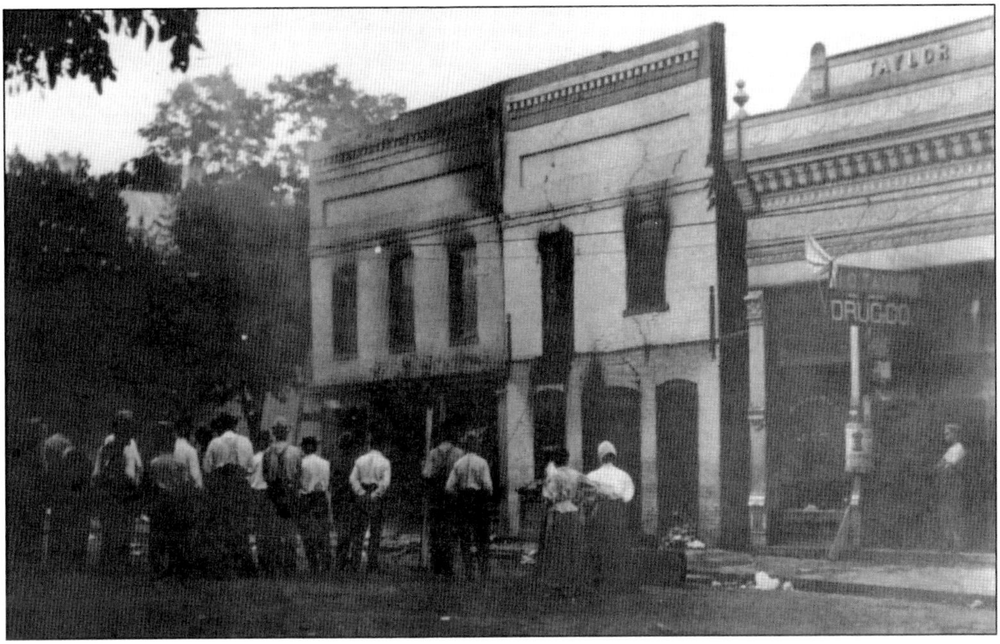

A fire in early October 1908 destroyed a section of businesses along the south side of Boone's Lick Road. Jones Tobacco Shop and Marx Butcher Shop were destroyed, while Taylor Drug suffered some damage. The local Warrenton Banner offices were upstairs, and with the fire, many early issues of Warren County history were lost as well. The buildings, at the corner of Boone's Lick Road and East Street, were first replaced by the three-story Odd Fellows building. That building was replaced in the late 20th century by a modern Commerce Warren County Bank building. The incident led to the purchase of Warrenton's first fire department automobile.

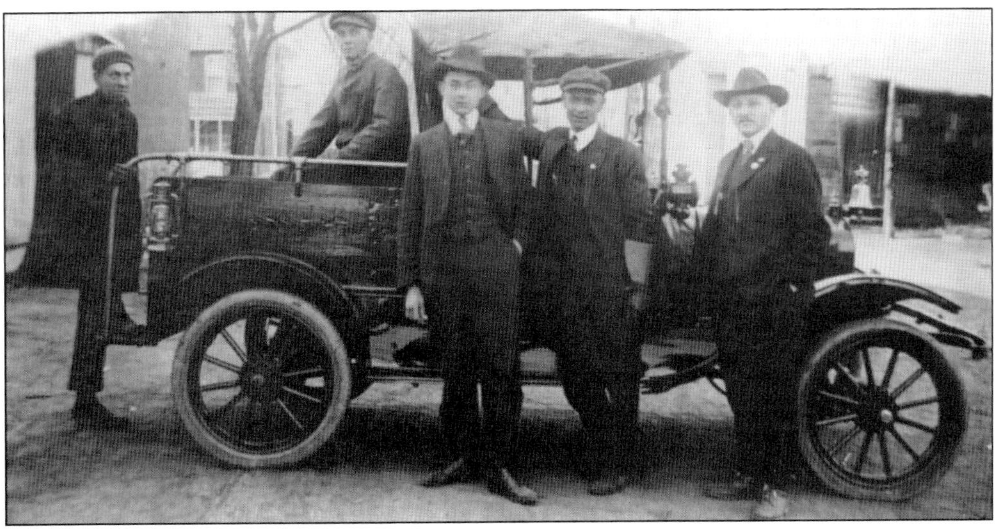

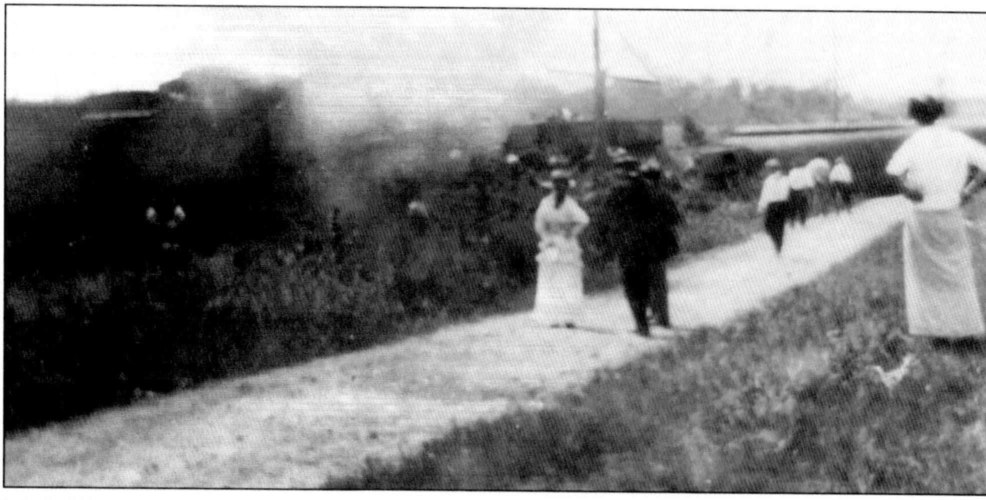

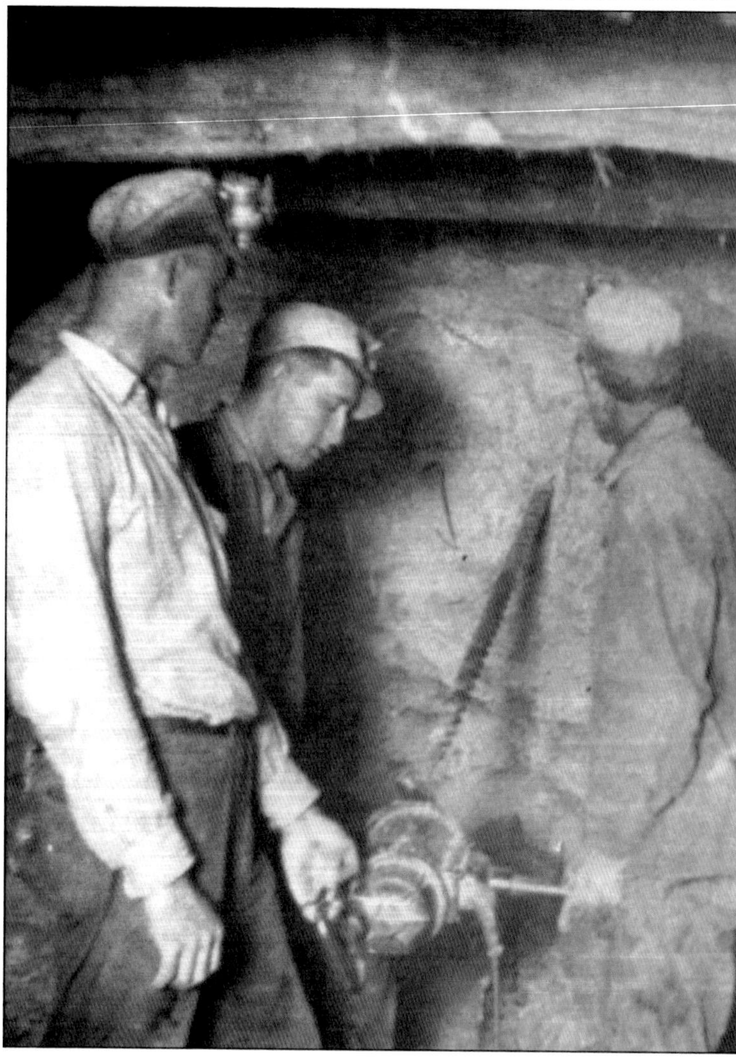

Other calamities were the train wrecks that occurred occasionally on the St. Louis, Kansas City & North Missouri Railroad, which later became known as the Wabash. The Wabash crossed Warren County from Wright City to Pendleton following the early Boone's Lick Trail prior to the arrival of today's Interstate 70. Coal mining took place in locations south of Truesdale and north of Warrenton and may have been a larger industry than many realized.

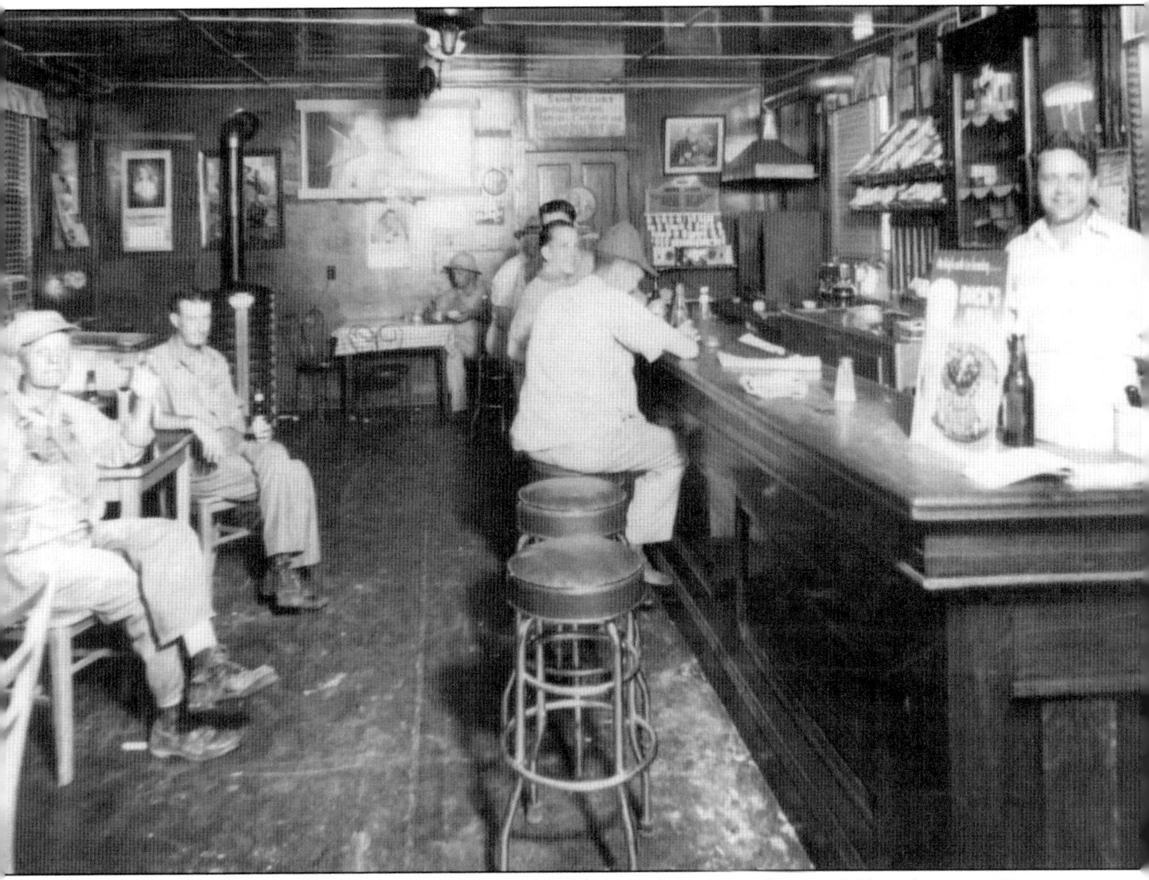

After a hard day's work in 1948, a visit to Andy's Place in Marthasville would hit the spot. From left to right are Pap Suhre, Lawrence Strubbe (at the table), two unidentified, Hugo Joerling, Harold Fortmann, Harvy Gardyne, and Emil Hilgedick (behind the bar).

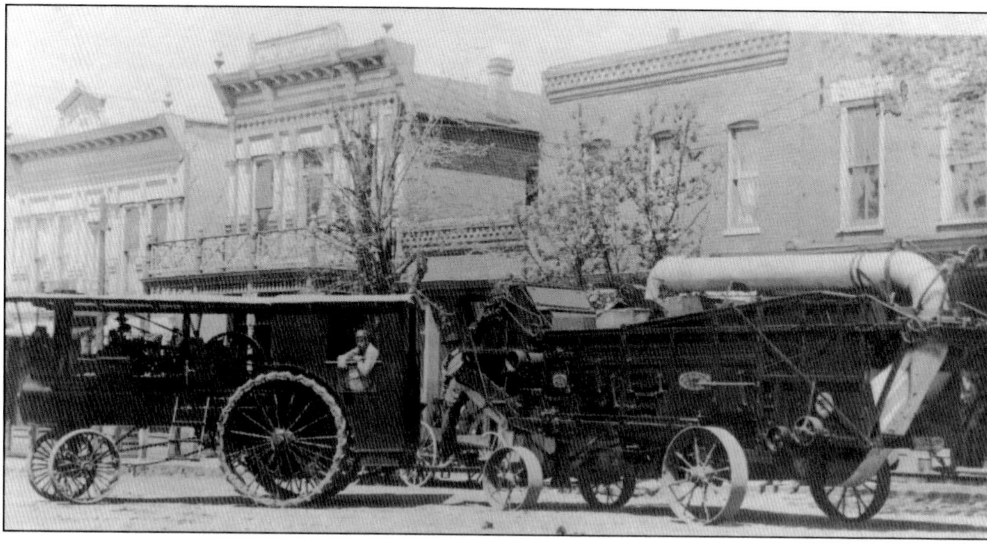

Warren County has always had a large amount of rural landscape. As seen in the image above, farmers Eli (in window) and Frank Dieckman (standing on the separator tongue) were proud of their modern threshing machine in 1909. Farmers like Fredric H. Vahle, who was born in Germany in 1877 to Fredric William Vahle and Frederica Ruwe, took great pride in their barns. From left to right below are Lydda Vahle (on her horse), her father Fredric, her sister Sadie, and hired hand Willie Hagemann.

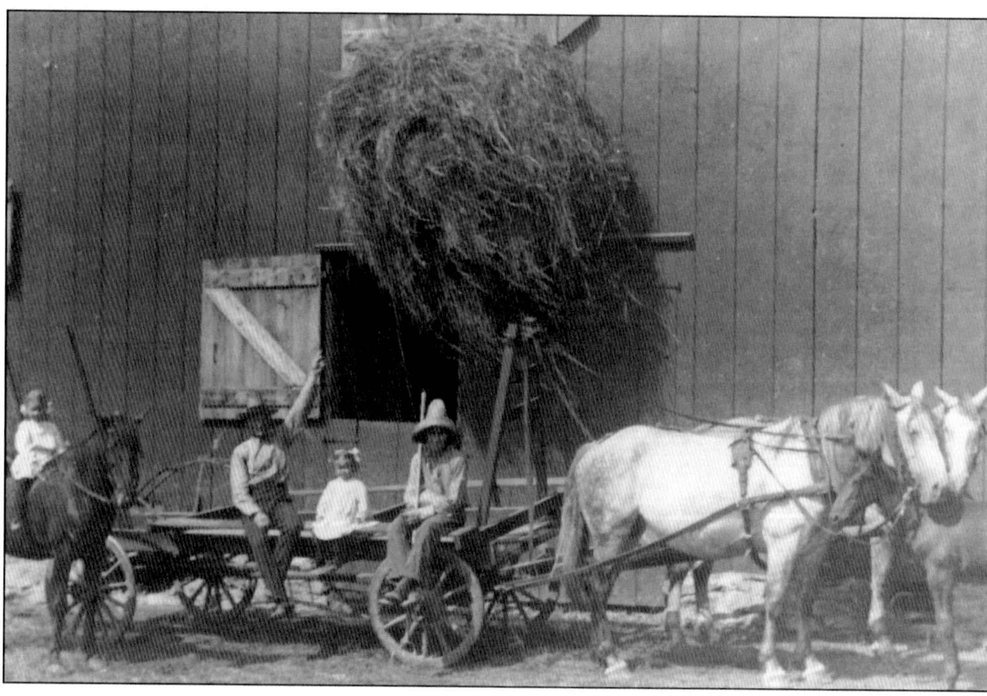

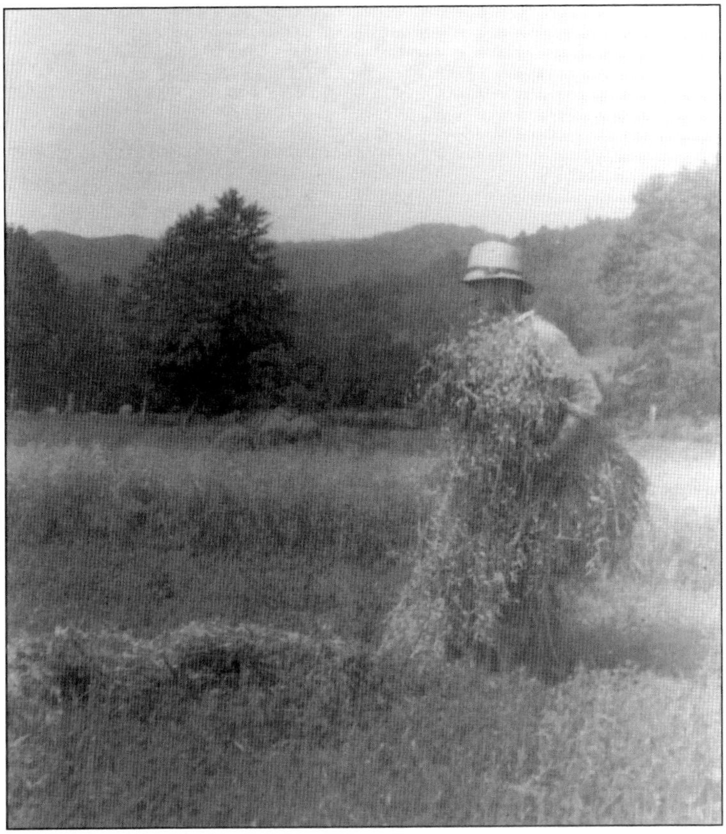

Gone are the days of hand bundling, as Victor Wehmeyer, son of Hemran and Henrietta (Koelling) Wehmeyer, is doing on his farm in near Pinckney. Below, Carroll Dieckman could drive the team of horses home at the age of nine, having been born and raised on the farm.

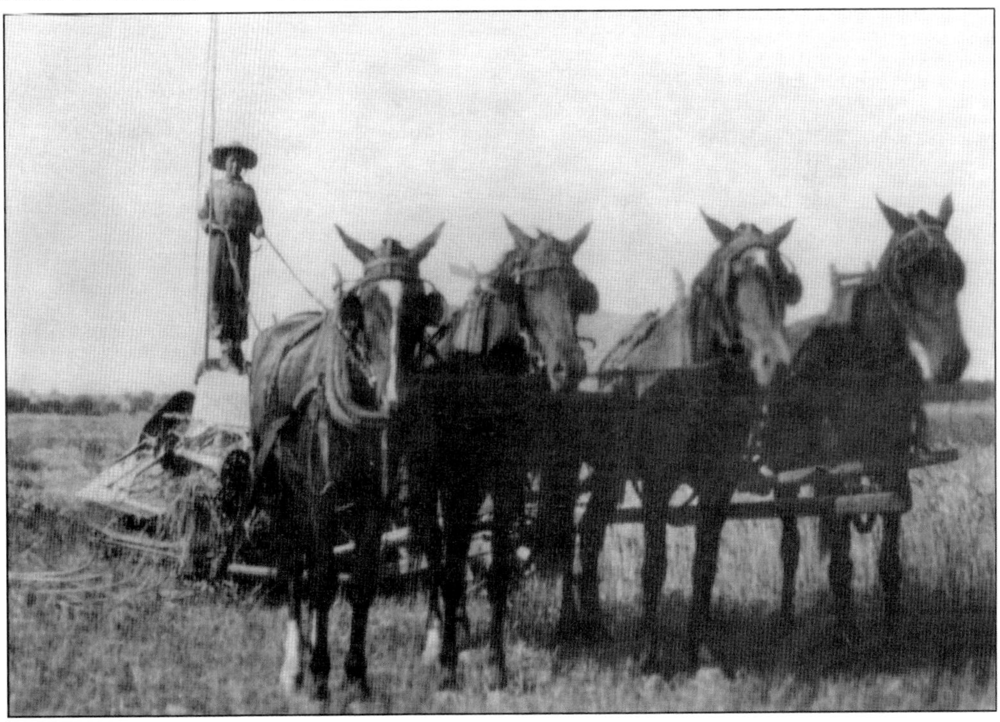

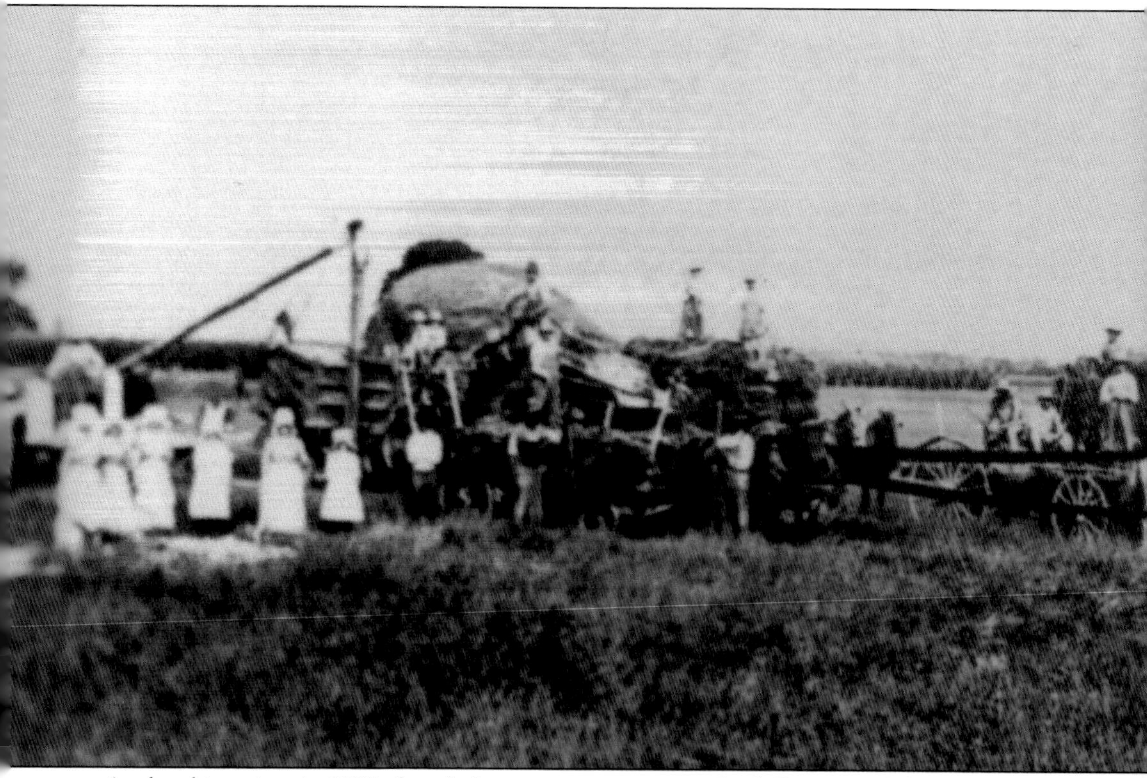

At threshing time in 1895, the whole community was involved. Everyone did their part, either on the big rigs or in the kitchen preparing the several meals, as the work was strenuous. Everyone worked at one farm until the tasks were completed, then moved on to the next farm, neighbor

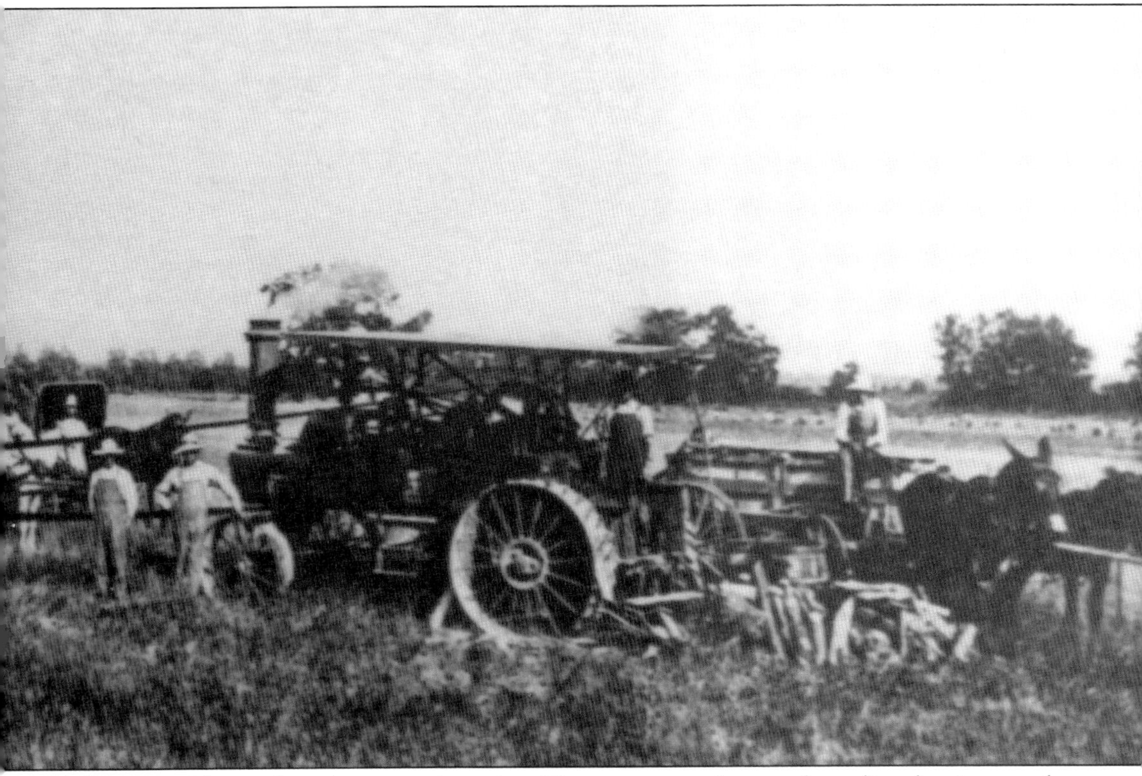

helping neighbor with real cooperative spirit. The process was long and grueling, but in a good year, the profits were high.

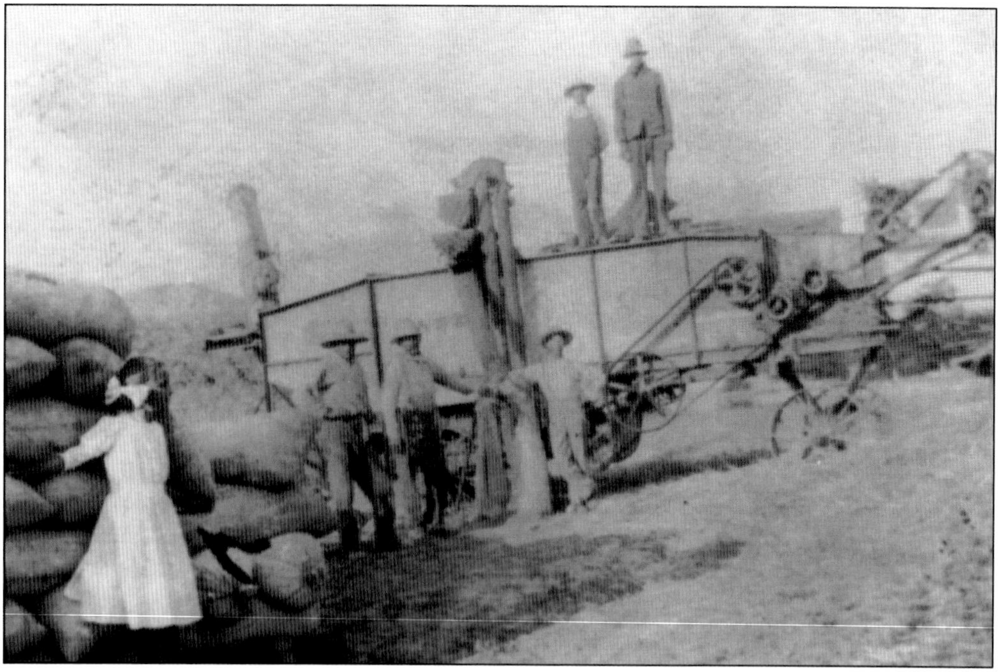

Seen above, Darby Meyer's threshing machine filled the sacks that are stacked to the left. In the image below, youngsters proudly show off their sheep at Frank Nordwald's farm. Activities like this were part of the county's 4-H clubs, providing hands-on training and leadership development for the children in rural families.

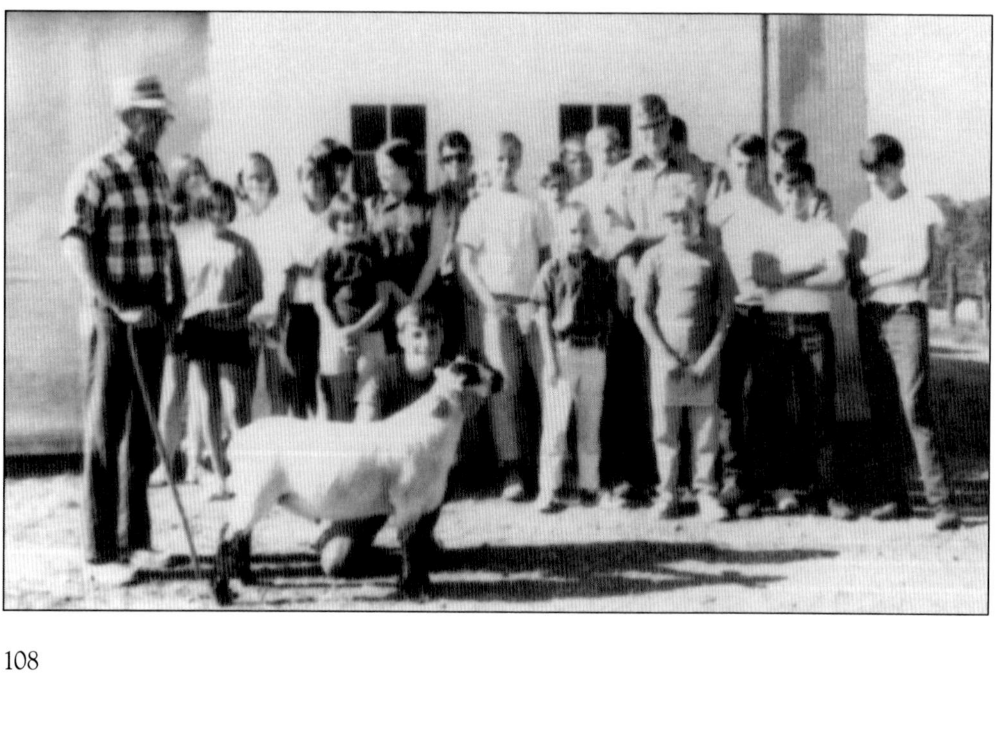

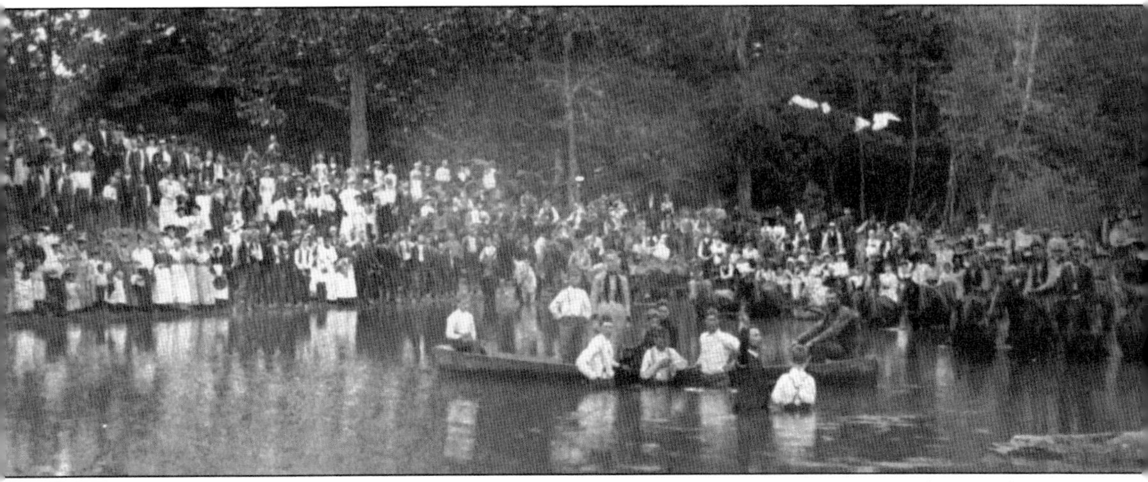

The Palmyra Baptist Church was organized near the Jones School in the Camp Branch Township. In the late 1890s, Elder S.L. Palmer preached for 18 evenings, resulting in 12 professions of faith and six baptisms. Huge camp meetings like this were held in various locations all over the county. This one is believed to be at Big Creek on the Yeater Branch.

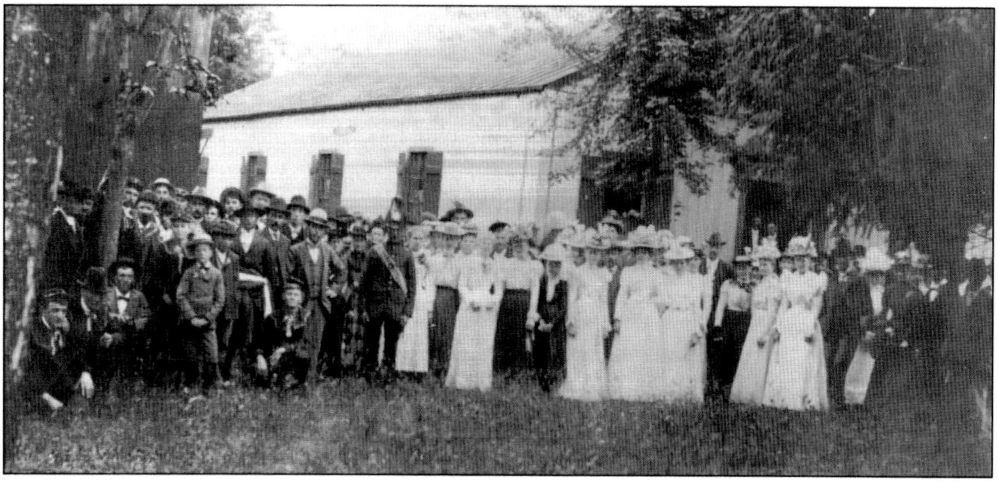

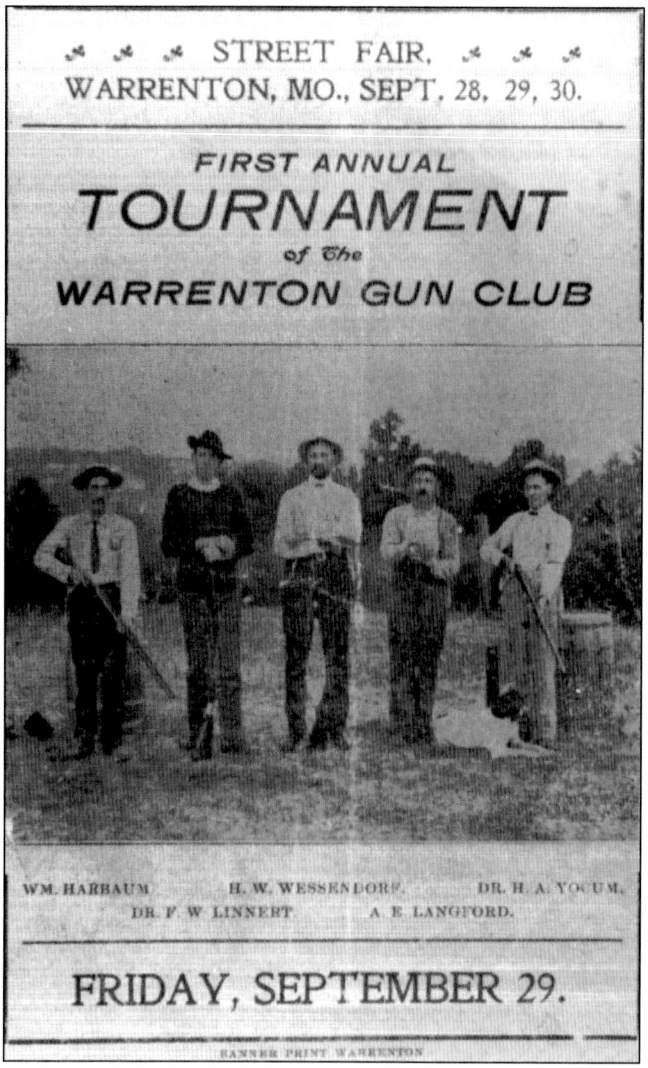

STREET FAIR,
WARRENTON, MO., SEPT. 28, 29, 30.

FIRST ANNUAL
TOURNAMENT
of The
WARRENTON GUN CLUB

WM. HARBAUM H. W. WESSENDORF. DR. H. A. YOCUM.
DR. F. W LINNERT. A. E. LANGFORD.

FRIDAY, SEPTEMBER 29.

BANNER PRINT WARRENTON

With the German immigrants came their customs from the old world. The Schützenfest, held by the local Schützen Verein, or shooting club, was held on the first Sunday after Easter every year. For many years, it was held at Brandt's Store, three miles east of Warrenton. Then it was moved to its eventual site located on Schützenground Road. An old-fashioned shooting festival took place, complete with the target of a large carved wooden eagle that represented the king of their former homeland, Germany. The festival's winner would announce his favorite young lady, and she would be located and escorted to the festival. After her arrival, a dance was held and honors bestowed on the best shot and his girlfriend, making them king and queen of the festival. Later, she would embroider their names and the year on a long sash that was passed on to the next year's winning recipients. At left is a ticket to the First Annual Tournament of the Warrenton Gun Club on September 29 in Warrenton.

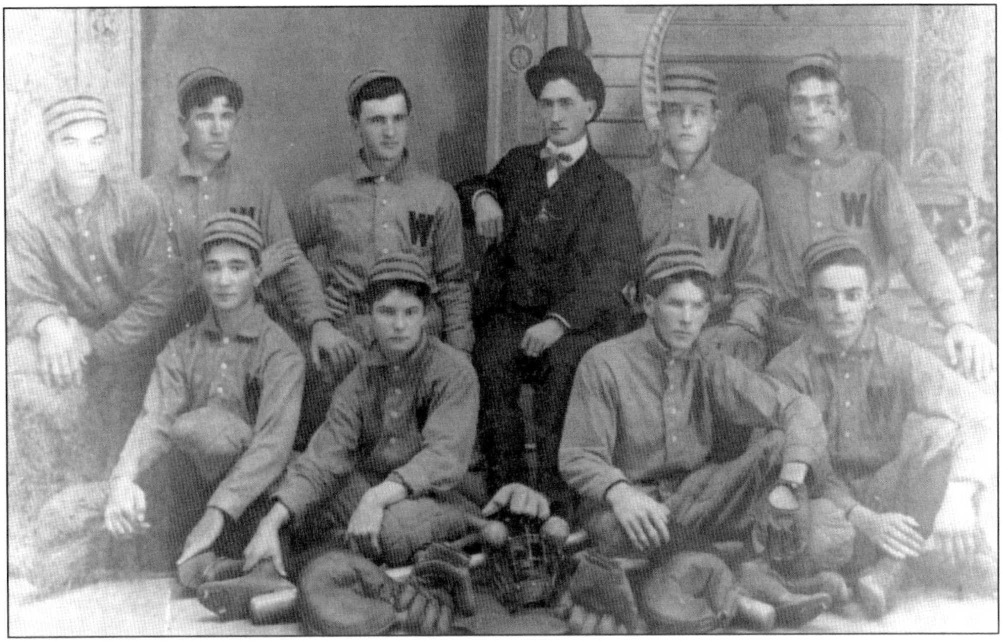

Another of life's pleasures in Warren County was a picnic to watch the Warrenton baseball team, which was established in 1893. Each town had its own team, and the rivalry was hot. The image below was captured when the men of Warren County turned out during the call for troops at the beginning of World War I. This was taken at Kelly's field near the Truesdale depot, where many summer afternoon baseball games had been played.

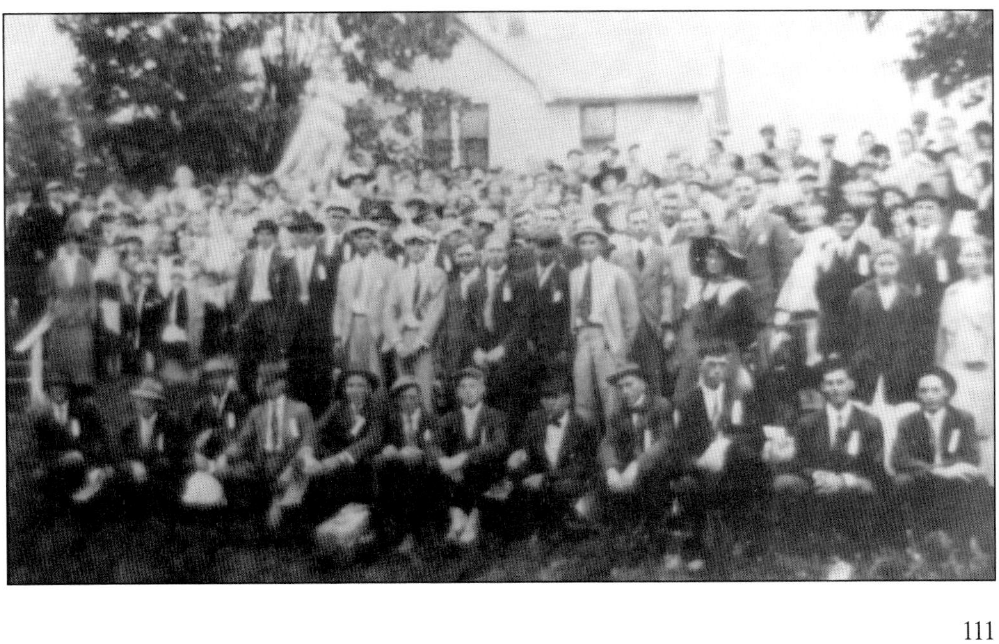

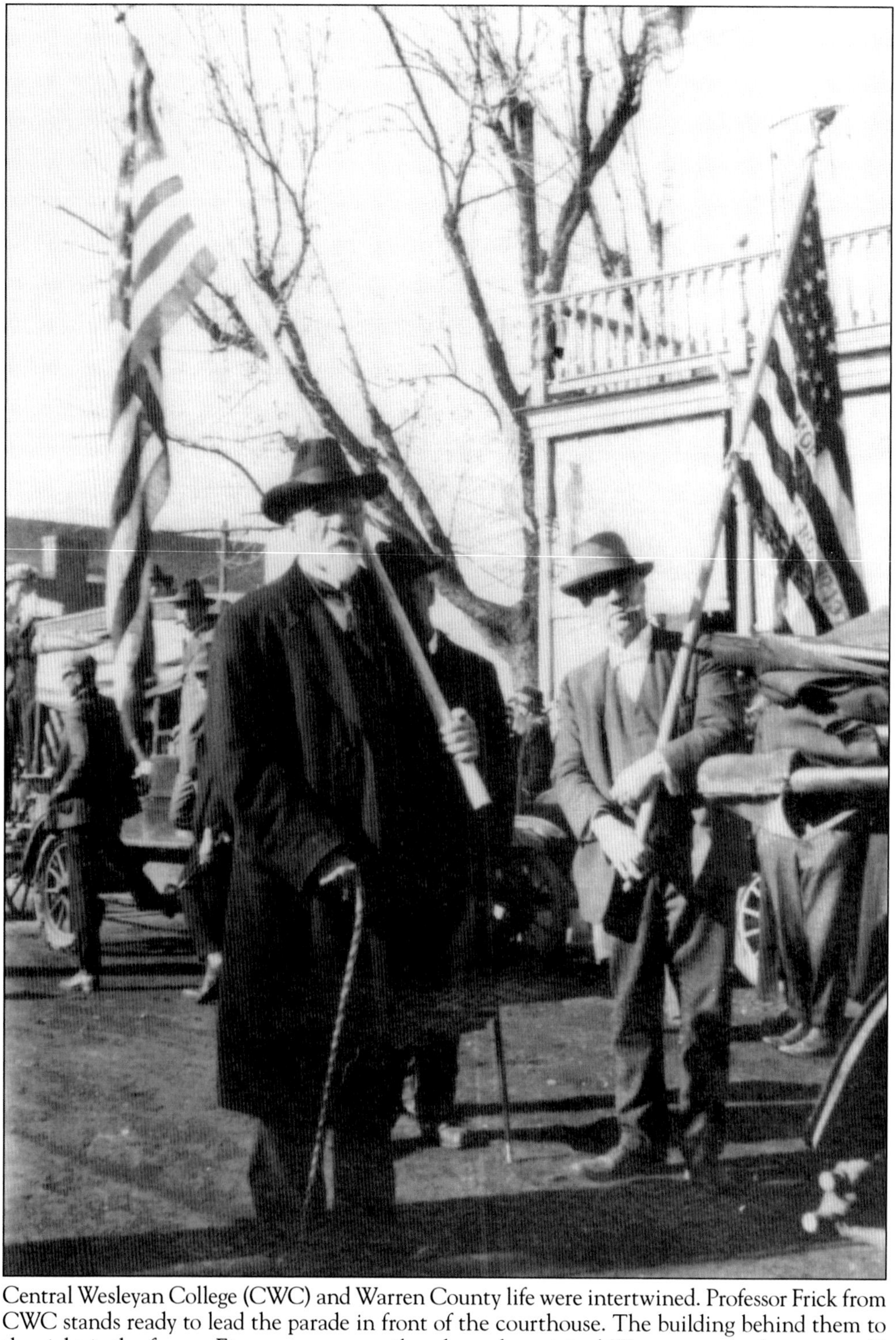

Central Wesleyan College (CWC) and Warren County life were intertwined. Professor Frick from CWC stands ready to lead the parade in front of the courthouse. The building behind them to the right is the former Eisenstein mercantile, where the original Warrenton city lots were sold when it was Ford & Munson Mercantile.

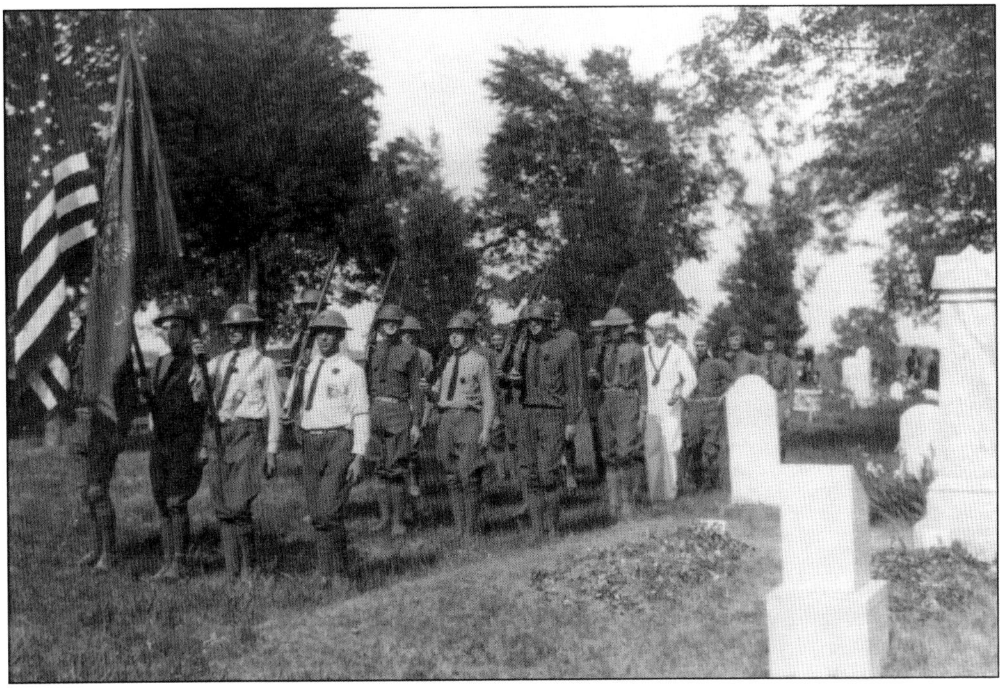

The veterans in these photographs honored the fallen heroes of Warren County with a parade from Warrenton's business district out to the city cemetery. Veterans of every war, including the Revolutionary and Civil Wars, were commemorated with a 21-gun salute.

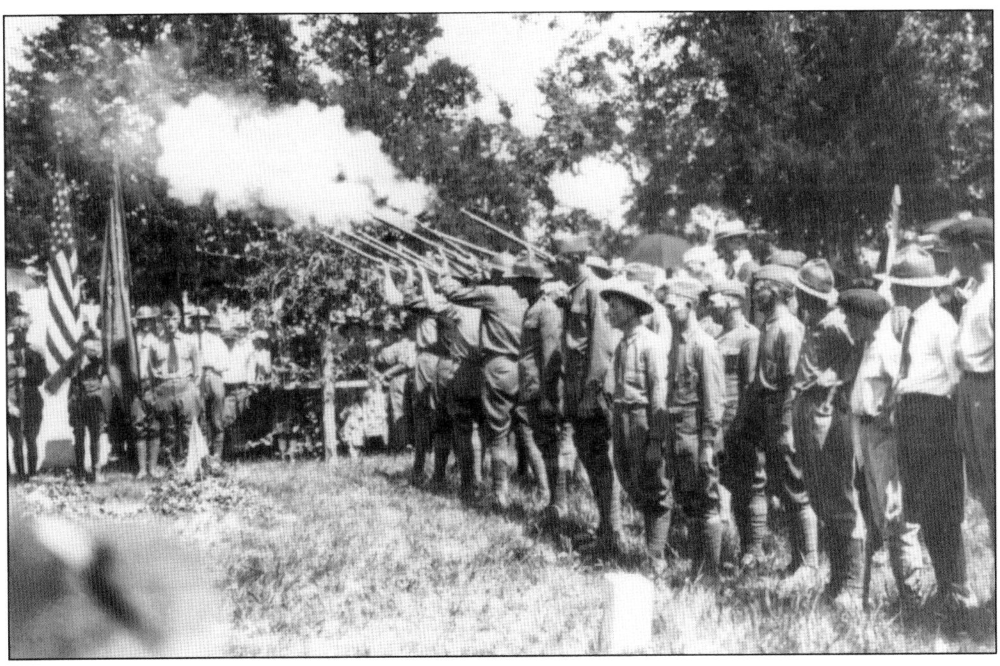

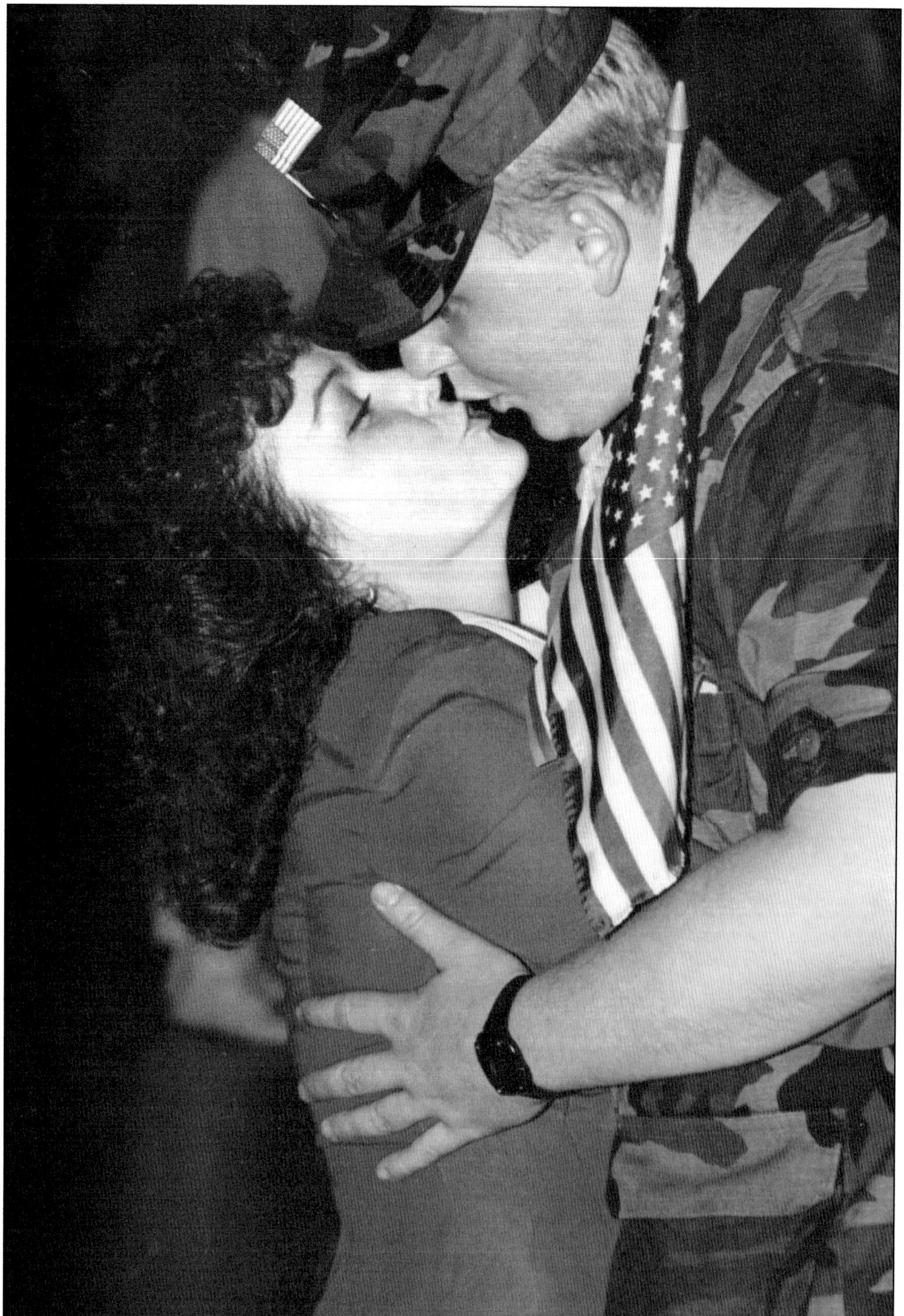

In 1991, Robert Haug of the 3175th US Military Police Battalion received a warm welcome home from his wife, Cheryl. The battalion's headquarters were at Warrenton.

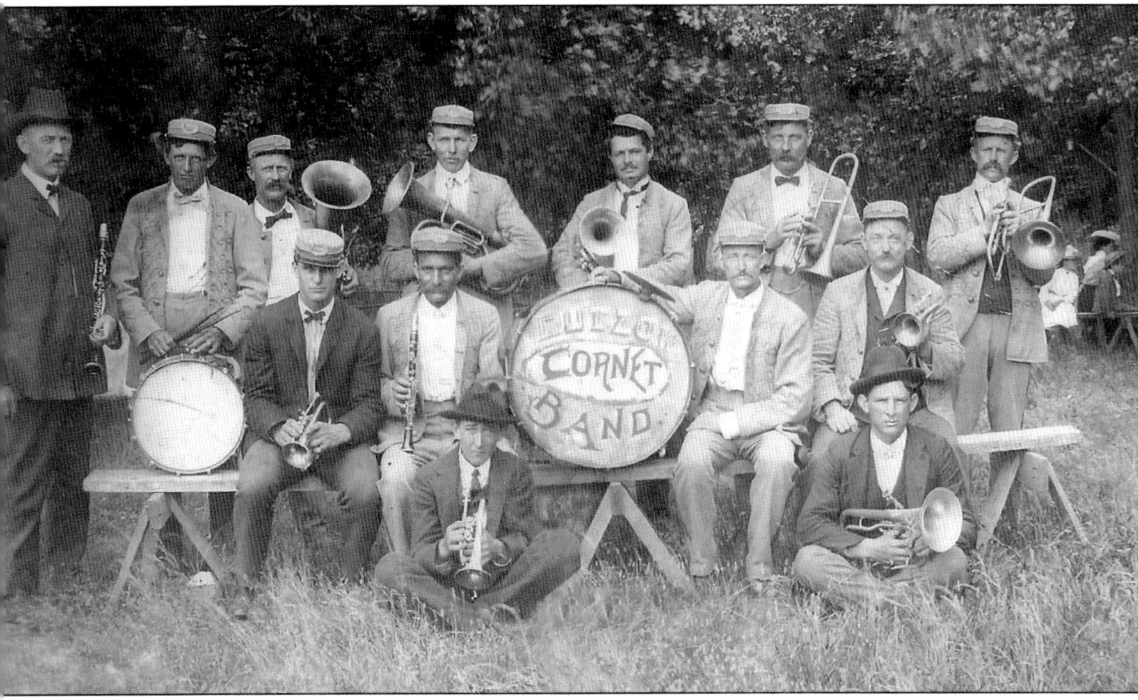

The Dutzow Coronet Band members in the image above include, from left to right, (first row) Ed Feldmann and Gus Berg; (second row) Fritz Dickhaus, Ben Nagel, August Riefenberg, and Charles Rexroth; (third row) Professor Husler, Anton Diermann, Otto Hinnah, Henry Rohe, George Schulz, John Schopp, and Alvin Dickhaus. Every one of their families were early German immigrants to Warren County and had brought many of their customs and traditions with them.

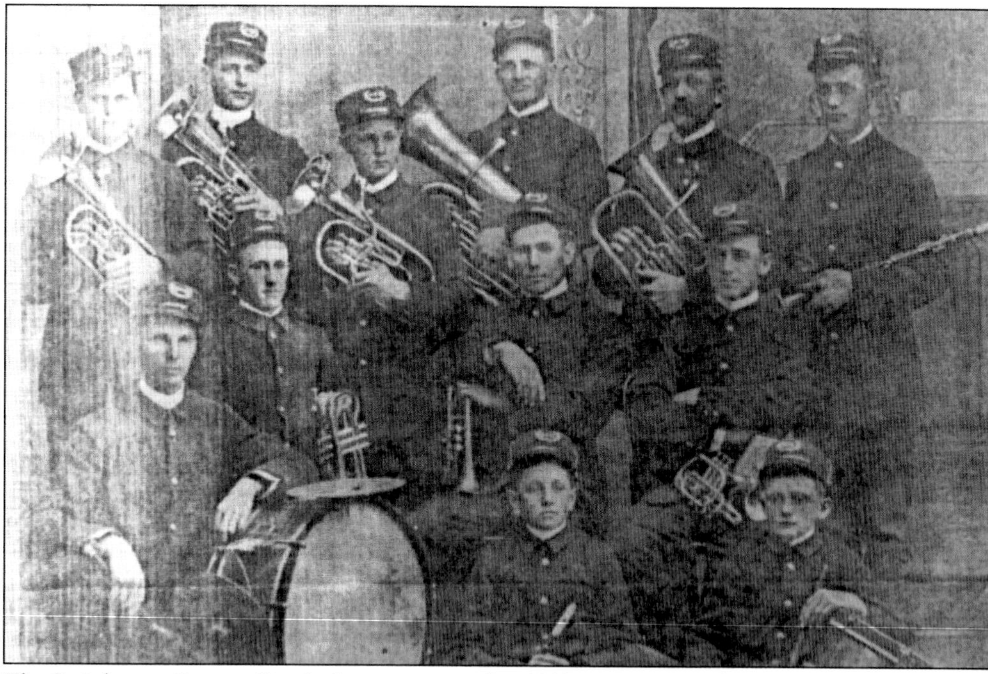

The Steinhagen Concert Band, above, organized in 1893 was very popular; it entertained everyone at the county fair, street festivals, and the Old Settlers Reunion. Members were, from left to right, (first row) Julius and Theo Hollmann; (second row) John Vogt, Louis Fieth, Fred Tebbe, and August Hollmann; (third row) Edward Meine, August Vogt, Henry Reese, Edwin Hollmann, Henry Hollmann, and Herman Hollmann. The Hopewell Cornet Band, below, formed on June 13, 1901, and entertained everyone in the southwest corner of the county.

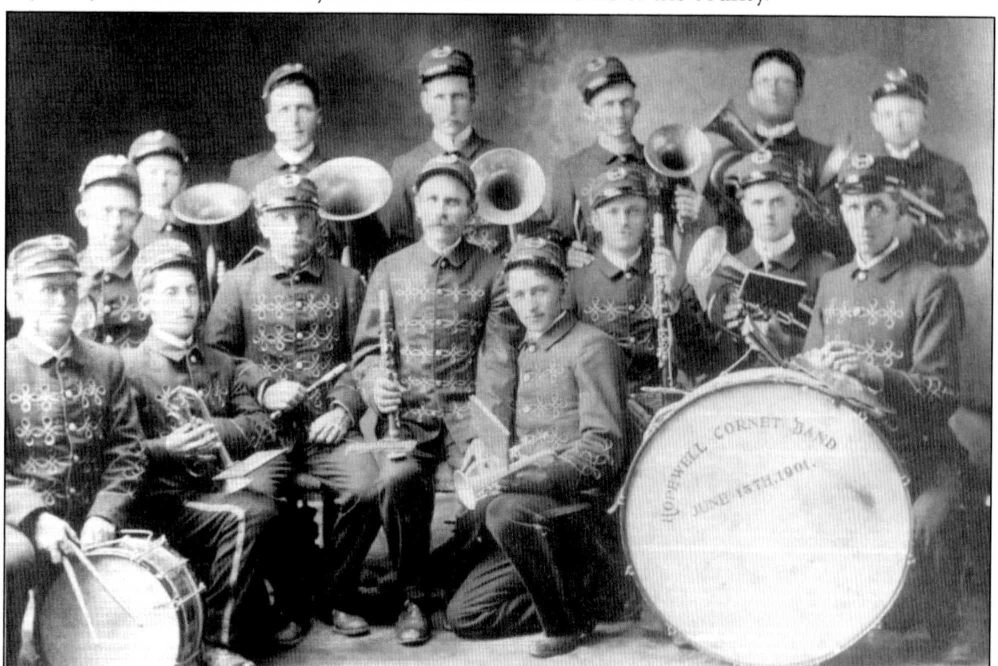

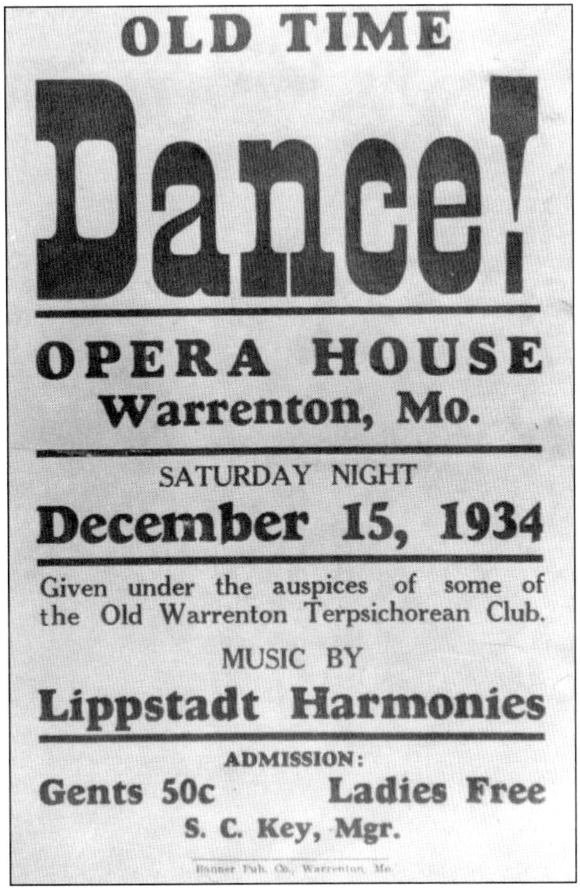

The poster advertising the Old Time Dance says that the Saturday night dance was 50¢ for "gents," but that ladies were admitted free in December 1934 at the Opera House in Warrenton. The Lippstadt Harmonies, as seen in the image below, from left to right, are Homer Sprick, Clarence Petersmeyer, Evelyn Koelling, William Koelling, Virgil Struebbe, and Inez Petersmeyer. They were one of the more popular musical groups that played around the county.

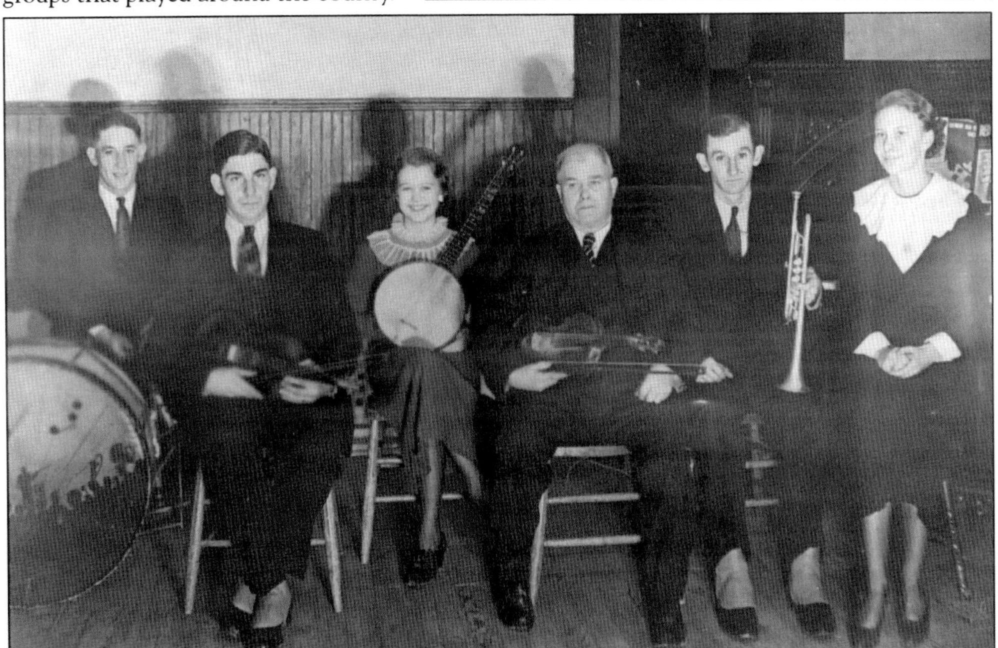

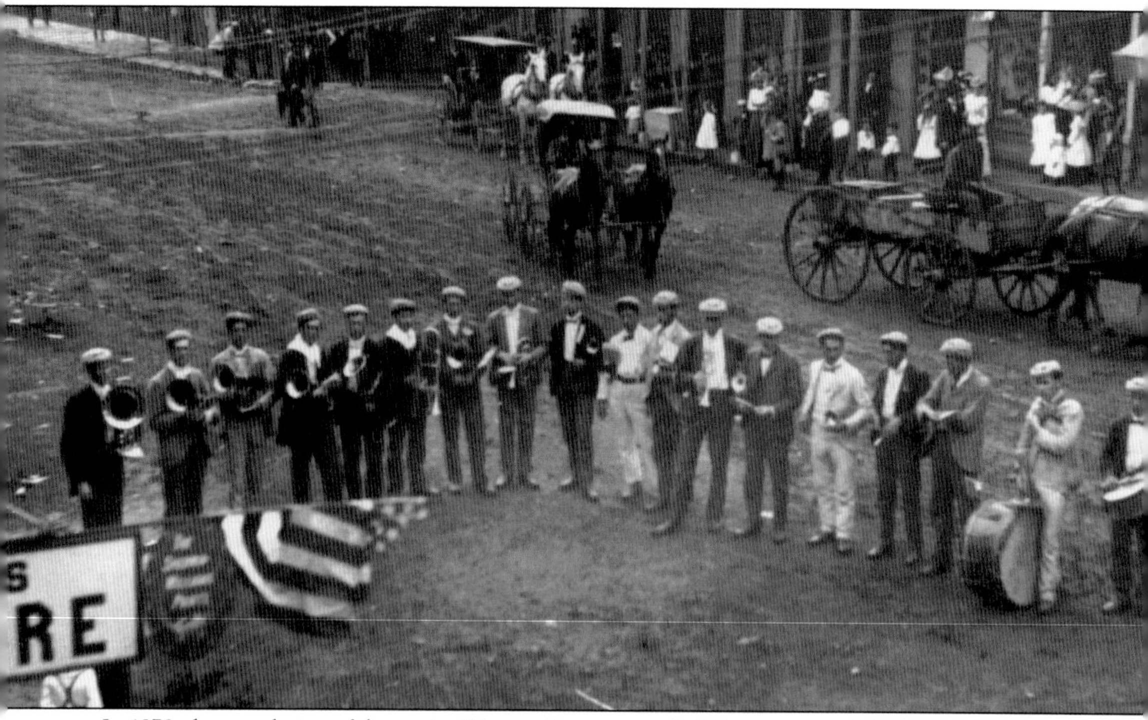

In 1870, the population of the entire Warren County was 10,105 persons, and the town of Warrenton was large enough to support its own popular brass band. This photograph by local photographer F.W. Buente shows the band, organized in 1868, playing in front of Harold Sander's Central Hotel with Prof. Roy Drake directing. Some members are John Middelkamp, John Cullom, W.A. Jones, James Riddle, W.L. Morsey, James Teasse, Charles Peers, William H. Delvanthal, N.M. McFadden, R. Ritter Jr., and R.B. Speed, but they are not identified in the picture.

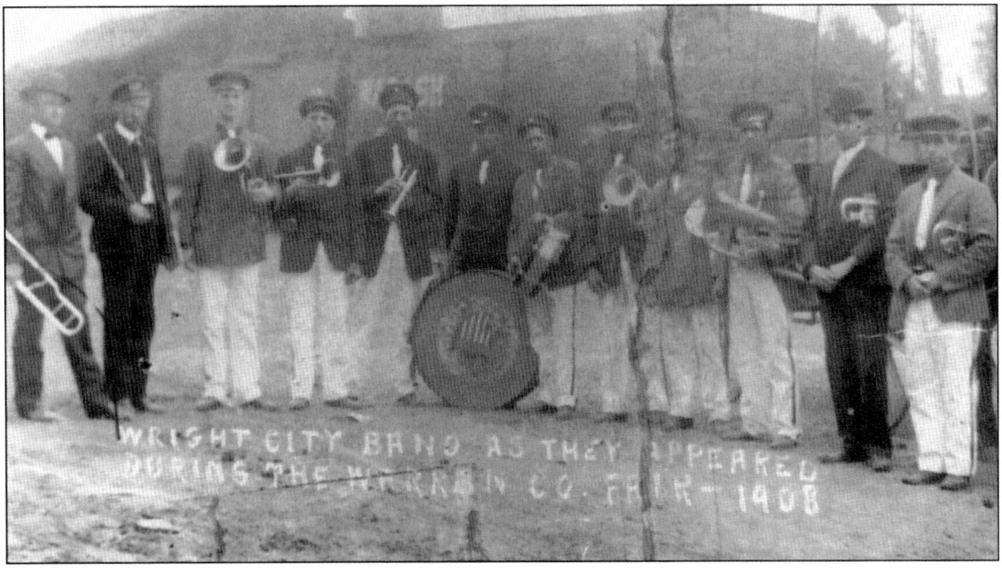

Brass bands were still popular in 1908, as these photographs of the Wright City Band show. The image above shows the band playing for arrivals at the train station, and the photograph below is of the Warren County Fair parade. In 1906, a group of Wright City businessmen organized the Warren County Fair. An agricultural fair had been in existence in the late 19th century but wasn't being held anymore.

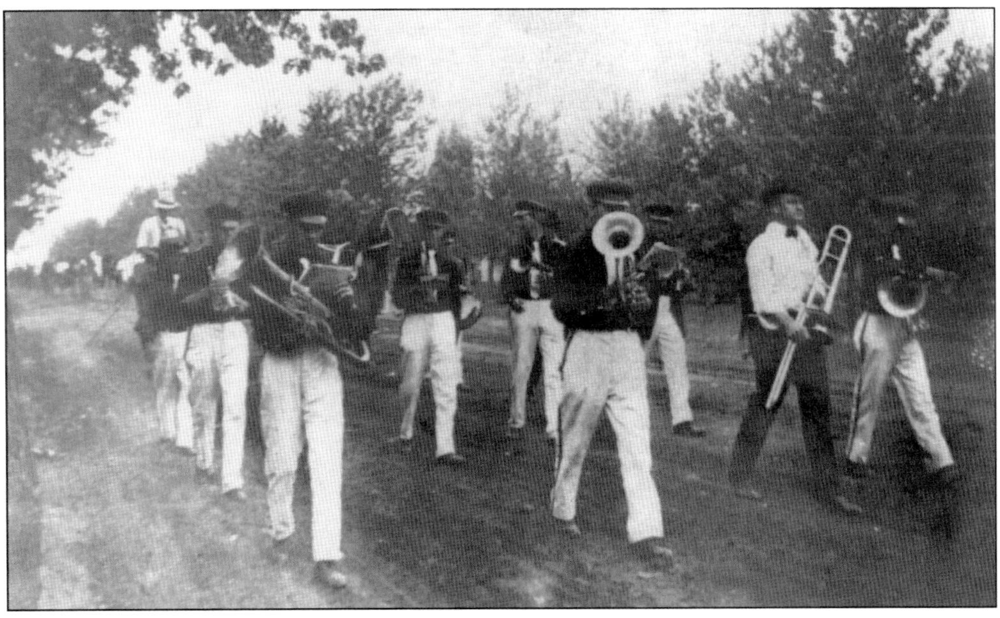

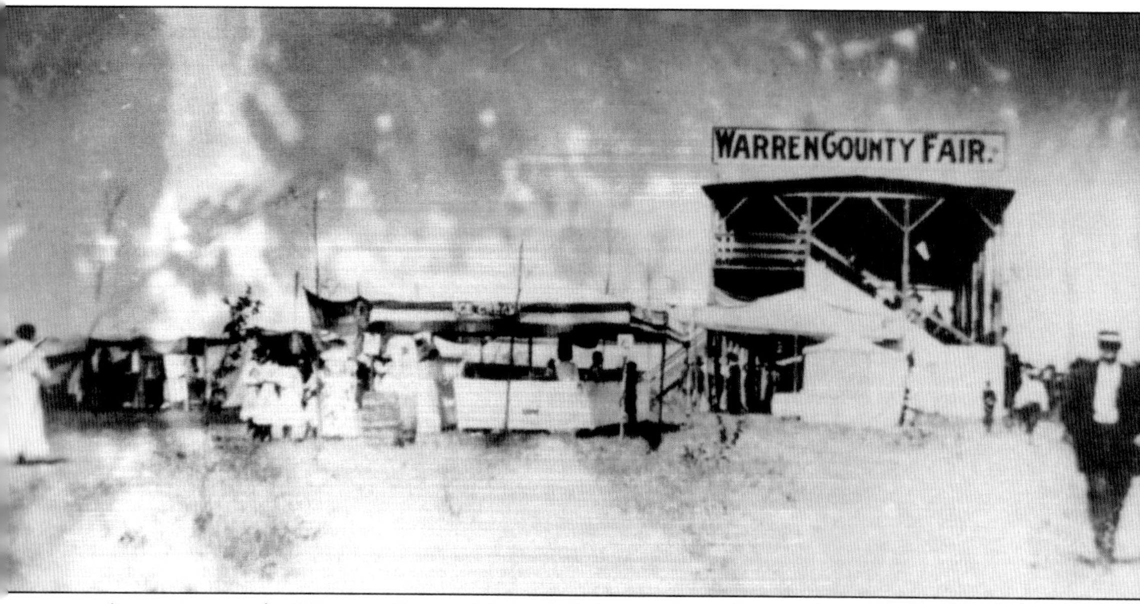

Attractions at the Warren County fair included agriculture, livestock, and implement displays, but horse racing was the big attraction. The first fair was scheduled for Tuesday, September 10, 1907, but a downpour stalled the event for one day. The site where the fair was first held is today Dickroeger Park, next to the south outer road along Interstate 70.

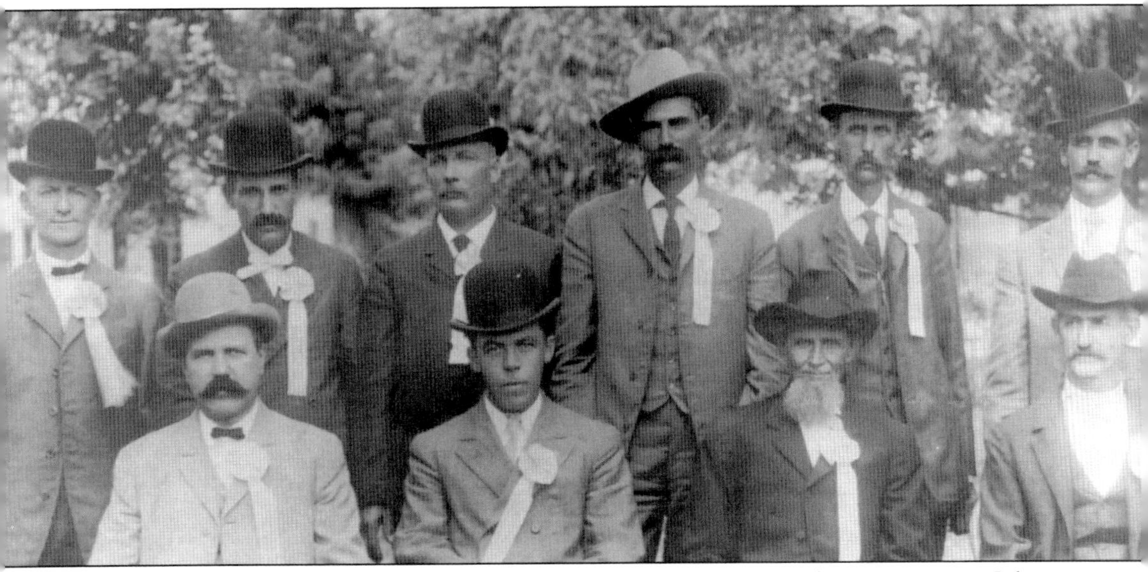

The Warren County Fair Board was, from left to right, (first row) George Blattner, treasurer; Julius H. Stegen, secretary; Judge Eversmeyer, first vice president; and William Heidtman, president; (second row) Gus W. Schape; Florence R. Ober; Herman H. Strathman; Judson S. Casner; Emil W. Dickroeger; and F.W. Schnadt, second vice president.

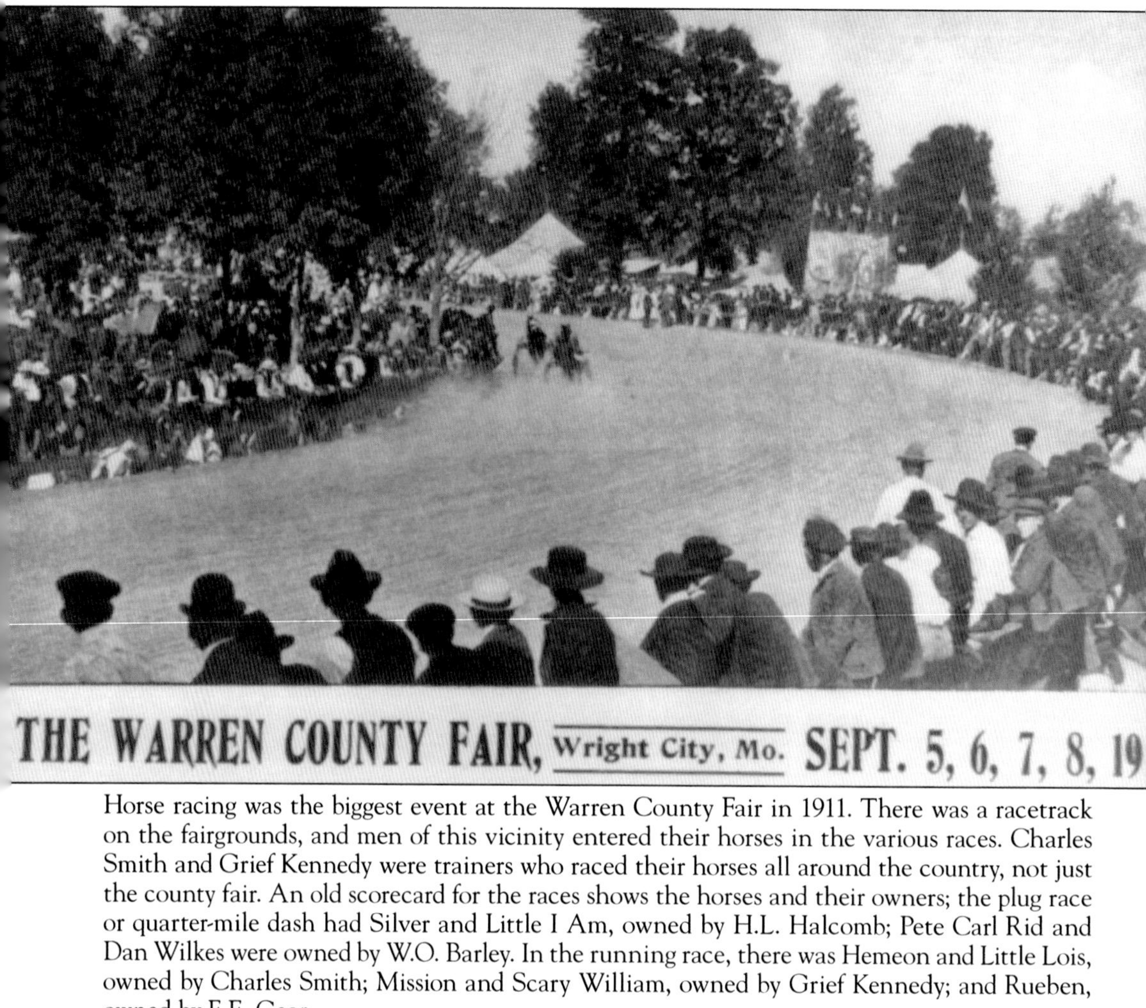

Horse racing was the biggest event at the Warren County Fair in 1911. There was a racetrack on the fairgrounds, and men of this vicinity entered their horses in the various races. Charles Smith and Grief Kennedy were trainers who raced their horses all around the country, not just the county fair. An old scorecard for the races shows the horses and their owners; the plug race or quarter-mile dash had Silver and Little I Am, owned by H.L. Halcomb; Pete Carl Rid and Dan Wilkes were owned by W.O. Barley. In the running race, there was Hemeon and Little Lois, owned by Charles Smith; Mission and Scary William, owned by Grief Kennedy; and Rueben, owned by E.E. Gear.

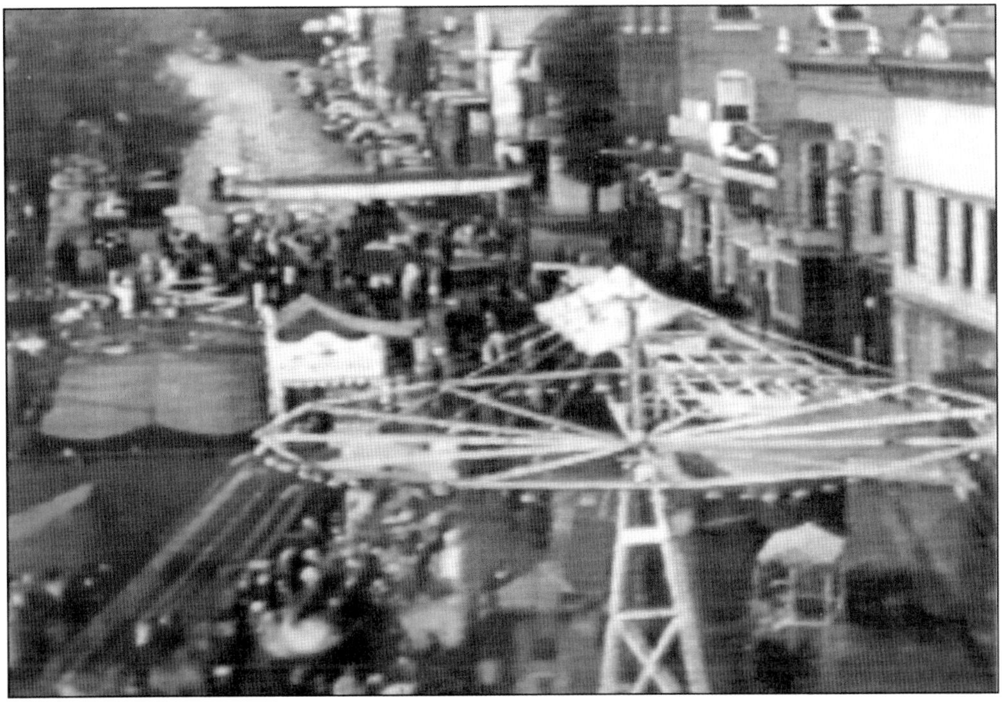

On August 26–29, 1937, Warren County celebrated its centennial. Though the county was officially 104 years old, the Depression had caused the celebration to be delayed. Here, Tom Terry, inside the wagon, plays his organ for local youths' dancing enjoyment. Boone's Lick Road was closed, and carnival rides lined the street. Sitting atop the Ferris wheel facing east gave the participant an unusual perspective on Main Street.

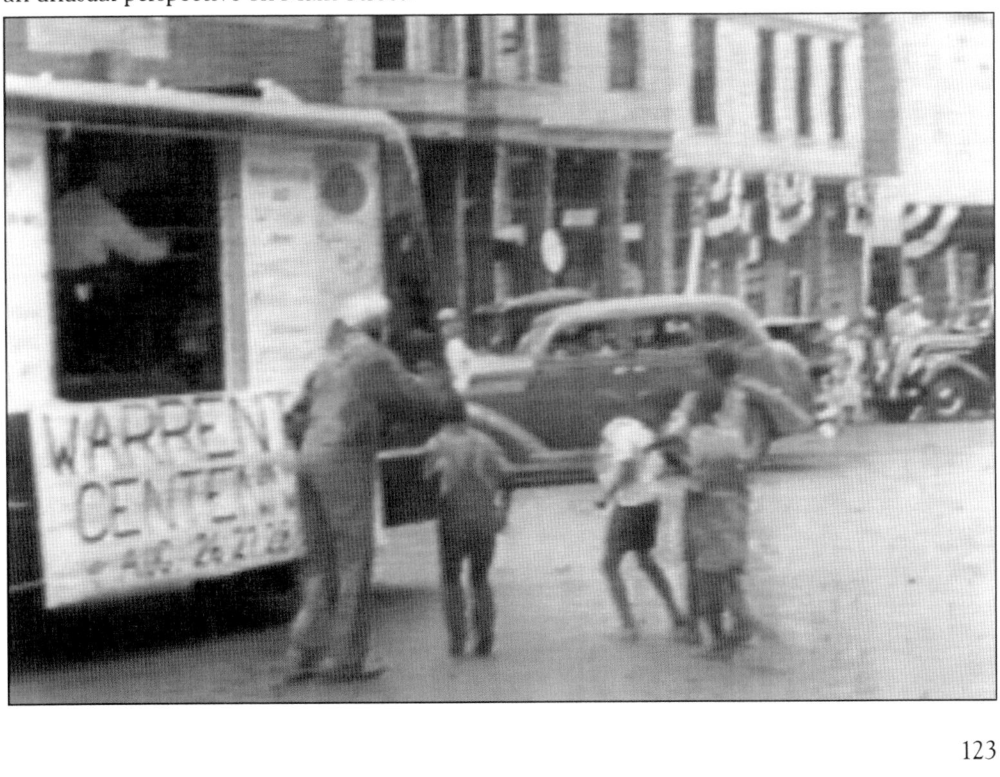

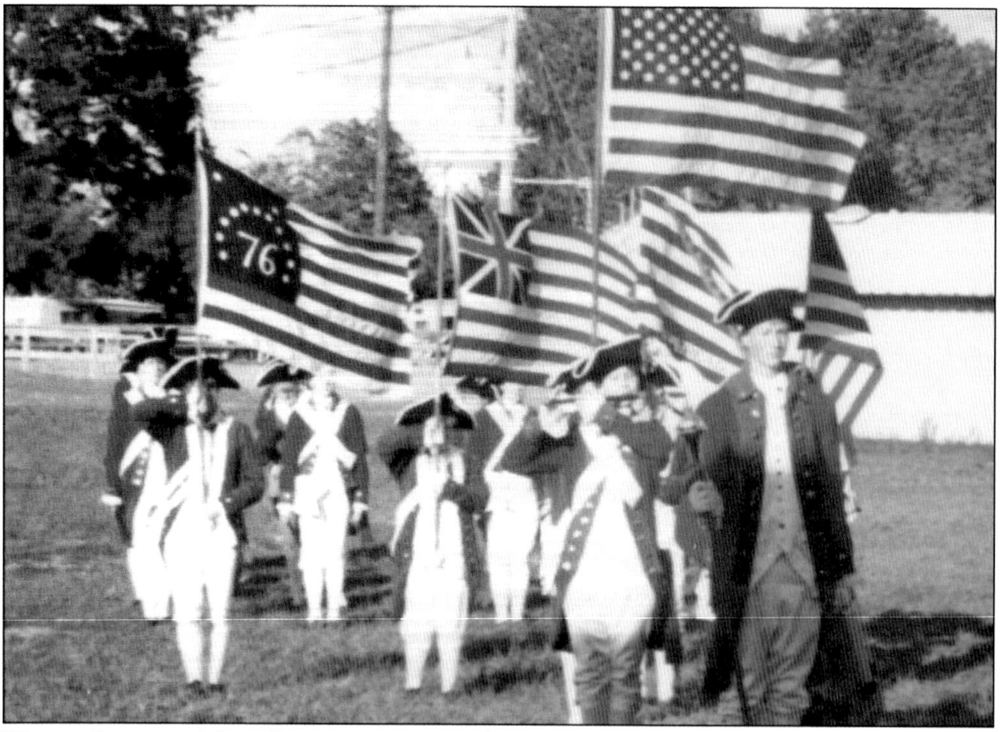

Warren County celebrated its sesquicentennial September 17–20, 1987, with most of its events at the Warren County Fairgrounds. The Warrenton Area Chamber of Commerce, the Warren County Historical Society, and the Warren County Fair Association sponsored the event. The event included a rededication of the gravesite of pioneer settler Daniel Boone and ceremonies held in front of the Warren County Courthouse. At the Warren County Fairgrounds, two miles north of Warrenton, the four-day celebration included a play called *The Warren County Follies*, portraying 150 years of history. The play had a cast of over 100 and was narrated by Wendell Roehrs, R-III school superintendent; Fred Vahle, president of the Warren County Historical Society; and Rev. David Richardson, pastor of the United Methodist church.

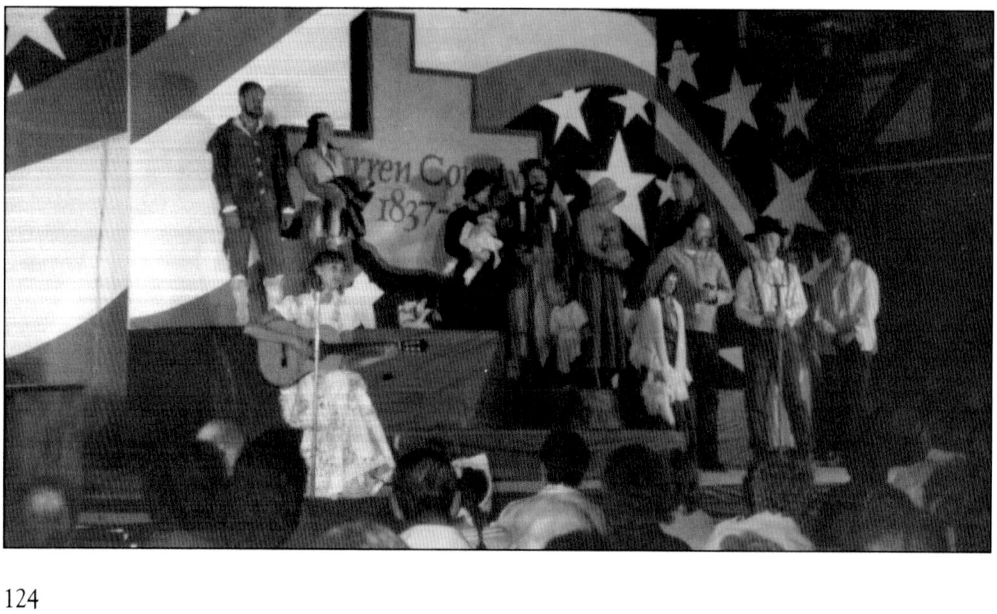

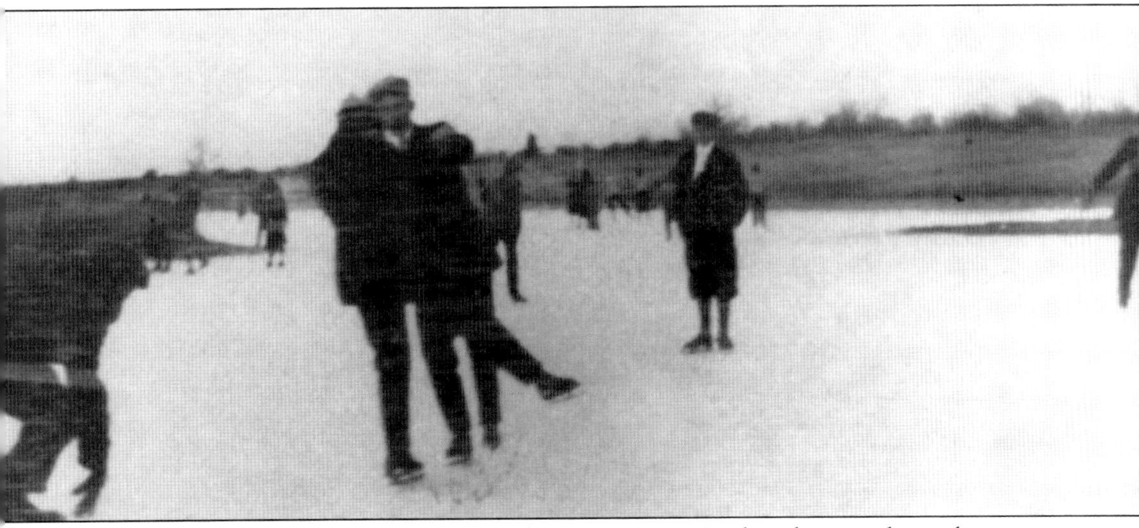

Warren County residents enjoyed winter and summer sports. In this photograph are skaters on Spoede brothers' pond, located west of Truesdale. Even though the pond was shallow and froze quickly, it was U-shaped, requiring one to be very careful of the cattails. The Spoede brothers were taxidermists and were famous for their fine collection of 250 birds, many which would have been seen here on the pond throughout the year.

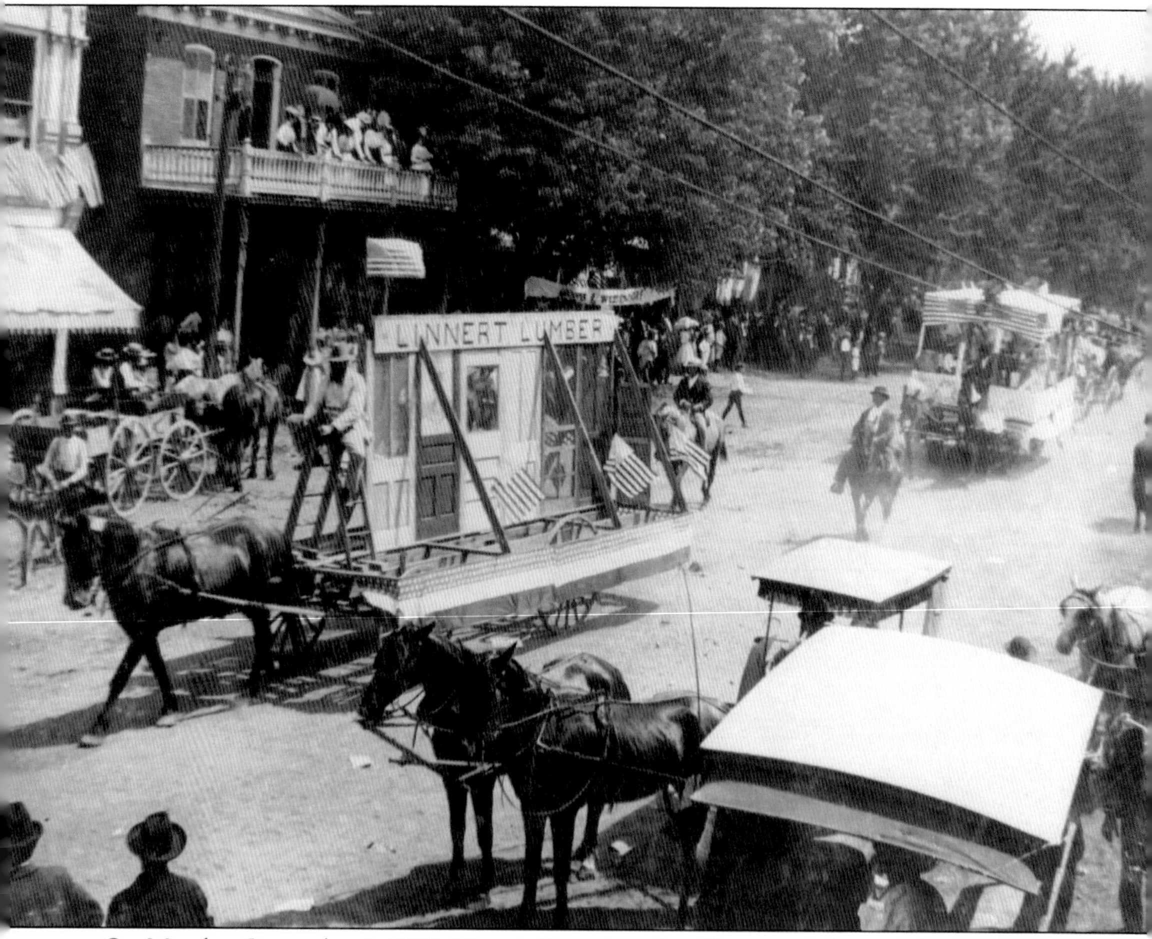

On Monday, September 1, 1902, Howe's Great London Shows and Sanger's Trained Animal Expositions arrived in town. A parade down Main Street was captured by local photographer Dr. Frank Linnert. Dr. Linnert was the town's dentist, and he also ran a photography studio. His office was located above the store of Schaper and Wessendorf. His father, Hermann Linnert, seen on the ladder, owned the lumberyard on the south side of Boone's Lick Road across from where Troy Road comes in.

BIBLIOGRAPHY

An Illustrated Historical Atlas of Warren County, Missouri. Philadelphia: Edwards Brothers, 1877.

Flucke, John W. *Evangelical Pioneers.* St. Louis: Eden Publishing House, 1931.

Keeven, Dorris. *A Window through Time, Pictorial History of Warren County.* Warrenton: Warren County Tribune, 1991.

———. *History of Warren County: A Compilation of Various Articles.* Warrenton: Warren County Tribune and the Warrenton News Journal, 1992.

Krome, Virginia. *The History of Wright City.* St. Louis: Missouri Historical Society, unpublished.

Reprint of the Warren County Section of History of St. Charles, Montgomery, and Warren Counties, Missouri. Warrenton: Warren County Historical Society, 1993.

Schowengerdt, Margaret. *Historic Sites of Warren County.* Warrenton: Warren County Historical Society, 1976.

Tolzmann, Don Heinrich. *Missouri's German Heritage.* Milford, OH: Little Miami Publishing Company, 2006.